A STUDY GUIDE AND R. ⟋ W9-CCP-213

THE
WESTERN
EXPERIENCE

VOLUME I   TO 1715

A STUDY GUIDE AND READINGS FOR

THE WESTERN EXPERIENCE

VOLUME I   TO 1715

FIFTH EDITION

Mortimer Chambers
University of California, Los Angeles
Raymond Grew
University of Michigan
David Herlihy
Brown University
Theodore K. Rabb
Princeton University
Isser Woloch
Columbia University

Prepared by
Dennis Sherman
John Jay College of Criminal Justice
City University of New York

McGRAW-HILL, INC.

New York St. Louis San Francisco Auckland Bogotá Caracas
Hamburg Lisbon London Madrid Mexico Milan Montreal
New Delhi Paris San Juan São Paulo Singapore Sydney Tokyo Toronto

To Marvin, Eva, Raymond, and Pat

A Study Guide and Readings for
THE WESTERN EXPERIENCE: Volume I: To 1715

1 2 3 4 5 6 7 8 9 0 DOH DOH 9 0 9 8 7 6 5 4 3 2 1

ISBN 0-07-010622-3

This book was set in Baskerville by Delphin Typographers, Inc.
The editors were David Follmer, Niels Aaboe, and Scott Amerman;
the production supervisor was Leroy A. Young.
The cover was designed by Karen K. Quigley.
R. R. Donnelley & Sons Company was printer and binder.

ABOUT THE AUTHOR

Dennis Sherman is Professor of History at John Jay College of Criminal Justice, the City University of New York. He received his B.A. (1962) and J.D. (1965) from the University of California at Berkeley and his Ph.D. (1970) from the University of Michigan. He was Visiting Professor at the University of Paris (1978–1979; 1985). He received the Ford Foundation Prize Fellowship (1968–1969, 1969–1970), a fellowship from the Council for Research on Economic History (1971–1972), and fellowships from the National Endowment for the Humanities (1973–1976). His publications include *A Short History of Western Civilization,* Seventh Edition, 1990 (co-author), *Western Civilization: Images and Interpretations,* Third Edition, 1991, a series of introductions in the Garland Library of War and Peace, and several articles and reviews on nineteenth-century French economic and social history in American and European journals.

CONTENTS

INTRODUCTION

I. What Is History?

A. Definition.

History is the record of the human past. It includes both the more concrete elements of the past such as our wars, governments, and creations, and the more elusive ones such as hopes, fantasies, and failures over time. Historians study this human past in order to discover what people thought and did, and then they organize these findings into a broad chronological framework. To do this, they look at the records humans have left of their past, the most important of which are written. Although nonwritten records, such as artifacts, buildings, oral traditions, and paintings, are also sources for the study of the human past, the period before written records appear is usually considered "pre-history."

B. The Purposes of History.

History can be used for various purposes. First, a systematic study of the past helps us to understand human nature; in short, history can be used to give us an idea of who we are as human beings. Second, it can be used to gain insights into contemporary affairs, either through a study of the developments that have shaped the present or through the use of analogies to related circumstances of the past. Third, societies use history to socialize the young, that is, to teach them how to behave and think in culturally and socially appropriate ways.

C. Orientation.

Historians approach the study of history from two main perspectives: the humanities and the social sciences. Those with a humanities orientation see history as be ng made up of unique people, actions, and events, which are to be studied both for their intrinsic value and for the insights they provide about humans in a particular set of historical circumstances. Those with a social science orientation look for patterns in human thought and behavior over time. They focus on comparisons rather than on unique events and are more willin to draw conclusions related to present problems. The authors of *The Western Experience,* Fifth Edition, use both perspectives.

D. Styles.

In writing history, historians traditionally use two main styles: narrative and analytic. Those who prefer the narrative style emphasize a chronological sequence of events. Their histories are more like stories, describing the events from the beginning to the end. Historians who prefer the analytic style emphasize explanation. Their histories deal more with topics, focusing on causes and relationships. Most historians use both styles but show a definite preference for one or the other. The authors of *The Western Experience* stress the analytic style.

E. Interpretations.

Some historians have a particular interpretation or philosophy of history, that is, a way of understanding its meaning and of interpreting its most important aspects. Marxist historians, for example, argue that economic forces are most important, influencing politics, culture, and society in profound ways. They view history organically, following a path in relatively predictable ways. Their interpretations are occasionally pointed out in *The Western Experience*. Most historians are not that committed to a particular philosophy of history, but they do interpret major historical developments in certain ways. Thus, for example, there are various groups of historians who emphasize a social interpretation of the French Revolution of 1789, while there are others who argue that the Revolution is best understood in political and economic terms. The authors of *The Western Experience* are relatively eclectic; they use a variety of interpretations and often indicate major points of interpretive disagreement among historians.

F. Common Concerns.

The style, orientation, and philosophy of most modern historians are not at one extreme or the other. Moreover, the concerns they share outweigh their differences. They all want to know what happened, when it happened, and how it happened. While the question of cause is touchy, historians all want to know why something happened, and they are all particularly interested in studying change over time.

II. The Historical Method.

A. Process.

1. *Search for Sources:* One of the first tasks a historian faces is the search for sources. Most sources are written documents, which include everything from gravestone inscriptions and diaries to books and governmental records. Other sources include buildings, art, maps, pottery, and oral traditions. In searching for sources, historians do not work at random. They usually have something in mind before they start, and in the process, they must decide which sources to emphasize over others.

2. *External Criticism:* To test the genuineness of the source, historians must engage in external criticism. This constitutes an attempt to uncover forgeries and errors. Some startling revisions of history have resulted from an effective criticism of previously accepted sources.

3. *Internal Criticism:* A source, though genuine, may not be objective, or it may reveal something that was not apparent at first. To deal with this, historians subject sources to internal criticism by such methods as evaluating the motives of the person who wrote the document, looking for inconsistencies within the source, and comparing different meanings of a word or phrase used in the source.

4. *Synthesis:* Finally, the historian creates a synthesis. He or she gathers the relevant sources together, applies them to the question being investigated, decides what is to be included, and writes a history. This oversimplifies the process, for historians often search, criticize, and synthesize at the same time. Moreover, the process is not as objective as it seems, for historians select what they think is most important and what fits into their own philosophy or interpretation of history.

B. Categories.

Historians use certain categories to organize different types of information. The number and boundaries of these differ according to what each historian thinks is most useful. The principal categories are as follows:

1. *Political:* This refers to questions of how humans are governed, including such matters as the exercise of power in peace and war, the use of law, the formation of governments, the collection of taxes, and the establishment of public services.

2. *Economic:* This refers to the production and distribution of goods and services. On the production side, historians usually focus on agriculture, commerce, manufacturing, and finance. On the distribution side, they deal with who gets how much of what is produced. Their problem is supply and demand and how people earn their living.

3. *Social:* This is the broadest category. It refers to relations between individuals or groups within some sort of community. This includes the institutions people create (the family, the army), the classes or castes to which people belong (the working class, the aristocracy), the customs people follow (marriage, eating), the activities people engage in together (sports, drinking), and the attitudes people share (toward foreigners, commerce).

4. *Intellectual:* This refers to the ideas, theories, and beliefs expressed by people in some organized way about topics thought to be important. This includes such matters as political theories, scientific ideas, and philosophies of life.

5. *Religious:* This refers to theories, beliefs, and practices related to the supernatural or the unknown. This includes such matters as the growth of religious institutions, the formation of beliefs about the relation between human beings and God, and the practice of rituals and festivals.

6. *Cultural:* This refers to the ideas, values, and expressions of human beings as evidenced in aesthetic works, such as music, art, and literature.

In addition to organizing different types of information into categories, historians often specialize in one or two of these. For example, some historians focus on political history, whereas others are concerned with social-economic history. The best historians bring to bear on the problems that interest them, however specialized the problems may seem, data from all these categories.

III. Documents.

Historians classify written documents into two types: primary and secondary. Primary documents are those written by a person living during the period being studied and participating in the matter under investigation. A primary document is looked at as a piece of evidence that shows what people thought, how they acted, and what they accomplished. A secondary document is usually written by someone after the period of time that is being studied. It is either mainly a description or an interpretation of the topic being studied: the more descriptive it is, the more it simply traces what happened; the more interpretive it is, the more it analyzes the causes or the significance of what happened. There are numerous examples of primary and both kinds of secondary documents provided in this study guide.

IV. Periodization.

Historians cannot deal with all of history at once. One way to solve this is to break history up into separate periods. How this is done is a matter of discretion; what is important is the division of a time into periods that can be dealt with as a whole, without doing too much violence to the continuity of history. Typically, Western Civilization is divided into the Ancient World, the Middle Ages, the Renaissance and Reformation, the Early Modern World, the nineteenth century (1789–1914), and the twentieth century (1914–present), as illustrated by the section summaries in this study guide. There are a number of subdivisions that can be made within these periods. *The Western Experience* is divided into both periodic and topical chapters.

V. Study Aids.

A. Reading.

There is no way to get around reading—the more you read, the better you become at it. Thus the best advice is to read the assigned chapters. But there are some techniques that will make the task easier. First, think about the title of the book you are reading; often, it tells much about what is in the book. Second, read through the chapter headings and subheadings. Whatever you read will make more sense and will be more easily remembered if it is placed in the context of the section, the chapter, and the book as a whole. Third, concentrate on the first and last paragraphs or two of each chapter and each major section of the chapter. Often, the author will summarize in these areas what he or she wants to communicate. Finally, concentrate on the first sentence of each paragraph. Often, but not always, the first sentence is a topic sentence, making the point for which the rest of the paragraph is an expansion.

B. Note Taking.

1. *Reading Assignments:* While it is easier said than done, it is of tremendous advantage to take notes on reading assignments. Taking notes, if done properly, will help you to integrate the readings into your mind much more than simply reading them. Moreover, notes will ease the problem of review for papers, exams, or classroom discussions.

There are a number of ways to take notes. Generally, you should use an outline form, following the main points or headings of each chapter. Under each section of your outline you should include the important points and information, translated into your own words. After each section of a chapter ask yourself, "What is the author trying to say here, what is he trying to convey?" It may be easier to copy phrases or words used by the author, but it is much more effective if you can transform them into your own words. While facts, names, and dates are important, avoid simply making a list of them without focusing on the more general interpretation, development, or topic that the author is discussing. Indicate the kinds of evidence the author uses, what the author's interpretations are, and to what degree you agree with what he says (does it make sense to you?). Some students prefer to underline in the text and write notes in the margins. This is a less time-consuming, easier, and often useful method, but probably not as effective as outlining and using your own words to summarize each section. As with many things, it is the extra effort involved that leads to the more effective learning.

2. *Lectures and Classes:* Much of what has been said also applies to taking notes in class, except that it is more difficult. The trick is to write just enough to get the main points without losing track of what is going on in class. A couple of techniques might help. It is crucial to be ready at the beginning of class. Often, the point of a whole lecture or discussion is outlined in the first couple of minutes; missing it makes much of what you hear seem out of context.

Take notes. Putting this off often leads to a passive state of listening, and soon, daydreaming, at which point much of what is said will go in one ear and out the other. Concentrate on the major points the speaker is trying to make, not simply all the facts. Do not try to write down everything or to write in complete sentences; try to develop a method of writing down key words or phrases that works for you. Finally, try to go over your notes after class.

C. Writing.

There are three steps that should be taken before you actually start writing your paper. First, carefully read the question or topic you are to write on; at times, good papers are written on the wrong topic. If you are to make up a topic, spend some time on it. Think of your topic as a question. It should not be unanswerably broad (what is the history of Western Civilization?) or insignificantly narrow (when was toothpaste invented?). It will be something that interests you and that is easily researched. Second, start reading about the topic, taking notes on the main points. Third, after some reading, start writing an outline of the main points you want to make. Revise this outline a number of times, arranging your points in some logical way and making sure all your points help answer the question or support the argument you are making.

A paper should have three parts: an introduction, a body, and a conclusion. For a short paper, your introduction should be only a paragraph or two in length; for a long paper, perhaps one or two pages. In the introduction tell the reader what the general topic is, what you will argue about the topic, and why it is important or interesting. This is an extremely important part of a paper, often neglected by students. You can win or lose the reader with the introduction. You may find it easier to leave the introduction until after you have written the body of the paper, especially if it is difficult to get started writing. In the body, make your argument. Generally, make one major point in each paragraph, usually in the first sentence (topic sentence). The rest of the paragraph should contain explanation, expansion, support, illustration, or evidence for this point. In the paragraph, you should make it clear how this point helps answer the question. Your paragraphs should be organized in some logical order (chronological, from strongest to weakest point, categories). Finally, in the conclusion, tell the reader — in different words — what you have argued in the body of the paper, and indicate why what you have argued is important. The conclusion, like the introduction, is a particularly important and yet an often slighted part of a paper.

Most of the same suggestions for papers apply to essay exams. Even more emphasis should be placed on making sure you know what the question asks. Spend some time outlining your answer. As with papers, you should have an introduction, body, and conclusion, even if they are all relatively short. For each point you make, try to supply some evidence as support. Keep to the indicated time limits.

D. Class Participation.

Class participation is difficult for many students, yet there is no better way to get over this difficulty than to do it. Try and force yourself to ask questions or indicate your point of view when appropriate times arise. If this is particularly difficult for you, it may help to talk about it with other students or with the teacher privately.

E. Studying.

If you have a style of studying that works well for you, stick to it. If not, try to do three things: keep up with all your assignments regularly, work with someone else, and spend some extra time reviewing before exams.

VI. How to Use This Guide.

There is one chapter in this guide corresponding to each chapter in *The Western Experience*. Each chapter of the guide is divided into a number of sections.

Main Themes: The main themes of each chapter are introduced here. Part of the purpose in doing this is to emphasize the importance of not losing sight of the broader concerns of the chapter as you study its specific sections. By returning to these main themes and expanding upon them after you read the chapter, they can become a tool to help you grasp more firmly what the chapter is about.

Outline and Summary: Here, the chapter in the text is outlined and summarized. The outline headings are the same as those in the text. Under each heading, the main points, with supporting information, are indicated. Keep in mind that everything cannot be included in this summary. It is designed as a guide, summary, and supplement to the text.

Significant Individuals: Here, the principal historical figures mentioned in the text are listed with some brief biographical information. This is intended to be used in two ways: first, as a reference; and second, as an exercise. You should be able to state, briefly, who each person is and why that person is important. Emphasis should be placed on the significance of the person's thoughts or actions.

Chronological Diagram: This diagram is intended to be used as a reference. Note what different sorts of events are related chronologically. It is often useful to compare the chronological chart in one chapter with those in the preceding and succeeding chapters. On an even broader scale, this is done in the chronological diagrams contained in each section summary.

Map Exercise: In most chapters a map is provided with exercises that relate to some of the main concerns of the chapter. Standing alone and without directly using the text, some of these exercises are difficult. But by utilizing the maps already present in the text and in some cases specific sections of the text referred to in the exercise, they become easier. The purposes here are to help you get used to using maps, to emphasize the importance of geographic considerations in history, and to encourage you to picture developments described in the text in concrete, geographic terms.

Identification: Some of the most important developments or events in the chapter are listed here. For each, you should indicate what the development or event was, when it occurred, and what its significance was (why was it important?).

Problems for Analysis: These are designed to cover each of the main sections of the chapter. They require a combination of specific information and analysis. Working on these problems should give you a much stronger grasp on the materials and issues dealt with in each section of the chapter. In addition, you might use some of these problems to prepare for class discussions. They might help you formulate questions to ask in class or present a point of view that you find particularly interesting or irritating.

Documents: Each chapter contains some documents, usually at least one primary and one secondary document. Sometimes the secondary documents are more descriptive, but usually, they are quite interpretive. These documents complement each chapter in the text by suggesting a different perspective from which to view the same material, clarifying the author's point through the use of contrasting materials, and supporting aspects of the text with different primary or secondary materials. Many of the documents emphasize interdisciplinary perspectives, for example, those of the social sciences and humanities, and point out some of the interpretive debates in which historians engage. Each document is preceded by an introductory note and followed by some questions.

Great care should be taken in reading the secondary documents, particularly those which are interpretive. These reflect choices the author has made and the author's own particular understanding of what he or she is commenting upon. Rarely do historians unanimously agree on how to understand important historical developments; usually there are important differences of opinion. In evaluating these documents, look for certain things: Does the author supply evidence to support his or her views, and if so what sort of evidence? Does the author's argument make sense to you? Does the author seem to agree or disagree with the text at all points? How might one argue against the interpretation presented by the author? Does the author reveal any political or ideological preferences in the analysis presented? Does the author reveal the concerns of his or her own period of time when looking at the past?

Speculations: These constitute unusual, interesting questions. They may require you to put yourself back into history, compare the past with the present, or speculate on various historical alternatives. They might be used as a first step toward identifying a paper topic or developing a classroom debate. From aspects of the broader speculations, more specific historical problems could be identified, put into perspective, and dealt with.

Transitions: These relate the previous chapter, the present chapter, and the following chapter. One of the main purposes here is to help you avoid losing the continuity of history; each chapter in the text is integrally connected to what came before and what follows. Another purpose is to emphasize briefly the main arguments presented in the chapter; focusing on specific events can sometimes lead one to overlook the broader conclusions that are being made.

In addition to the chapters, there are six section summaries; these correspond to periods into which historians commonly divide Western history and to sections of the book often covered in an exam or a paper. Each contains Chronological Diagrams, Map Exercises, and Box Charts for you to fill in. Tabulating material from your reading notes on these charts (which you will need to reproduce in larger format in your notebook or on separate sheets of paper) will help you place individuals and events in a broader chronological framework, identify historical turning points, better understand developments that span long periods of time and several chapters, and distinguish important facts from less important ones. The charts should be particularly useful when you are reviewing for an exam.

Dennis Sherman

ONE
THE FIRST
CIVILIZATIONS

MAIN THEMES

1. Humans became food producers rather than food gatherers some 12,000 years ago with the development of agriculture, the essential step in the creation of complex civilizations.
2. As cities were established in the river valleys of Mesopotamia, the early Sumerian and Babylonian civilizations emerged.
3. Egyptians developed a prosperous, long-lasting, religious society along the Nile between about 3000 and 300 B.C..
4. After 1650 the Hittites established a powerful state in the Near East, but between 1250 and 1100, invaders utilizing iron weapons ended the Hittite domination and brought the Bronze Age to an end.
5. In Palestine, the Israelites developed a short-lived kingdom, but an enduring religious and cultural tradition was formed.
6. The Assyrians, followed by the Chaldeans, the Medes, and the Persians, established powerful unifying empires in the Near East.

OUTLINE AND SUMMARY

I. The Earliest Humans.

Homo sapiens have inhabited the earth for the last 350,000 years. Scholars now think that predecessors, including Homo erectus and perhaps Homo habilis, emerged between 1,500,000 and 1,800,000 years ago. Anthropologists differ on the earlier origins of human beings, which may extend to some 20 million years ago.

A. Human Beings as Food Gatherers.

For most of their existence, human beings got food by hunting and gathering. During this long period, known as the Old Stone Age or Paleolithic Age, men and women probably shared most tasks, but women may have supplied most of the food by gathering. Men may have specialized in hunting and defense, perhaps becoming politically and socially dominant. Cave paintings are the most striking documents from gathering societies.

1

B. Human Beings as Food Producers.

About 10,000 B.C. the Neolithic Revolution—the rise of agriculture—occurred. Perhaps caused by the need for new food supplies, this revolution led to long-term planning, cooperative efforts, division of labor, population increase, new technologies, and trade. This occurred first in the hills of the Near East. Between 9000 and 6000 B.C. villages with social organization, organized religion, and economic specialization appeared in the area. Women probably played crucial roles in the development of early agriculture and crafts.

II. The First Civilizations in Mesopotamia.

A. The Emergence of Civilization.

The rise of civilization in the urban areas of Mesopotamia involved a more complex political and legal system as well as greater specialization into military, domestic, and economic activities.

B. Sumer.

The first cities appeared in Sumer in southern Mesopotamia. By the beginning of the Bronze Age (about 3000 B.C.), there were a number of independent city-states in the area, Ur being the largest. The Sumerians organized themselves into classes (nobles and priests, commoners, and slaves) ruled by a king who was dependent for support upon the priests and nobles. They developed an efficient form of writing ("cuneiform"), some of which reveals that the Sumerians speculated about causes and tried to explain divine action. Some of their myths formed a background for later traditions (Homer's *Odyssey*) and religious themes (biblical accounts of Creation). Some of their most important accomplishments include the development of law codes, manufacturing (metal work), and mathematical notation.

C. Sargon, and the Revival of Ur.

Weakened by continual warfare, the Sumerian cities fell to the invading Akkadians under the warlord Sargon after 2371. The Sumerians regained control after the dissolution of the Akkadian kingdom around 2230. The first law codes date from this Third Dynasty of Ur.

D. Ebla in Syria.

Recent evidence indicates that a complex urban culture, Ebla, formed during the third millennium B.C. in northern Syria. Some of its unusual features include elected kings and an unusually "lay" society.

E. The Babylonian Kingdom.

Toward the end of the third millennium B.C. a Semitic people, the Amorites, succeeded the Sumerians, eventually forming the powerful kingdom of Babylonia under Hammurabi (1792–1750). The Code of Hammurabi reveals much about Babylonian laws and politics as well as about social and sexual divisions within Babylonian society.

F. Mesopotamian Culture.

Records indicate that Mesopotamians developed relatively complex mathematics, astronomy, and astrology and at least partially diagnosed and treated disease from a rational, regulated basis.

III. Egyptian Society.

A. The Nile River.

The Nile River was central to the long-lasting Egyptian civilization. The only inhabitable area for the Egyptians was close to the Nile, making defense and social control comparatively easy. Thanks to yearly overflows produced by floods, Egyptians were able to develop agricultural systems that supplied more than sufficient quantities of food.

B. The List of Rulers.

Between about 3000 and 332 there were thirty-one dynasties of kings in Egypt. In earliest times, Egypt was divided into Upper and Lower kingdoms, probably reflecting differing ethnic and linguistic origins.

C. The Old Kingdom.

Around 3000, Menes unified Egypt. During the Old Kingdom (2700–2200) the king acquired absolute power as owner of the land and as a living god. Between about 2600 and 2500 the Old Kingdom reached its peak. The great pyramids at Giza were constructed. Toward the end of the period the kings were forced to share some of their power with priests.

D. The Middle Kingdom.

After a period of instability, the Middle Kingdom, based in Thebes, arose. Amen-Re became the Egyptian national god.

E. Egyptian Culture.

1. *Religion:* The king and a number of associated and lesser gods presided over Egyptian civilization. Egyptians believed in a relatively pleasant life after death and devoted much effort in preparation for it. The arts of embalming and pyramid building testify to this.

2. *Maat:* The Egyptians were perhaps the first to think abstractly about ethical qualities, as indicated by their belief in *maat,* or "right order."

3. *Art and Writing:* Most of the surviving Egyptian art is religious, characterized by optimistic scenes of Egyptian life. The Egyptians developed their pictorial and phonetic form of writing (hieroglyphics) and writing material (papyri).

4. *Literature:* Egyptians produced a variety of religious myths (the *Book of the Dead*), "instructions" on how to get ahead in the world, love poems, and fables.

5. *Mathematics and Medicine:* Egyptians mastered the art of surveying in order to deal with the changing Nile. Their accomplishments in multiplication and division were relatively elementary. In medicine, they went beyond magic by using an empirical approach to illness.

F. The Invasion of the Hyksos.

Around 1720 the invasion of the Hyksos ended the Middle Kingdom. By about 1570 Egyptian warriors drove the Hyksos out and initiated the New Kingdom.

G. Hatshepsut and the New Kingdom.

The New Kingdom was established after 1570, when the Hyksos were expelled from Egypt. Rulers such as the extraordinary woman, Hatshepsut, and Thutmose III established a powerful military state. Tribute, slaves, trade, and prosperity resulted.

H. Akhnaton's Religious Reform.

King Amenhotep IV (Akhnaton) attempted a major religious reform, which was connected with efforts to overcome the power of priests and bureaucrats, by sponsoring the worship of Aton over the traditional god Amen-Re. Religiously, he was, at best, temporarily successful; but politically, his authority disintegrated. He was succeeded by more traditional pharaohs such as Ramses II, who reestablished Amen-Re, gained political dominance within Egypt, reasserted Egyptian control in Palestine, and continued the construction of massive monuments.

I. A View of Egyptian Society.

From slaves and peasants at the bottom to priests and kings at the top, Egyptian society survived for some 3,000 years. Relatively liberal in the scope given to women, it was a religious, prosperous society characterized by a positive attitude toward life in the next world.

IV. The Early Indo-Europeans.

After 5000 B.C. Indo-Europeans—groups of linguistically related peoples probably originating in southern Russia—began spreading across Europe and parts of Asia.

A. The Hittite Kingdom.

Hittites were among the Indo-Europeans who invaded Babylonia. By 1650, Hittites established a powerful society in northwest Turkey. Over the next 400 years, they expanded to become the most formidable state in the Near East. The king acted as general. Their society was patriarchal and somewhat feudal.

B. Close of the Bronze Age.

The period between 1250 and 1100 was one of upheaval in the Near East, probably brought on by the iron age. The use by invaders of iron for weapons broke up the Hittite kingdom. Moreover, the use of iron, which was cheaper and more available than bronze, meant that more people could acquire the power that weapons brought.

V. Palestine.

The cultural and religious continuity of the Israelites since ancient times is indicated by attitudes in the modern state of Israel and by the monotheistic roots of modern religions.

A. Canaanites and Phoenicians.

The Canaanites preceded the Israelites in Palestine. By about 1200 the Canaanites were forced into Phoenicia, and these Phoenicians soon became a sophisticated urban and commercial power with extraordinary naval expertise.

B. The Old Testament as a Historical Source.

The Old Testament can serve as a useful, though not literal, historical document. The writers of the Old Testament creatively used traditional materials and emphasized one god and humans' relationship to him in forming their history of the Israelites.

C. The Early Israelites.

Between about 1800 and 1200, Israelite tribes migrated into various parts of the Near East and Egypt. Around 1200 Moses unified many of these tribes with some Canaanites under a jealous god, Yahweh, and a complex code of ethically based laws. Women were severely restricted in early Israelite society.

D. The Israelite Monarchy.

The Israelite tribes successfully invaded Canaanite territory and eventually unified and formed a central government under a line of strong kings (Saul, David, and Solomon) between 1020 and 920. After the autocratic and extravagant Solomon, the kingdom split into two parts—the northern, eventually conquered by Assyria in 722, and the southern, finally falling in 586 to the Chaldeans. The

Israelites were tragically dispersed, though later, they managed to obtain partial independence in Palestine for occasional periods.

E. The Faith and the Prophets.

Over time, Judaism was shaped by a series of social critics (prophets)—who emphasized corruption, moral reform, and a redeeming Messiah—and a series of scholars—who organized the sacred writings of Judaism.

F. The Jewish Legacy.

Through their traditions and religious beliefs, the Jewish culture became the most influential in the ancient Near East.

VI. The Near Eastern Empires.

The Assyrians were the first to unify politically the Near East. They were followed by the Persians.

A. The Assyrian State.

The militaristic Assyrians conquered most of the Near East between about 900 and 700. They ruled their vast empire both directly and indirectly, extracting tribute everywhere. Their language, Aramaic, became established throughout the area. Their cultural legacy remains in their art (reliefs at Nineveh) and cuneiform texts.

B. The Chaldeans and the Medes.

The Assyrians fell to the Chaldeans, based in Babylon, and the Medes, located further east. The Chaldeans are best known for their superb astronomers and for their capital city, with its lavish temples built by Nebuchadnezzar. The Medes established their kingdom around 650, but it soon fell to the Persians.

C. The Persian Empire.

King Cyrus (559–530) formed the Persian Empire by conquering the Medes to the north, the Lydians to the west, and the Chaldeans to the south. His successor, Cambyses, conquered Egypt in 525. Darius (521–486) divided the empire effectively into some twenty provinces ruled by satraps. He linked his empire together with a system of roads and adopted the Lydian invention of coinage, crucial for the subsequent development of trade.

D. Zoroastrianism.

The Persian priest and reformer Zarathustra (Zoroaster) profoundly influenced Persian religion during the 500s. A contemporary of the Israelite prophets, the early Greek philosophers, the Indian Buddha, and the Chinese philosopher Confucius, Zoroaster taught a dualistic religion, which held that there was a supreme god of truth opposed by an evil spirit. This would prove to be a popular, long-lasting, and influential religion.

Experiences of Daily Life: Building a Pyramid.

Using relatively simple methods of construction, Egyptians skillfully and laboriously constructed their massive pyramids.

SIGNIFICANT INDIVIDUALS

Kings

Sargon (2371–2316), Akkad.
Ur-Nammu (2113–2096), Ur.
Hammurabi (1792–1750), Babylonia.
Suppiluliumas (ca. 1380–1340),
   Hittite.
Amenhotep IV (1369?–1353?),
   Egypt.
Ramses II (1292–1225), Egypt.

Saul (ca. 1020), Israel.
David (1010?–960?), Israel.
Solomon (960?–920?), Israel.
Ashurbanipal (668–627?), Assyria.
Nebuchadnezzar (604–562), Chaldea.
Cyrus (559–530), Persia.
Croesus (580?–546), Lydia.
Darius (521–486), Persia.

Religious Leaders

Moses (ca. 1200), Israelite prophet.

Zarathustra (Zoroaster) (ca. 600),
   Persian priest and reformer.

CHRONOLOGICAL DIAGRAM

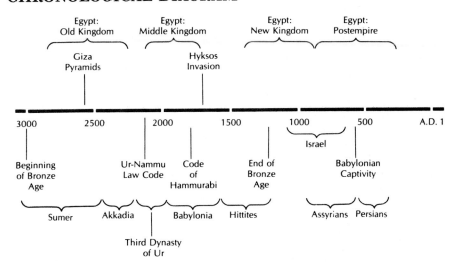

IDENTIFICATION

Homo sapiens	ziggurat
Bronze Age	cuneiform
Code of Hammurabi	Amen-Re
Ebla	Aton
maat	Indo-European
hieroglyphics	Zoroastrianism

PROBLEMS FOR ANALYSIS

I. Early Humans.

1. Why was the development of agriculture so crucial for the establishment of civilization? What advantages do food producers have over food gatherers?

II. The First Civilizations in Mesopotamia.

1. In what ways was the rise of Sumerian cities a significant development in Western history? Describe the characteristics of Sumerian civilization.
2. How has analysis of cuneiform inscriptions and codes revealed much about Babylonian politics, society, and culture?

III. Egyptian Society.

1. Compare Egyptian civilization with Mesopotamia. What role did the Nile play in the development of Egyptian civilization?
2. What do Egyptian attitudes toward life after death reveal about the Egyptian religion and attitudes toward life in general?

IV. The Early Indo-Europeans.

1. In what ways were the Hittites unique, and in what ways did they adapt to conditions in areas they conquered?

V. Palestine.

1. How useful is the Old Testament as a historical document? Explain.
2. How did the religion and culture of the Israelites become so influential in Western civilization?

VI. The Near Eastern Empires.

1. Using examples from the Assyrians and Persians, explain how Near Eastern kings were able to hold their vast empires together.

MAP EXERCISE

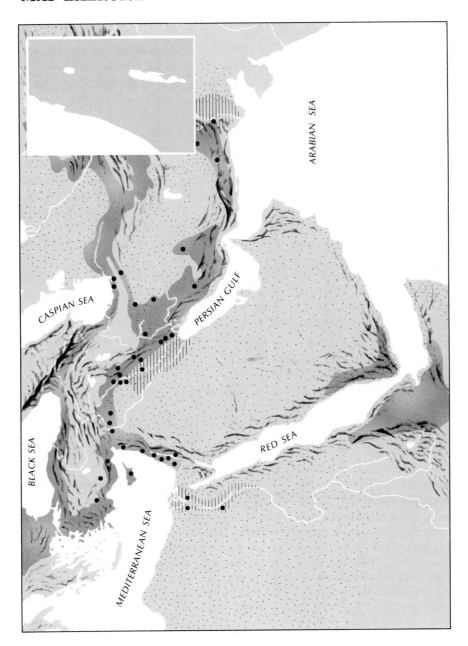

1. Indicate the approximate boundaries of Egypt, the Assyrian Empire, the Hittite kingdom, the Hebrew kingdom, and the Persian Empire at their heights.
2. Indicate the main river valleys in the area.
3. Indicate the location of some early agricultural sites.

DOCUMENTS

An Egyptian Prince

Noble families were powerful in Egypt and had considerable military and administrative responsibilities. This is described in the following tomb inscription of Ameni (Amenemhet), a prince of a leading noble family who lived in the early years of the Middle Kingdom (ca. 1950 B.C.).

First Expedition

I followed my lord when he sailed southward to overthrow his enemies among the four barbarians. I sailed southward, as the son of a count, wearer of the royal seal, and commander in chief of the troops of the Oryx nome, as a man represents his old father, according to [his] favor in the palace and his love in the court. I passed Kush, sailing southward, I advanced the boundary of the land, I brought all gifts; my praise, it reached heaven. Then his majesty returned in safety, having overthrown his enemies in Kush the vile. I returned, following him, with ready face. There was no loss among my soldiers.

Second Expedition

I sailed southward, to bring gold ore for the majesty of the King of Upper and Lower Egypt, Kheperkere (Sesostris I), living forever and ever. I sailed southward together with the hereditary prince, count, oldest son of the king, of his body, Ameni. I sailed southward, with a number, 400 of all the choicest of my troops, who returned in safety, having suffered no loss. I brought the gold exacted of me; I was praised for it in the palace, the king's-son praised god for me.

Third Expedition

Then I sailed southward to bring ore, to the city of Coptos, together with the hereditary prince, count, governor of the city and vizier, Sesostris. I sailed southward with a number, 600 of all the bravest of the Oryx nome. I returned in safety, my soldiers uninjured; having done all that had been told me.

Ameni's Able Administration

I was amiable, and greatly loved, a ruler beloved of his city. Now, I passed years as ruler in the Oryx nome. All the imposts of the king's house passed through my hand. The gang-overseers of the crown possessions of the shepherds of the Oryx nome gave to me 3,000 bulls in their yokes. I was praised on account of it in the palace each year of the loan-herds. I carried all their dues to the king's house; there were no arrears against me in any office of his. The entire Oryx nome labored for me.

Ameni's Impartiality and Benevolence

There was no citizen's daughter whom I misused, there was no widow whom I oppressed, there was no [peasant] whom I repulsed, there was no shepherd whom I repelled, there was no overseer of serf-laborers whose people I took for (unpaid) imposts, there was none wretched in my community, there was none hungry in my time. When years of famine came I plowed all the fields of the Oryx nome, as far as its southern and northern boundary, preserving its people alive and furnishing its food so that there was none hungry therein. I gave to the widow as (to) her who had a husband; I did not exalt the great above the small in all that I gave. Then came great Niles, possessors of grain and all things, (but) I did not collect the arrears of the field.[1]

1. Ameni is most proud of what kinds of deeds?
2. What were the main military and administrative tasks of Ameni?

The Code of Hammurabi

Hammurabi was the leading ruler of Babylonia. This eighteenth-century ruler is most famous for his legal codes, which regulated almost all aspects of life. The following are selections from those codes.

8. If a patrician has stolen ox, sheep, ass, pig, or ship, whether from a temple, or a house, he shall pay thirtyfold. If he be a plebeian, he shall return tenfold. If the thief cannot pay, he shall be put to death.

. . .

14. If a man has stolen a child, he shall be put to death.
15. If a man has induced either a male or female slave from the house of a patrician, or plebeian, to leave the city, he shall be put to death.

. . .

21. If a man has broken into a house he shall be killed before the breach and buried there.
22. If a man has committed highway robbery and has been caught, that man shall be put to death.
23. If the highwayman has not been caught, the man that has been robbed shall state on oath what he has lost, and the city or district governor in whose territory or district the robbery took place shall restore to him what he has lost.

. . .

25. If a fire has broken out in a man's house and one who has come to put it out has coveted the property of the householder and appropriated any of it, that man shall be cast into the self-same fire.

. . .

108. If the mistress of a beer-shop has not received corn as the price of beer or has demanded silver on an excessive scale, and has made the measure of beer less than the measure of corn, that beer-seller shall be prosecuted and drowned.

. . .

117. If a man owes a debt, and he has given his wife, his son, or his daughter for the money, or has handed someone over to work it off, the hostage shall do the work of the creditor's house, but in the fourth year he shall set them free.

. . .

129. If a man's wife be caught lying with another, they shall be strangled and cast into the water. If the wife's husband would save his wife, the king can save his servant.

. . .

141. If a man's wife, living in her husband's house, has persisted in going out, has acted the fool, has wasted her house, has belittled her husband, he shall prosecute her.

---

[1] James Henry Breasted, *Ancient Records of Egypt,* Vol. I (Chicago: University of Chicago Press, 1906), pp. 251–253.

If her husband has said, "I divorce her," she shall go her way; he shall give her nothing as her price of divorce. If her husband has said, "I will not divorce her," he may take another woman to wife; the wife shall live as a slave in her husband's house.

. . .

215. If a surgeon has operated with the bronze lancet on a patrician for a serious injury, and has cured him, or has removed with a bronze lancet a cataract for a patrician, and has cured his eye, he shall take ten shekels of silver.
216. If it be a plebeian, he shall take five shekels of silver.
217. If it be a man's slave, the owner of the slave shall give two shekels of silver to the surgeon.
218. If a surgeon has operated with the bronze lancet on a patrician for a serious injury, and has caused his death, or has removed a cataract for a patrician, with the bronze lancet, and has made him lose his eye, his hands shall be cut off.[2]

1. What social and legal distinctions were there between people and between classes?
2. Characterize the Babylonian legal system. What role would a judge play in this system?

Primitive and Civilized Humans

In the following selection, the well-known anthropologist Franz Boas distinguishes the mind of primitive humans from that of civilized humans. Note the assumed definitions of "primitive" and "civilized."

The difference in the mode of thought of primitive man and that of civilized man seems to consist largely in the difference of character of the traditional material with which the new perception associates itself. The instruction given to the child of primitive man is not based on centuries of experimentation, but consists of the crude experiences of generations. When a new experience enters the mind of primitive man, the same process which we observe among civilized man brings about an entirely different series of associations, and therefore results in a different type of explanation. A sudden explosion will associate itself in his mind, perhaps, with tales which he has heard in regard to the mythical history of the world, and consequently will be accompanied by superstitious fear. The new, unknown epidemic may be explained by the belief in demons that persecute mankind; and the existing world may be explained as the result of transformations, or by objectivation of the thoughts of a creator.

When we recognize that neither among civilized nor among primitive men the average individual carries to completion the attempt at causal explanation of phenomena, but only so far as to amalgamate it with other previous knowledge, we recognize that the result of the whole process depends entirely upon the character of the traditional material. Herein lies the immense importance of folk-lore in determining the mode of thought. Herein lies particularly the enormous influence of current philosophic opinion upon the masses of the people, and the influence of the dominant scientific theory upon the character of scientific work.

[2]C. H. W. Johns, *Babylonian and Assyrian Laws, Contracts and Letters* (New York: Scribner's, 1904), pp. 44–66.

It would be vain to try to understand the development of modern science without an intelligent understanding of modern philosophy; it would be vain to try to understand the history of medieval science without a knowledge of medieval theology; and so it is vain to try to understand primitive science without an intelligent knowledge of primitive mythology. "Mythology," "theology" and "philosophy" are different terms for the same influences which shape the current of human thought, and which determine the character of the attempts of man to explain the phenomena of nature. To primitive man — who has been taught to consider the heavenly orbs as animate beings; who sees in every animal a being more powerful than man; to whom the mountains, trees and stones are endowed with life or with special virtues — explanations of phenomena will suggest themselves entirely different from those to which we are accustomed, since we still base our conclusions upon the existence of matter and force as bringing about the observed results.[3]

1. How does the mind of the primitive human reflect the environment?
2. What are the principal characteristics that distinguish the mind of the primiive human from that of the civilized human?

Sumerian Religion

This selection incorporates primary material to support an interpretation of Sumerian religious beliefs and practices.

The gods preferred the ethical and moral to the unethical and immoral, according to the Sumerian sages, and practically all the major deities of the Sumerian pantheon are extolled in their hymns as lovers of the good and the just, of truth and righteousness. Indeed, there were several deities who had the supervision of the moral order as their main functions: for example, the sun-god, Utu. Another deity, the Lagashite goddess named Nanshe, also played a significant role in the sphere of man's ethical and moral conduct. She is described in one of her hymns as the goddess

> Who knows the orphan, who knows the widow,
> Knows the oppression of man over man, is the orphan's mother,
> Nanshe, who cares for the widow,
> Who seeks out (?) justice (?) for the poorest (?).
> The queen brings the refugee to her lap,
> Finds shelter for the weak.

In another passage of this hymn, she is pictured as judging mankind on New Year's Day; by her side are Nidaba, the goddess of writing and accounts, and her husband, Haia, as well as numerous witnesses. The evil human types who suffer her displeasure are

> (People) who walking in transgression reached out with high hand, ... ,
> Who transgress the established norms, violate contracts,
> Who looked with favor on the places of evil, ... ,
> Who substituted a small weight for a large weight,
> Who substituted a small measure for a large measure,

[3] Franz Boas, *The Mind of Primitive Man* (New York: Macmillan, 1938), copyright 1938 by Macmillan Publishing Co., Inc., renewed 1966 by Franziska Boas Nicholson.

> Who having eaten (something not belonging to him) did not say "I have
>   eaten it,"
> Who having drunk, did not say "I have drunk it," . . . . ,
> Who said "I would eat that which is forbidden,"
> Who said "I would drink that which is forbidden."

Nanshe's social conscience is further revealed in lines which read:

> To comfort the orphan, to make disappear the widow,
> To set up a place of destruction for the mighty,
> To turn over the mighty to the weak . . . . ,
> Nanshe searches the heart of the people.

Unfortunately, although the leading deities were assumed to be ethical and moral in their conduct, the fact remained that, in accordance with the world view of the Sumerians, they were also the ones who in the process of establishing civilization had planned evil and falsehood, violence and oppression — in short, all the immoral and unethical modes of human conduct. Thus, for example, among the list of *me*'s the rules and regulations devised by the gods to make the cosmos run smoothly and effectively, there are not only those which regulate "truth," "peace," "goodness," and "justice," but also those which govern "falsehood," "strife," "lamentation," and "fear." Why, then, one might ask, did the gods find it necessary to plan and create sin and evil, suffering and misfortune, which were so pervasive that one Sumerian pessimist could say, "Never has a sinless child been born to his mother"? To judge from our available material, the Sumerian sages, if they asked the question at all, were prepared to admit their ignorance in this respect; the will of the gods and their motives were at times inscrutable. The proper course for a Sumerian Job to pursue was not to argue and complain in face of seemingly unjustifiable misfortune, but to plead and wail, lament and confess, his inevitable sins and failings.

But will the gods give heed to him, a lone and not very effective mortal, even if he prostrates and humbles himself in heartfelt prayer? Probably not, the Sumerian teachers would have answered. As they saw it, gods were like mortal rulers and no doubt had more important things to attend to; and so as in the case of kings, man must have an intermediary to intercede in his behalf, one whom the gods would be willing to hear and favor. As a result, the Sumerian thinkers contrived and evolved the notion of a personal god, a kind of good angel to each particular individual and family head, his divine father who had begot him, as it were. It was to him, to his personal deity, that the individual sufferer bared his heart in prayer and supplication, and it was through him that he found his salvation.[4]

1. Characterize the Sumerian image of the gods.
2. Why were personal gods so important to the Sumerians?

SPECULATIONS

1. Explain what you think prompted people to initiate the first civilizations. How do you explain the development of civilizations in different places during the same period of time?

[4]S. N. Kramer, *The Sumerians* (Chicago: University of Chicago Press, 1963).

2. What are the advantages and disadvantages of civilization? Use examples from Egyptian or Near Eastern civilizations.
3. Given the historical conditions of the time, if you were a Persian king in the year 550, how would you organize your empire? Why?

TRANSITIONS

In "The First Civilizations," the nature and beginnings of Western Civilization in the Near East and Egypt are examined. The development of agriculture in these river valleys was the crucial step allowing greater numbers of people to support themselves, enabling the production of surplus food, facilitating specialization, and stimulating the growth of more complex societies. These changes were furthered through the growth of cities and imperial expansion, consolidating the transition to civilized conditions. Early civilizations discovered different ways to deal with the problems of how people relate to each other and to divine forces. Some of the peoples in this area, such as the Egyptians, Assyrians, and Persians, developed large and long-lasting societies, while others, such as the Israelites, left a more influential religious and ethical heritage.

In "The Foundations of Greek Civilization," the focus will shift north to Greece, where a highly urbanized and extraordinarily sophisticated civilization developed.

TWO
THE FOUNDATIONS
OF GREEK CIVILIZATION

MAIN THEMES

1. Early Greek civilization was dominated by Crete (the Minoan civilization) and independent city-states (most prominently, Mycenae). This age was brought to a close by the Dorian invasions around 1100, which ushered in a Dark Age of some 300 years.
2. Greek civilization revived after 800, as indicated by the flowering of Homeric epic poetry, the establishment of numerous Greek colonies, the development of an unusual set of religious beliefs, and the creation of uniquely Hellenistic literature and art.
3. Greek political, social, and economic life was centered around the *polis*, whose organization and government evolved into different forms over time, as exemplified by the contrasting Spartan and Athenian experiences.

OUTLINE AND SUMMARY

I. Early Greece.

Between about 3000 to 1100 Bronze Age kingdoms rose and flourished in the Greek world.

A. Cretan Civilization.

Brought to light by the excavations of Sir Arthur Evans at Knossos, Cretan (Minoan) civilization flourished between 2600 and 1200. Crete became a thriving maritime power that traded throughout the eastern Mediterranean and reached its height between 1500 and 1400. Its buildings were extraordinarily sophisticated (Palace of Minos, plumbing), its art unusually colorful and graceful (pottery), and its culture especially peaceful (sports, dancing, games). Women played an important role in Cretan society. Their Linear A and Linear B writing tablets have survived, and the latter have been deciphered and evidence a Greek influence toward the civilization's end. Around 1380 some sort of violent disaster, perhaps the combined effects of earthquakes and rebellions, engulfed Cretan cities; thereafter the Greek city of Mycenae rose in power and prosperity.

B. Mycenaean Civilization (ca. 1600–1100 B.C.).

The mountainous geography helped split the Greeks (the Hellenes) into independent political communities. The proximity of the sea and natural harbors probably turned them into sailors and traders. By 1600 Greeks had established a number of prosperous city-states; until its fall around 1100, Mycenae was the most prominent. As revealed by excavated graves and monuments and by Linear B tablets, Mycenae was a rich, warlike kingdom. The other city-states were probably independent under their own kings, though they once seem to have formed a league against Troy, a prosperous city in Asia Minor. Excavations of Troy by Schliemann support at least parts of Homer's accounts of the Greek expedition against Troy. The Mycenaean Age was brought to a close around 1100 by invaders, perhaps Dorians, ending forever the domination of palace-centered kings. From 1100 to 800, Greece entered a Dark Age, her culture disintegrating to the point of a loss of writing skills.

II. The Greek Renaissance (ca. 800–606 B.C.).

Greek culture and civilization revived after the Dark Age.

A. Epic Poetry.

The Dark Age followed the collapse of the Mycenaean world. After 800 the Greeks gained a new sense of optimism and adventure, as indicated by the appearance of epic poetry ascribed to Homer: the *Iliad* and the *Odyessey*. Scholars disagree over who wrote these poems; perhaps one or two poets united several sagas into these two epics. The Homeric epics would provide the prime inspiration for Greek literature and would influence authors in subsequent civilizations.

B. Greek Religion.

The Homeric epics reveal the nature of Greek religion. Greek gods were anthropomorphic beings with distinct personalities who intervened actively in human affairs. Greek religion did not include a rigorous religious code of behavior or a separate priestly class. Religion served to support the life of individual cities. It also supported a common Panhellenic culture throughout Greece, as did the Panhellenic games and the Delphic oracle.

C. Colonization.

Between 750 and 600 Greeks, perhaps because of a growing population and limited resources, established colonies throughout the Mediterranean. This resulted in growing trade and prosperity and the adaptation of foreign influences, such as the Phoenician alphabet.

D. Archaic Literature.

Greek poets adapted the legacy of the Homeric epics to create a more personal literature, as with Hesiod's *Work and Days*, Sappho's lyric poetry, and Pindar's choral odes.

E. Archaic Greek Art.

Although influenced by other cultures, the Greeks developed their own Hellenistic pottery, sculpture, and architecture. This can be seen in the changed style of vase painting, the freestanding marble statue, and the public temple.

III. The Polis.

A. Government and Economic Life.

The independent city-state, the *polis*, consisted of a city built around a citadel (*akrópolis*), the surrounding area of farms, and its community of citizens. In the early *poleis* local kings were powerful, but by 700 they had generally been replaced by landowning oligarchies who governed through assemblies. In the seventh and sixth centuries, political power spread to the poorer classes, as indicated by new legal codes. At this time, also, "tyrants" such as Cypselus emerged to challenge the rule of the aristocrats. Economic life was predominantly agricultural, but homeland Greeks often relied on trade and colonization to feed themselves. Manual labor was looked down upon by citizens; slaves and foreigners were relied on, particularly for craft and industrial labor. Most major public expenses were assigned to the rich.

B. Life in the Polis.

Although Greek city-states had influential landed families, there was no hereditary nobility. Social mobility was relatively fluid. Women in Greek literature and religion, such as Penelope, Clytemnestra, Antigone, and Athena, were relatively free and respected. In Greek society women played more limited roles—in the middle classes primarily as housewives, in the lower classes often as low-status workers. Home life was simple and inexpensive. Civil life was an extension of personal life; Greeks spent much of their free time in public places and were often expected to contribute to public affairs.

C. Sparta.

Sparta, the leader of the Dorian states in the Peloponnesus, became a rigid, militaristic oligarchy in the seventh century, in response to population problems and in order to control the numerous Messenians it subjected to farming. Spartan society was strictly divided into pure Spartans, Periokoi (other citizens of lower rank), and helots (conquered Messenians and other near slaves). Sparta rigorously trained its children, avoided foreign contacts, and did not encourage development of the arts. Yet it became an interesting political model and a symbol of tenacity and strength.

D. Athens.

Athens, an unusually large and commercial polis, experimented politically more than any other city-state. Before 683, Athens was ruled by a king and his advisers. Over the next 200 years there were various reforms, usually resulting in increasing participation by male citizens in public affairs. Institutions, such as the Areopagus and the board of archons, broadened in the 600s. In 621 Draco instituted legal reforms. Reacting to growing agricultural problems, Solon instituted a series of reforms in 594 that freed peasants from agricultural debts, prevented civil war, and ended privileges based on birth (but not property). In the middle of the sixth century Pisistratus seized power, weakened the power of the aristocracy, encouraged industry and trade, and initiated a program of public works. Around 508 Cleisthenes instituted far-reaching reforms, reorganizing Athens socially and politically. More male citizens became directly involved in government and the judicial system, often holding important offices through rotation of service or election by lot.

Experiences of Daily Life: The Greek Agora.

In Greek cities such as Athens, the agora, a sacred open space, served as a civic center or main public square.

SIGNIFICANT INDIVIDUALS

Political Leaders

Lycurgus, a legendary Spartan lawgiver.

Draco (ca. 621), Athenian lawgiver.

Solon (638?–559?), Athenian lawgiver.

Pisistratus (590?–527), Athenian tyrant.

Cleisthenes (ca. 508), Athenian lawgiver.

Poets

Homer (8th century?), epic poet.

Hesiod (ca. 700), epic poet.

Sappho of Lesbos (ca. 600), lyric poet.

Pindar of Thebes (518–438), lyric poet.

Archaeologists

Sir Arthur Evans (1851–1941), excavations in Crete.

Heinrich Schliemann (1822–1890), excavations in Troy, Mycenae.

IDENTIFICATION

Palace of Minos

Linear B

Trojan War

Dorian invasions

the *Iliad*

Panhellenic games

polis

"tyrants"

helots

archons

Cleisthenes' *demokratia*

Council of 500

CHRONOLOGICAL DIAGRAM

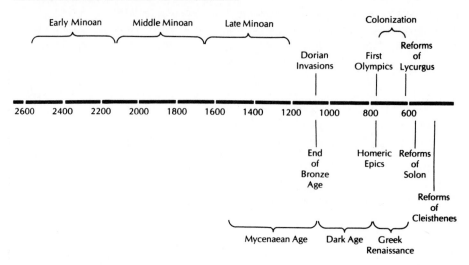

MAP EXERCISE

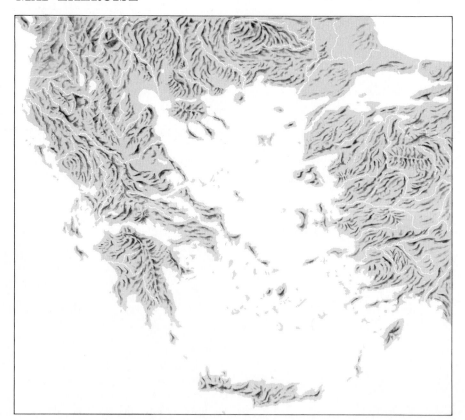

1. Indicate the approximate location of Mycenae, Crete, Troy, Sparta, Athens, Ionia, Miletus, Peloponnesus, Attica, and the Aegean Sea.
2. Compare this map with the one in Chapter 1. Describe the geographic differences and indicate how these might relate to differences between the societies of the Near East and those of Greece.

PROBLEMS FOR ANALYSIS

I. Early Greece.

1. Compare the Cretan and Mycenaean civilizations. What evidence is there of contact between these two civilizations?
2. In what ways did Greece enter a Dark Age between 1100 and 800? Was this an unmitigated disaster? Why?

II. The Greek Renaissance.

1. Analyze the religious and cultural importance of the Homeric epics.
2. In what ways did colonization lead to significant changes in Greek economic, social, and political life?
3. Analyze some of the main themes of Archaic literature.

III. The Polis.

1. What was the significance of Greek attitudes toward various kinds of work? How did these attitudes affect Greek social and cultural life?
2. Analyze the position of women in Greek society.
3. Compare Sparta and Athens. What were the advantages and disadvantages of the various political and social choices these two city-states made?
4. Trace the development of more democratic institutions in Athens. What were the main problems in shaping this development?

DOCUMENTS

Seventh-Century Sparta

Much of what we know about seventh-century Sparta comes from later sources. One of the fullest of these is a study of Lycurgus written by the Greek biographer Plutarch (A.D. 46?–120?). In the following excerpt, Plutarch describes changes in the system of property initiated by Lycurgus.

> A second and bolder political enterprise of Lycurgus was a new division of the lands. For he found a prodigious inequality, the city overcharged with many indigent persons, who had no land, and the wealth centred in the hands of a few. Determined, therefore, to root out the evils of insolence, envy, avarice, and luxury, and those

distempers of a state still more inveterate and fatal, I mean poverty and riches, he persuaded them to cancel all former divisions of land, and to make new ones, in such a manner that they might be perfectly equal in their possessions and way of living. Hence, if they were ambitious of distinction they might seek it in virtue, as no other difference was left between them but that which arises from the dishonour of base actions and the praise of good ones. His proposal was put in practice. . . .

After this, he attempted to divide also the movables, in order to take away all appearance of inequality; but he soon perceived that they could not bear to have their goods directly taken from them, and therefore took another method, counterworking their avarice by a stratagem. First he stopped the currency of the gold and silver coin, and ordered that they should make use of iron money only, then to a great quantity and weight of this he assigned but a small value; so that to lay up ten *minae,* a whole room was required, and to remove it, nothing less than a yoke of oxen. When this became current, many kinds of injustice ceased in Lacedaemon. Who would steal or take a bribe, who would defraud or rob, when he could not conceal the booty; when he could neither be dignified by the possession of it, nor if cut in pieces be served by its use? For we are told that when hot, they quenched it in vinegar, to make it brittle and unmalleable, and consequently unfit for any other service. In the next place, he excluded unprofitable and superfluous arts: indeed, if he had not done this, most of them would have fallen of themselves, when the new money took place, as the manufactures could not be disposed of. Their iron coin would not pass in the rest of Greece, but was ridiculed and despised; so that the Spartans had no means of purchasing any foreign or curious wares; nor did any merchant-ship unlade in their harbours. There were not even to be found in all their country either sophists, wandering fortune-tellers, keepers of infamous houses, or dealers in gold and silver trinkets, because there was no money. Thus luxury, losing by degrees the means that cherished and supported it, died away of itself: even they who had great possessions, had no advantage from them, since they could not be displayed in public, but must lie useless, in unregarded repositories.[1]

1. What social and economic problems were such reforms designed to solve?
2. What might be the economic and social consequences of such reforms?

An Athenian Gentleman

Xenophon was a fifth-century Athenian aristocrat who served as a soldier and statesman and was an associate of Socrates. In the following selection from *Oeconomicus,* Xenophon describes the everyday life of a successful Athenian gentleman.

"Why, then, Socrates, my habit is to rise from bed betimes, when I may still expect to find at home this, that, or the other friend whom I may wish to see. Then, if anything has to be done in town, I set off to transact the business and make that my walk; or if there is no business to transact in town, my serving boy leads on my horse to the farm; I follow, and so make the country road my walk, which suits my purpose quite as well or better, Socrates, perhaps, than pacing up and down the colonnade [in the city]. Then when I have reached the farm, where mayhap some of my men are planting

[1] Henry Morley, ed., *Ideal Commonwealths* (London: George Routledge and Sons, 1890), pp. 19–21.

trees, or breaking fallow, sowing, or getting in the crops, I inspect their various labors with an eye to every detail, and whenever I can improve upon the present system, I introduce reform.

"After this, usually I may mount my hourse and take a canter. I put him through his paces, suiting these, so far as possible to those inevitable in war—in other words, I avoid neither steep slope, nor sheer incline, neither trench nor runnel, only giving my uttermost heed the while so as not to lame my horse while exercising him. When that is over, the boy gives the horse a roll, and leads him homeward, taking at the same time from the country to town whatever we may chance to need. Meanwhile I am off for home, partly walking, partly running, and having reached home I take a bath and give myself a rub—and then I breakfast—a repast that leaves me neither hungry nor overfed, and will suffice me through the day." [2]

1. Describe the economic concerns of this Athenian gentleman.
2. What social and economic distinctions are shown here to exist in Athens?

Athenian Values

The Greek historian Herodotus traveled throughout the ancient world. In the following account he recreates a meeting between the Athenian lawmaker Solon and the sixty-century Lydian king Croesus, who was of great reputed wealth.

30. On this account, as well as to see the world, Solon set out upon his travels, in the course of which he went to Egypt to the court of Amasis, and also came on a visit to Croesus at Sardis. Croesus received him as his guest, and lodged him in the royal palace. On the third or fourth day after, he bade his servants conduct Solon over his treasuries, and show him all their greatness and magnificence. When he had seen them all, and, so far as time allowed, inspected them, Croesus addressed this question to him, "Stranger of Athens, we have heard much of your wisdom and of your travels through many lands, from love of knowledge and a wish to see the world. I am curious therfore to inquire of you, whom, of all the men that you have seen, you consider the most happy?" This he asked because he thought himself the happiest of mortals: but Solon answered him without flattery, according to his true sentiments, "Tellus of Athens, sire." Full of astonishment at what he heard, Croesus demanded sharply, "And wherefore do you deem Tellus happiest?" To which the other replied, "First, because his country was flourishing in his days, and he himself had sons both beautiful and good, and he lived to see children born to each of them, and these children all grew up; and further because, after a life spent in what our people look upon as comfort, his end was surpassingly glorious. In a battle between the Athenians and their neighbours near Eleusis, he came to the assistance of his countrymen, routed the foe, and died upon the field most gallantly. The Athenians gave him a public funeral on the spot where he fell, and paid him the highest honours.

". . . For assuredly he who possesses great store or riches is no nearer happiness than he who has what suffices for his daily needs, unless luck attend upon him, and so he continue in the enjoyment of all his good things to the end of life. For many of the wealthiest men have been unfavoured of fortune, and many whose means were moderate, have had excellent luck. Men of the former class excel those of the latter but in

---

[2] Xenophon, "Oeconomicus," trans. H. G. Dakyns, in *Readings in Ancient History* (Boston: Allyn and Bacon, 1912), p. 271.

two respects; these last excel the former in many. The wealthy man is better able to content his desires, and to bear up against a sudden buffet of calamity. The other has less ability to withstand these evils (from which, however, his good luck keeps him clear), but he enjoys all these following blessings: he is whole of limb, a stranger to disease, free from misfortune, happy in his children, and comely to look upon. If, in addition to all this, he end his life well, he is of a truth the man of whom you are in search, the man who may rightly be termed happy. Call him, however, until he die, not happy but fortunate. Scarcely, indeed, can any man unite all these advantages: as there is no country which contains within it all that it needs, but each, while it possesses some things, lacks others, and the best country is that which contains the most; so no single human being is complete in every respect—something is always lacking. He who unites the greatest number of advantages, and retaining them to the day of his death, then dies peaceably, that man alone, sire, is, in my judgment, entitled to bear the name of 'happy.' But in every matter we must mark well the end; for oftentimes God gives men a gleam of happiness, and then plunges them into ruin."

1. What does this selection reveal about Greek values?
2. How does Herodotus perceive Croesus and, by implication, Near Eastern civilization?

Slavery in Greece

In the following selection, M. I. Finley interprets the role played by slaves in Greek civilization.

Now we observe that a sizable fraction of the population of the Greek world consisted of slaves, or other kinds of dependent labour, many of them barbarians; that by and large the elite in each city-state were men of leisure, completely free from any preoccupation with economic matters, thanks to a labour force which they bought and sold, over whom they had extensive property rights, and, equally important, what we may call physical rights; that the condition of servitude was one which no man, woman, or child, regardless of status or wealth, could be sure to escape in case of war or some other unpredictable and uncontrollable emergency. It seems to me that, seeing all this, if we could emancipate ourselves from the despotism of extraneous moral, intellectual, and political pressures, we would conclude, without hesitation, that slavery was a basic element in Greek civilization.

. . . With little exception, there was no activity, productive or unproductive, public or private, pleasant or unpleasant, which was not performed by slaves at some times and in some places in the Greek world. The major exception was, of course, political: no slave held public office or sat on the deliberative and judicial bodies (though slaves were commonly employed in the "civil service," as secretaries and clerks, and as policemen and prison attendants). Slaves did not fight as a rule either, unless freed (although helots apparently did), and they were very rare in the liberal professions, including medicine.[4]

---

[3] Herodotus, *The Persian Wars,* trans. George Rawlinson (New York: Random House, 1942), pp. 16–19.

[4] M. I. Finley, "Was Greek Civilization Based on Slave Labour?" *Historia,* VIII (Wiesbaden, Germany: Franz Steiner Verlag, 1959).

1. Is it fair to conclude that slavery was a basic element in Greek civilization? Why?
2. Was slavery in ancient Greece based solely on racial discrimination? Explain.

Law in the Polis

In the following selection, M. I. Finley deals with law and freedom as they evolved in ancient Greece.

> The question then arises, if the *polis* had such limitless authority, in what sense were the Greeks free men, as they believed themselves to be? Up to a point their answer was given in the epigram, "The law is king." Freedom was not equated with anarchy but with an ordered existence within a community which was governed by an established code respected by all. That was what had been fought for through much of the archaic period, first against the traditional privilege and monopoly of power possessed by the nobility, then against the unchecked power of the tyrants. The fact that the community was the sole source of law was a guarantee of freedom. On that all could agree, but the translation of the principle into practice was another matter; it brought the classical Greeks up against a difficulty which has persisted in political theory without firm resolution ever since. How free was the community to alter its established laws? If the laws could be changed at will, and that means by whichever faction or group held a commanding position in the state at any given moment, did that not amount to anarchy, to undermining the very stability and certainty which were implicit in the doctrine that the law was king? [5]

1. In what sense were the Greeks free people?
2. Considering the issues raised in this selection, and the material on the political evolution of Greece, how free was the community to alter its established laws?

SPECULATIONS

1. How do you explain the development of such an extraordinary civilization by the Greeks? Do you think much of the credit belongs to some sort of Greek "spirit," or were geographic factors more important?
2. Should Greek civilization before 500 be considered superior to Near Eastern civilizations, or simply different? How do you evaluate this?

TRANSITIONS

In "The First Civilizations," the origins of Western Civilization in the Near East and Egypt were examined.

In "The Foundations of Greek Civilization," focus is shifted to the Aegean area. The Greeks viewed the world and human affairs in extraordinarily natural,

[5] M. I. Finley, *The Ancient Greeks* (New York: The Viking Press, 1963), pp. 41–42.

rational, and secular terms. Greek philosophy helped create a common cultural tradition for the Western experience. Living in independent city-states, Greeks experienced changing political forms, democracy eventually spreading to an unprecedented degree. The evolution of Greek civilization, from the Minoans and Mycenaeans to the Spartans and Athenians, is traced, with emphasis on the later political developments in Athens and cultural accomplishments.

In "Classical and Hellenistic Greece," developments in Greece and the Near East during the fifth, fourth, and third centuries will be examined.

THREE
CLASSICAL AND
HELLENISTIC GREECE

MAIN THEMES

1. The Greeks unified themselves and gained stunning victories over the invading Persians, thereby preserving their independence.
2. After the Persian Wars, Athens rose to dominance in the Greek world, attaining its height during the Age of Pericles.
3. The Peloponnesian War proved disastrous for Athens and many other Greek city-states.
4. Philip II and Alexander III took advantage of the disunity among the Greek city-states and brought Macedonia to dominance in Greece. Alexander III led a force that conquered the Persian Empire
5. Athens produced extraordinarily creative dramatists, historians, architects, sculptors, and philosophers during the Classical Age (500–323).
6. The period between the death of Alexander and that of Cleopatra is called the Hellenistic Age, a period in which Greeks transformed their culture and institutions in the wider, cosmopolitan environment of the East.

OUTLINE AND SUMMARY

I. *The Challenge of Persia.*

By about 500, most Greek states were no longer ruled by kings.

A. *Invasions of Greece (490 and 480–479 B.C.).*

Angered by Athenian support of the Ionian Revolt (499), Darius of Persia attacked the Athenians at Marathon and Athens in 490. He suffered stinging losses. For the next decade Darius and his successor, Xerxes, planned and prepared for a much greater attack. Meanwhile Athens, at the urging of Themistocles, built up its navy and allied itself with some thirty city-states under Spartan leadership. The first battle was at Thermopylae in 480, a costly Persian victory.

B. *Greek Victory.*

The Persians burned an abandoned Athens but succumbed to the strategy of Themistocles, who led the Greeks to a stunning naval victory at Salamis. In 479 the Greeks decisively defeated the Persian army at Plataea and then at Mycale in Asia Minor.

II. The Supremacy of Athens.

During the half century following the Persian Wars, Athens dominated the Greek world politically and commercially, while domestically its democratic institutions flourished.

A. The Athenian Empire.

In 478–477, a number of city-states, under the leadership of Athens, formed a confederation — the Delian League — for protection and continued war against Persia. By the 450s the league had succeeded against Persia and evolved into the Athenian Empire, with Athens being the beneficiary of contributions to the treasury.

B. The Age of Pericles.

Athens reached her height during the Age of Pericles (459–429). Pericles, an aristocratic leader who functioned as champion of the masses, focused on Sparta rather than Persia as the threat of the future, rebuilt the Acropolis, strengthened the Athenian Empire through aggressive imperialism, and encouraged further democratization of the Athenian judicial system.

III. The Peloponnesian War (427–404 B.C.).

A. The War Years.

In the 430s provocative actions by the Athenians led the Peloponnesian League, headed by Sparta, to declare a preventive war on Athens. Lasting for almost thirty years, the Peloponnesian War pitted the dominant Greek naval power, the Athenian Empire, against the dominant Greek land power, the Peloponnesian League. Years of indecisive but costly struggle and missed opportunities for peace were ended in 413, when Athens lost a crucial naval and land battle in an ambitious expedition against Syracuse, in Sicily. Athens fought on for nine more years until it was decisively beaten by Sparta. Athens lost its empire, most of its navy, and much of its trade. Political leadership and vitality were diminished. Athenian intellectuals became pessimistic, particularly about democracy, as is revealed in its political philosophy. In general, the Greek poleis were weakened by a long-lasting loss of manpower and leadership.

IV. The Rise of Macedonia.

A. The Era of Hegemonies.

During the 300s, the Greek city-states, principally Athens, Thebes, and Sparta, fought among themselves for dominance, each experiencing gains and losses.

B. The Monarchs of Macedonia.

By 338, Philip II, through clever use of aggression and diplomacy, had led Macedonia to dominance over most of the important Greek city-states (with the exception of Sparta). After his assassination in 336, his son Alexander carried out his plans to invade Persia. By the time of his death in 323, Alexander had defeated the decaying Persian Empire and established his rule from Egypt and Greece in the West to the Indus River in the East.

V. Classical Greek Culture.

A. Greek Drama.

Athens was preeminent culturally in the Classical Age of Greece (500–323). Drawing on familiar tales and characters in mythology, Greek dramatists embodied religion and culture in their works. The finest dramatists dealt with such themes as the nature of justice (Aeschylus, the *Oresteia*), enduring psychological complex (Sophocles, *Oedipus the King*), and how the inner workings of a person's mind and emotions shape individual destiny (Euripides, *Medea*).

B. Comedy.

Aristophanes (*Knights*) satirized political and social life in his comedies, providing us with insights into everyday life in classical Athens.

C. Historical Writing.

The Greeks produced the first serious analytic historian in the person of Herodotus. He compared Greek and Persian cultures to explain the Persian Wars. Thucydides (*History of the Peloponnesian War*) became the standard among ancient historians, analyzing the Peloponnesian War as a coldly realistic pursuit of power and depicting the decline of Athens after Pericles' death.

D. Art and Architecture.

Architecture and sculpture became the leading art forms of the fifth century. Architects perfected the proportions and details of the temple. Sculpture became progressively more realistic and humanistic, as exemplified by the statuary and decorative frieze of the Parthenon.

E. Philosophy.

The Greeks developed philosophy—the attempt to use reason to discover why things are as they are. The first Greek philosophers were citizens of Miletus, an extraordinarily commercial and wealthy city, whose location in Ionia enabled it to have direct contact with the ideas and achievements of the Near East. Milesians such as Thales and Anaximander developed answers to the question "What exists?" by pointing to common primal elements. Others, such as Pythagoras of Samos, turned to the study of numbers to answer this question.

F. The Sophists and Socrates.

The first fifth-century philosophers were Sophists, who emphasized the study of homo sapiens and how intellectual activity could be turned to practical advantage.

Their ideas were an attack on accepted beliefs. Socrates (469–399) combined a reasoned pursuit of the truth through relentless questioning (the Socratic method) with ethics, thereby making him a critic of the Sophists.

G. Plato and Aristotle.

Socrates' pupil Plato (428–347) dealt with some of the most profound issues of political philosophy, the theory of knowledge, and the nature of reality. He proposed a utopian state (*The Republic*), which would be strictly ordered and ruled by philosopher kings. His pupil Aristotle (384–322) had encyclopedic interests. Most importantly, his approach was empirical, drawing generalizations from large numbers of facts and observations (*Politics, Ethics*). After Aristotle, Greek philosophy became narrower in focus.

VI. The Hellenistic Age (323–30 B.C.).

A. Dissolution of Alexander's Empire.

From the death of Alexander to that of Cleopatra in Egypt two centuries later, the Greeks and their culture spread in the East (Hellenization). Alexander's empire was carved up into three kingdoms ruled by descendents of three of his generals: Macedonia under the Antigonids, Egypt under the Ptolemies, and western Asia under the Seleucids. Many Greek city-states, supported by defensive leagues (Aetolian, Achaean), were able to acquire considerable independence. Continual warfare typified the next two centuries, as did the dominance of Greeks in leadership positions.

B. Economic Life.

The Greeks, supported by Hellenistic kings and bankers, brought talent and capital into the economic life. They helped improve transportation facilities and expand the size of commercial and industrial enterprises. They introduced new crops and techniques in agriculture. As a result, the Hellenistic states experienced economic growth. Yet, all did not benefit from this new prosperity; most of the wealth went into the hands of the upper classes, and mainland Greece lost much of its commercial prosperity.

C. Hellenistic Cities.

Cosmopolitan cities of unprecedented size, such as those in western Asia and Alexandria in Egypt, dominated Hellenistic civilization as centers of government, trade, and culture. In these cities Greeks established modified forms of their temples, theaters, gymnasiums, schools, language, and political institutions. The age was characterized by the cosmopolitanism of Hellenistic cities and growing professionalism.

D. Literature, Art, and Science.

Poetry became much more lyrical and individualistic. Scholarship, especially around the library in Alexandria, grew in importance. Architecture and sculpture became grandiose, emotional, and realistic (Altar of Zeus in Pergamum). Advances were made in science that would not be surpassed for centuries (Euclid, geometry; Archimedes, mathematics and physics; Aristarchus, mathematics and astronomy).

E. Philosophy and Religion.

Philosophy, mainly for the intellectual elite, was to be dominated by Epicureanism and Stoicism, both of which were individualistic. Epicurus (341–270) believed that people should avoid anxiety by leading pleasurable, tranquil lives. For the most part, this meant withdrawal and avoidance of physical and mental pain rather than self-indulgence. Zeno (335–263), and later, the Stoics, emphasized universal brotherhood and the virtues of tolerance, patience in adversity, self-discipline, and justice toward the less fortunate members of the human race—a philosophy that was influential among the educated into Roman times. For the masses, Eastern religions came to dominate, especially ritualistic and emotional mystery cults centering on the worship of a redeeming savior and deities, such as Yahweh. Christianity grew from these Persian and Jewish origins.

Experiences of Daily Life: Slavery

Slavery was common and accepted in the ancient world. Slaves were usually acquired by conquest, and their conditions of life and options for freedom varied greatly. Slavery declined during the later Roman Empire.

SIGNIFICANT INDIVIDUALS

Political Leaders

Darius (521–486), king of Persia.
Xerxes (486–465), king of Persia.
Pericles (490?–429), Athenian statesman.
Alcibiades (450–404), Athenian statesman.

Philip II (359–336), king of Macedonia.
Alexander III (336–323), king of Macedonia.
Darius III (336–330), king of Persia.

Dramatists

Aeschylus (525?–456), Athenian.
Sophocles (496?–406), Athenian.

Euripides (480?–406?), Athenian.
Aristophanes (448?–385?), Athenian.

Historians

Herodotus (484?–425?), Greek.

Thucydides (455?–399?), Athenian.

Philosophers

Thales of Miletus (640?–546), scientist.

Anaximander of Miletus (611?–547?), astronomer.

Pythagoras of Samos (ca. 530), mathematician.

Protagoras (5th century), Greek Sophist.

Socrates (469–399), Athenian.

Plato (428–347), Athenian.

Aristotle (384–322), Athenian.

Zeno (335–263), Greek.

Epicurus (341–270), Greek.

Astronomers

Aristarchus (3rd century), Greek.

Hipparchus (190?–after 126), Greek.

Eratosthenes (275?–194?), Greek.

Ptolemy of Alexandria (ca. A.D. 140), Greek.

Others

Demosthenes (385?–322), Athenian orator.

Theocritus (3rd century), Greek poet.

Euclid (ca. 300), Greek geometer.

Archimedes (287?–212), Greek mathematician.

CHRONOLOGICAL DIAGRAM

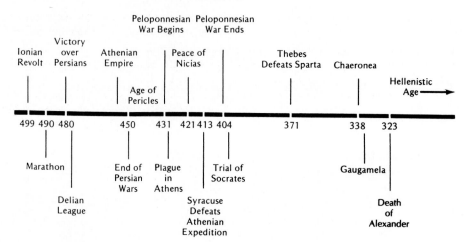

IDENTIFICATION

Ionian Revolt

Salamis

Delian League

Peloponnesian League

the *Oresteia*

Melian Dialogue

Sophists

Socratic method

The Republic
Idealism
Hellenization

Stoicism
Epicureanism
mystery cults

MAP EXERCISE

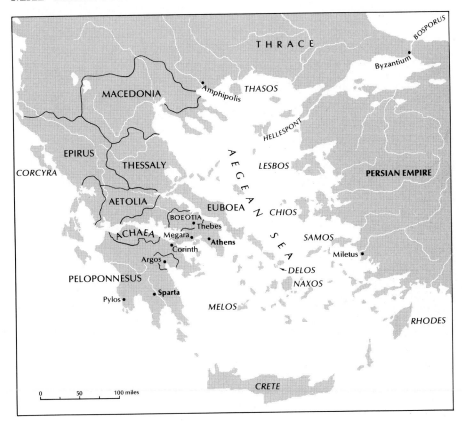

1. Indicate (by shading) the principal Athenian and Spartan allies during the Peloponnesian War.

PROBLEMS FOR ANALYSIS

I. *The Challenge of Persia.*

1. How do you explain the Greek victory over the Persians, despite the overwhelming odds?

II. The Supremacy of Athens.

1. How was Athens able to rise to such a position of leadership in the Greek world? How did its role in the Persian Wars contribute to this? How important was Pericles?

III. The Peloponnesian War.

1. Considering that Athens survived and remained independent, what was so particularly disastrous about the Peloponnesian War?

IV. The Rise of Macedonia.

1. "The Macedonian conquest of Greece was really a blessing in disguise." Do you agree? Explain.

V. Classical Greek Culture.

1. In what ways does Greek drama reflect characteristics of Greek culture as well as universal human problems?
2. Trace the evolution of Greek philosophy from its beginnings in the seventh century B.C. to Aristotle in the fourth century B.C. What historical trends in Athenian life does this evolution reflect?

VI. The Hellenistic Age.

1. Compare the Classical Age with the Hellenistic Age. What are the main differences?
2. How did the spread of Greeks into the East affect those areas? What were the economic and cultural consequences of Hellenization?
3. Some people argue that literature, art, science, and philosophy did not decline after the fourth century, but that they simply turned to other styles and concerns equally legitimate as those of the earlier period. Do you agree?

DOCUMENTS

Athens at Its Height

Athens' greatest historian, Thucydides, reported a eulogy delivered by the Athenian leader Pericles following the early campaigns of the Peloponnesian War. As part of this funeral oration, Pericles explains to his fellow Athenians the things that made Athens so great and worthy of pride.

> But what was the road by which we reached our position, what the form of government under which our greatness grew, what the national habits out of which it sprang; these are questions which I may try to solve before I proceed to my panegyric upon

these men; since I think this to be a subject upon which on the present occasion a speaker may properly dwell, and to which the whole assemblage, whether citizens or foreigners, may listen with advantage.

Our constitution does not copy the laws of neighbouring states; we are rather a pattern to others than imitators ourselves. Its administration favours the many instead of the few; this is why it is called a democracy. If we look to the laws, they afford equal justice to all in their private differences; if to social standing, advancement in public life falls to reputation for capacity, class considerations not being allowed to interfere with merit; nor again does poverty bar the way, if a man is able to serve the state, he is not hindered by the obscurity of his condition. The freedom which we enjoy in our government extends also to our ordinary life. There, far from exercising a jealous surveillance over each other, we do not feel called upon to be angry with our neighbour for doing what he likes, or even to indulge in those injurious looks which cannot fail to be offensive, although they inflict no positive penalty. But all this ease in our private relations does not make us lawless as citizens. Against this fear is our chief safeguard, teaching us to obey the magistrates and the laws, particularly such as regard the protection of the injured, whether they are actually on the statute book, or belong to that code which, although unwritten, yet cannot be broken without acknowledged disgrace.

Further, we provide plenty of means for the mind to refresh itself from business. We celebrate games and sacrifices all the year round, and the elegance of our private establishments forms a daily source of pleasure and helps to banish the spleen; while the magnitude of our city draws the produce of the world into our harbour, so that to the Athenian the fruits of other countries are as familiar a luxury as those of his own.

If we turn to our military policy, there also we differ from our antagonists. We throw open our city to the world, and never by alien acts exclude foreigners from any opportunity of learning or observing, although the eyes of an enemy may occasionally profit by our liberality; trusting less in system and policy than to the native spirit of our citizens; while in education, where our rivals from their very cradles by a painful discipline seek after manliness, at Athens we live exactly as we please, and yet are just as ready to encounter every legitimate danger.

. . . We cultivate refinement without extravagance and knowledge without effeminacy; wealth we employ more for use than for show, and place the real disgrace of poverty not in owning to the fact but in declining the struggle against it. Our public men have, besides politics, their private affairs to attend to, and our ordinary citizens, though occupied with the pursuits of industry, are still fair judges of public matters; for, unlike any other nation, regarding him who takes no part in these duties not as unambitious but as useless, we Athenians are able to judge at all events if we cannot originate, and instead of looking on discussion as a stumbling-block in the way of action, we think it an indispensable preliminary to any wise action at all. [1]

1. Suppose this was the only document about fifth-century Athens that survived. What conclusions would you draw from it about Athens, its institutions, and its people? Considering other information you have about fifth-century Athens, how accurate would your conclusions be?
2. Do you think that Pericles, a general and a politician, is being unrealistically boastful or justly proud? Why?

[1] Thucydides, "History of the Peloponnesian War," trans. Richard Crawley, in Brian Tierney, Donald Kagan, and L. Pearce Williams, eds., *Great Issues in Western Civilization,* Vol. I, 2nd edition (New York: Random House, 1972), pp. 68–69.

Conformity and the Supernatural in Greece

Most historians understandably stress the intellectual and scientific accomplishments of the ancient Greeks, above all, their extraordinary use of reason. In the following selection, Finley Hooper puts this into the more ordinary historical context of the supernatural and the demand to conform, which typified everyday life for most Greeks.

A frequently repeated exaggeration about the ancient Greeks is that statement that they made a religion out of reason. The statement is dangerously misleading because it fails to emphasize two points which may be of interest in the continuing debate over the role of the intellectual in a popular democracy. To begin with, only a small minority of Greeks ever abandoned the magical, mythological and supernatural common beliefs in favor of a speculative approach toward the universe around them or their own behavior in it. Speculation about the origin of all that exists, the conflict between being and becoming and the essence of virtue, is not a popular pastime. The vast majority of human beings in all places at all times have spent most of their existence in the honorable but routine process of making a living. The majority of the Greeks were no exception and they never gave up their belief in a god of the winds or a god of the sea. They lived, as do most Greeks in the modern world, by instinct, habit and faith. . . .

Secondly, the minority, insofar as it gave expression to views contrary to accepted beliefs, was no more popular in Greece than such a minority has ever been anywhere. At the height of the Periclean democracy in the fifth century, the philosopher Anaxagoras was driven from the city on the charge of atheism. There may have been some politics involved, but even if the charge of atheism was a smokescreen for the real reason, it was apparently calculated to win popular support.

Much more agreeable to the popular viewpoint were the comedies of Aristophanes, which pictured the sophistic intellectuals of the fifth century as undermining the moral structure of society by their persistent doubts and endless quibbling. Aristophanes in his play the *Clouds* presented Socrates as just such a man and his caricature of Socrates is thought to have contributed to the downfall of history's best known freethinker.

. . . For a brief time in certain cities, Athens especially, an atmosphere was provided wherein a tolerated minority of men were free to pursue their doubts and speculations and to keep alert the minds of other men. That they were generally tolerated does not mean that they were liked. Nor were they disliked only for their ideas. Their own persistent quarrelsomeness and frequent obnoxiousness had something to do with it.

This emphasis on the correlation between individual expression and the variety of thought is not intended to suggest that Greek creative works were only produced by those who broke with established convictions. The great dramatic poets, Aeschylus and Sophocles, treated the traditional themes in a respectful and meaningful manner. The building of temples, theaters, and much Greek statuary was a reflection of the desire to honor and offer worship to the gods. Their beauty was inspired by a faith common to a whole people. Yet the traditional and accepted does not of itself admit the diversity which is best gained through tolerance of the experimental, the unusual and the unorthodox. The history of rationalism in Greece is an intellectual tradition and not a popular one. [2]

---

[2] Finley Hooper, *Greek Realities* (New York: Charles Scribner's Sons, 1967), pp. 124–125. Reprinted by permission of Wayne State University Press. Copyright © Wayne State University Press.

1. If this description is correct, then how do you explain both the "tolerance" and the fact of such extraordinary rationalism and nonconformity that characterized Greek civilization?
2. Does this mean that the average Greek of the fifth century was more or less the same as the average Persian or Egyptian of the same period? Why?

SPECULATIONS

1. How does the civilization of fifth- and fourth-century Athens compare with our own? In which would you rather live? Why?
2. Whether or not Alexander had high ideals behind his conquests, he and his followers should be praised, for they infused relatively backward civilizations with more advanced Greek institutions and ideals. Do you agree? Why?
3. It is a mistake to be so admiring of the ancient Greeks. We think highly of their civilization only because it resembles our own in some ways, and we overlook the fact that it was based upon slave labor, the subjection of women, and almost perpetual warfare. Do you agree? Why?

TRANSITIONS

In "The Foundations of Greek Civilization," the evolution of Greek civilization from Minoan and Mycenaean origins to the development of diversified city-states by the end of the sixth century was traced.

In "Classical and Hellenistic Greece," the unexpected victory of the Greeks over the invading Persians brought glory and prosperity but also created a problem of leadership in the Greek world. This led to the long and costly war between Athens and Sparta, which so weakened the Greeks that during the fourth century Philip II and Alexander the Great were able to conquer the Greeks. During these two centuries Greek intellectual and artistic achievements peaked. The victories of Alexander in the East caused an expansion of Greek culture and a fusion of cultures into a new Hellenistic civilization.

In "The Roman Republic," the development of Roman civilization through the first century B.C. will be traced. During this period political dominance over the Mediterranean will shift westward, the Romans ultimately conquering the various parts of the Hellenistic world while absorbing aspects of its culture.

FOUR
THE ROMAN REPUBLIC

MAIN THEMES

1. Through a number of long wars, a series of internal struggles, and a system of confederation, the Romans unified the Italian peninsula under their rule. Plebeians struggled with the long-dominant patricians for political power.
2. Wars and interventions in Africa, Spain, Greece, and Asia Minor made Rome the supreme Mediterranean power.
3. In their religion and culture, Romans were heavily influenced by the Greeks, but they developed their own rites and literature.
4. Between 133 and 31, Rome experienced a slow revolution marked by the rise of powerful men, such as Sulla, Pompey, and Julius Caesar, resulting in the fall of the Republic.
5. Octavian defeated his competitors and brought the Republic to an end.

OUTLINE AND SUMMARY

I. The Unification of Italy (to 264 B.C.).

A. Geography of Italy.

Mountains divide Italy into numerous small valleys. The richest areas are in the center of the country and the Po River valley in the north.

B. The Origins of Rome.

Rome, founded about 625, was at first under the control of the already established Etruscans. The sophisticated Etruscan civilization, influenced by contact with Greeks, flourished until the fourth century, when the Romans, who first freed themselves around 500, finally absorbed it.

C. The Early Constitution.

The Roman Republic was based on an unwritten constitution of customary laws. Rule was divided between the elected magistrates (consuls), the Senate, and the assemblies. However, the family was the real location of power in Roman society.

D. The Struggle of the Orders (494–287 B.C.).

Roman citizens were divided into the patricians, an aristocratic order with a base of power in the Senate, and the plebeians, the majority, who had a right to vote in the assemblies. In a series of struggles, the plebeians gradually gained concessions from the patricians and acquired more influence over Roman political institutions. But for the most part it was wealthy plebeians that gained office and who, along with patricians in the Senate, controlled the more popular institutions.

E. Early Expansion of Rome.

In a series of long and costly wars, sometimes marked by defeats, Rome gained control of the Italian peninsula by 265.

F. The Roman Federation.

Rome effectively administered conquered territory through a system of confederation, which allowed some communities full citizenship, others partial citizenship, and still others allied status.

II. The Age of Imperialism (264–133 B.C.).

A. The Punic Wars.

Between 264 and 146, three wars with Carthage, the major power in the western Mediterranean, established Rome as an imperial power. The second Punic War (219–202) was most significant, as Rome, led by Scipio, defeated Hannibal and took over most of Carthage's territories. In the third Punic War (149–146), Rome destroyed Carthage.

B. Rome's Eastern Wars.

Rome began to intervene in Greece. Philip V of Macedonia brought on the first of four wars with Macedonia when he allied with Hannibal.

1. *Warfare in Asia Minor:* Conflict between Greece and the Syrian Empire in 192 led to Roman intervention and success in Asia Minor.

2. *Annexation of Greece and Asia Minor:* Further wars led Rome to annex Macedonia and Greece in 146. Some twenty years later Rome came into possession of its first Asian province in Pergamum.

C. The Nature of Roman Imperialism.

Thanks to a number of external threats, Rome succeeded in forming alliances with other peoples, which eventually led to the unification of the Italian peninsula. Further perceived threats and a practice of avoiding interference in the internal affairs of subject allies enabled Rome to pursue a ruthless policy of imperialism.

1. *Provincial Administration:* The Senate appointed provincial governors with almost absolute powers. Usually their rule was effective; taxes from these provinces supported Rome.

2. *The Roman Family:* The father was considered the absolute owner of the whole family, with women most praised for their obedience and domestic virtues. Over time, women gained some behind-the-scenes political importance.

3. *Religion:* Within Roman households, the father acted as a priest in the worship of household gods. Public religion was closely connected with the interests of the state. The Romans adapted Greek mythology, giving Greek deities Roman names. Groups of priests ensured respect for custom and order in religious rites.

4. *Earlier Roman Literature:* The Romans, most influenced by Greek literature, developed their own Latin literature. Ennius (239–169), the first to translate the Greek tragedies, was the founder of Latin literature. Dramatists (Plautus and Terence) wrote comedies based on the Greek New Comedy. The Greek Polybius was the most important Hellenistic historian, providing our most reliable guide to earlier Roman history.

III. The Roman Revolution (133–27 B.C.).

A. The Changing World of Italy.

The wars with Carthage impoverished the Italian peasantry. An influx from the East of new wealth, new slaves, and new conditions of farming (specialization in wine) further undermined the position of the small farmer.

B. Strains on the Constitution.

In the 130s, Rome faced a decline in military manpower that was caused by the displacement of small farmers, and a slave revolt threatened grain shortages.

1. *Tiberius and Gaius Gracchus:* Between 133 and 121 these brothers sponsored policies of land redistribution and elevation of the equestrians (a middle class) to greater political power. Retaliation by the Senate led to an increasing number of political murders.

2. *Marius, the First Warlord:* Gaius Marius (157–86) was the first of a series of powerful generals who used his army to gain political power, thereby weakening the Republican system. Marius gained great stature as a successful general and created an army that for the first time included the poor and volunteers. He thus solved some of the problems of displaced farmers and recruitment, while also creating an army rewarded by and loyal to its commander.

3. *The War with the Italians:* Through a guerrilla war (91–88), some Italian tribes were partially successful in gaining citizenship.

4. *Senatorial Reaction Under Sulla:* After a civil war broke out, the Roman general Sulla conquered Rome in 82, became dictator, instituted political and legal reforms to bring back the power and prestige of the Senate, and then resigned from office.

5. *The Rise of Pompey:* Pompey, through successful campaigns from Spain in the West to Syria in the East, succeeded Sulla as Rome's most powerful general. As consul with Crassus, he took away some of the newly reacquired powers of the Senate.

6. *Cicero and Catiline:* Cicero, as consul, succeeded in frustrating a plot by

Catiline to undermine the constitution, but he failed to halt the slow dissolution of the Republic.

7. *The First Triumvirate:* In 59 Pompey combined with another general, Julius Caesar, and with the wealthy Crassus to form the First Triumvirate, which further weakened the power and prestige of the Senate.

8. *Caesar's Consulship and the Gallic War:* Between 58 and 50 Caesar expanded Roman territories by conquering Gallic tribes in modern France and Belgium.

9. *The Break Between Caesar and the Senate:* In 49 a faction of the Senate, fearing Caesar might destroy the Roman constitution, tried to strip Caesar of his command and to turn Pompey against him.

10. *Caesar's Invasion of Italy:* Challenged by the Senate, Caesar successfully invaded his own country and then decisively defeated Pompey in Greece. After spending some months in Egypt with Cleopatra, Caesar returned to Rome in 46.

11. *Caesar's Rule:* Caesar made himself dictator for life, instituted a series of reforms, and turned the Senate into his rubber stamp.

12. *The Death of Caesar:* In 44 Caesar was murdered by aristocratic conspirators led by Brutus and Cassius. This controversial man's career reveals the political weakness of the late Roman Republic.

13. *Literature in the Age of Revolution:* Lucretius (95–55) tried to spread Epicureanism through his poetry, while Catullus wrote more personal poems. The statesman Cicero (106–43) was the most versatile Latin writer of his time; he wrote elegant orations, essays, letters, and philosophic treatises while also pursuing a frustrating political career.

IV. The End of the Roman Republic.

A. The Victory of Octavian.

Caesar's adopted son, Octavian (Augustus), used his army to found an enduring autocracy.

1. *The Second Triumvirate:* Despite attempts by senators to reassert republican government, Octavian, Marc Antony, and Lepidus formed the Second Triumvirate in 43 and ruled for a number of years. Ultimately, the two major partners, Antony and Octavian, struggled for power. Octavian defeated Antony in 31. The following year Antony and Cleopatra took their lives before Octavian could capture them in Egypt, marking an end to the Hellenistic Age and the Roman Republic.

Experiences of Daily Life: Housing in Rome.

Most lower-middle-class Romans lived in fragile, crowded apartment houses.

SIGNIFICANT INDIVIDUALS

Political and Military Leaders

Hannibal (247–183), Carthaginian general.

Gaius Graccus (153–121), Roman statesman, tribune.

Gaius Marius (157–86), Roman
general.

Lucius Cornelius Sulla (138–78),
Roman general, dictator.

Pompey (106–48), general,
consul.

Marcus Licinius Crassus (115?–53),
general, consul.

Gaius Julius Caesar (100–44), general,
consul, dictator.

Marc Antony (83?–30), consul,
tribune, soldier.

Octavian (Augustus) (63 B.C.–A.D. 14),
consul, emperor.

Cleopatra (51–49, 48–30), queen of
Egypt.

Writers

Quintus Ennius (239–169), Latin
writer.

Lucretius (94–55), Latin poet.

Polybius (200?–118?), Greek historian.

Marcus Tullius Cicero (106–43),
Latin writer, politician.

CHRONOLOGICAL DIAGRAM

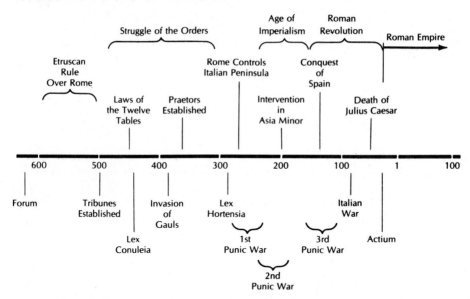

IDENTIFICATION

consul
Senate
Struggle of the Orders
tribune
Lex Canuleia
equestrians

Italian War
Tribal Assembly
amicitia
First Triumvirate
Actium

MAP EXERCISE

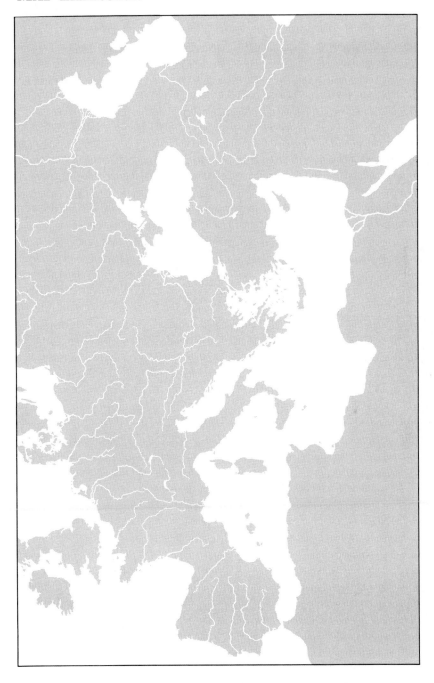

1. Indicate the main areas and dates of Roman expansion between 500 and 44 B.C.

PROBLEMS FOR ANALYSIS

I. The Unification of Italy.

1. Polybius called the Roman constitution a perfect blend of regal, aristocratic, and democratic elements. Do you agree? Explain.
2. How were the Romans able to hold their growing territories together during the early period of the Roman Republic?

II. The Age of Imperialism.

1. Trace the main steps by which Rome became an imperial power. What role did Rome's system of alliances and its method of provincial administration play in this?
2. Is it fair to say that the Romans simply copied Greek religion and literature, using the Latin language rather than Greek? Explain.

III. The Roman Revolution.

1. What were the fundamental strains and changes that undermined the foundations of the Roman Republic? How is this reflected in the developments concerning Tiberius and Gaius Gracchus?
2. What role did powerful generals play in the decline of the Republic? Use examples.
3. How did the Senate respond to threats? Did it simply give up, respond in kind, or pursue policies that further undermined its own authority?

IV. The End of the Roman Republic.

1. How was Octavian able to acquire supreme power over his competitors?
2. In what ways did Octavian's victory mark the end of the Roman Republic and the Hellenistic Age?

DOCUMENTS

The Roman Statesman

Marcus Tullius Cicero (106–43) was an orator, writer, and statesman during the later years of the Roman Republic. He idealized the traditional, conservative institutions of the Roman Republic, which he feared were in danger.

> But those whom Nature endowed with the capacity for administering public affairs should put aside all hesitation, enter the race for public office, and take a hand in directing the government; for in no other way can a government be administered or greatness of spirit be made manifest. Statesmen, too, no less than philosophers — perhaps even more so — should carry with them that greatness of spirit and indifference to outward circumstances to which I so often refer, together with calm of soul

and freedom from care, if they are to be free from worries and lead a dignified and self-consistent life. This is easier for the philosophers; as their life is less exposed to the assaults of fortune, their wants are fewer; and if any misfortune overtakes them, their fall is not so disastrous. Not without reason, therefore, are stronger emotions aroused in those who engage in public life than in those who live in retirement, and greater is their ambition for success; the more, therefore, do they need to enjoy greatness of spirit and freedom from annoying cares. . . . [1]

1. According to Cicero, what are the public obligations of the talented elite?
2. What role should wealth and emotion play in Roman politics?

Roman Values and Economic Life

Cato (234–149) was a Roman statesman who extolled the values and life of the early Roman Republic. The following is an excerpt from his work "On Agriculture."

It is true that business and banking sometimes are more profitable than farming, but farming is less hazardous than the former and more honorable than the latter. Our ancestors had the idea and put it into law that a thief should be fined twofold and a money lender fourfold. From this fact you may gather how far below the thief they rated the money lender. When they praised a good man, they called him a "good husbandman" and a "good farmer." A man so praised was supposed to have received the highest compliments. I look upon the merchant as an active man, devoted to making money, but, as I have just said, it is a hazardous and risky occupation. From the farmers, on the other hand, come the bravest men and the most vigorous soldiers; they are highly respected, have an assured livelihood, are looked upon with least envy, and are least inclined to plot evil. . . . [2]

1. Describe Cato's image of economic life during the Roman Republic.
2. How does Cato evaluate farming as compared to other occupations? Why?

Social Institutions

In this selection, M. I. Finley describes morals, marriage, and family life in Rome.

There was no puritanism in the Roman concept of morality. Marriage was a central institution but it had nothing sacramental about it. It was central because the whole structure of property rested on it and because both the indispensable family cult and the institution of citizenship required the orderly, regular succession of legitimate children in one generation after another. There were neither spinsters nor confirmed bachelors in this world. It was assumed that if one reached the right age—and many of course did not, given the enormously high rate of infant mortality—one would

---

[1] Cicero, *De Officiis* (i. 21), trans. Walter Miller (Cambridge, Mass.: Loeb Classical Library, Harvard University Press, 1913), p. 73.

[2] Cato, "On Agriculture," trans. Alfred P. Dorjahn, in Kevin Guinagh and Alfred P. Dorjahn, eds., *Latin Literature in Translation,* 2nd edition (New York: Longman Inc., 1952). Copyright © 1952 by Longman Inc. Previously published by David McKay Company, Inc. Reprinted by permission of Longman Inc.

marry. Society could not pursue its normal course otherwise. But the stress was always on the rightness of the marriage from a social and economic point of view, and on its legitimacy (and therefore also on the legitimacy of the offspring) from the political and legal point of view. If the relationship turned out also to be pleasant and affectionate, so much the better. It was taken for granted, however, that men would find comradeship and sexual satisfaction from others as well, and often only chiefly from others. They were expected to behave with good taste in this respect, but no more. [3]

1. Why was marriage so important in Rome? Why were there neither spinsters nor confirmed bachelors there?
2. How crucial were love and sex to marriage in Rome?

Causes for the Rise of Rome

In the following excerpt, C. Warren Hollister interprets the nature of the Roman Republic and the causes for some of the successes enjoyed during the early republican period.

Civil dedication was a hallmark of the early Roman. Devoted to the numerous gods of the city, the field, and the hearth, he was hard working, respectful of tradition, obedient to civil and military authority, and profoundly dedicated to the welfare of the state. The backbone of Old Rome was the small, independent farmer who worked long and hard to raise crops from his fields and remained always vigilant against raids by savage tribesmen from the surrounding hills. To men such as these life was intensely serious. Their stern sobriety and rustic virtues were exaggerated by Roman moralists writing in a later and more luxurious age, but there can be little doubt that the tenacious spirit and astonishing military success of early republican Rome owed much to the discipline and steadfastness of these simple citizen-farmers. As triumph followed triumph, as the booty of war flowed into Rome from far and wide, the character of her citizenry inevitably suffered; one of the great tragic themes of Roman history is the gradual erosion of social morality by wealth and power—and by the gradual expansion of huge slave-operated estates at the expense of the small farmer. But long before this process was complete the empire had been won. [4]

1. Why was the small, independent farmer so crucial to the rise and the decline of the Roman Republic?
2. Is the "tragic theme" of Roman history here solely an objective evaluation, or is it colored by the author's attitudes toward slavery?

SPECULATIONS

1. Suppose you were a Roman. Present arguments justifying Roman expansion as something more than ruthless territorial acquisition.

---

[3] M. I. Finley, *Aspects of Antiquity* (New York: The Viking Press, 1965), p. 133.

[4] C. Warren Hollister, *Roots of the Western Tradition* (New York: John Wiley and Sons, Inc., 1966), pp. 150–151.

2. What policies should the Senate have followed to prevent the fall of the Roman Republic? Do you think it would have been better if the Republic was preserved? Explain.
3. Compare the strengths and weaknesses of the Greeks and Romans.

TRANSITIONS

In "Classical and Hellenistic Greece," Greek civilization at its height as well as its spread and transformation in the East under Alexander and his successors were examined.

In "The Roman Republic," the Romans, driven by a desire to impose themselves on all others, supported by large reserves of manpower, and aided by an authoritarian view of life, succeeded in unifying most of the Mediterranean and European worlds under their rule. In the latter years of the Republic a revolution eliminated political freedom. Years of instability were finally brought to an end by Octavian, who effectively ended the Roman Republic.

In "The Empire and Christianity," the Roman Empire at its height, the growth of a new religion (Christianity), and the transformation and decline of the Empire will be examined.

FIVE
THE EMPIRE
AND CHRISTIANITY

MAIN THEMES

1. Octavian (Augustus) strengthened Roman administration over vast dominions and laid firm foundations for the Roman Empire.

2. Thanks to an effective government, a well-functioning, slave-based economy, and a sense of well-being among the elite, the two centuries after the death of Augustus were a period of relative peace, prosperity, and creative accomplishment.

3. In the third century the Empire experienced political instability, economic decline, social turmoil, and cultural disintegration.

4. Despite opposition from the government and from heretical divisions, the Christian Church formulated dogma and became established, effecting a cultural revolution in the classical world.

5. Although reforms by Diocletian and Constantine extended the life of the Empire, the Western Empire succumbed to a number of problems and fell—marking a turning point in history.

OUTLINE AND SUMMARY

I. The Founding of the Roman Empire.

A. The Rule of Augustus to A.D. 14.

Though appearing to return power to the Senate, Octavian actually turned the Republic into an Empire. Between 27 B.C. and his death in A.D. 14, Octavian established his system. He took direct command of vast provinces, ruling through assistants (legates). He had his name changed to Augustus and laid foundations for the deification of emperors. He instituted the payment of soldiers by the state rather than by the generals, solidified frontiers, and created an elite security force—the Praetorian Guard. A superb administrator and politician, Augustus managed these reforms with grace. His rule was marked by relative peace, prosperity, and cultural creativity. His system lasted for two centuries in the West and for much longer in the East.

II. The Empire at Its Height.

Three unifying elements made the Empire survive and work: the figure of the emperor; the civil servants and city councils; the army.

A. The Succesors of Augustus.

The Julio-Claudian emperors who succeeded Augustus until A.D. 68 were of low quality but managed to centralize power effectively. The Praetorian Guard started intervening in civil authority.

B. The Five Good Emperors.

From the end of the first century to the end of the second century, five capable emperors ruled Rome. Trajan led Rome to her furthest extension to the East in 116. During this period of prosperity, vast building projects were undertaken.

C. Roman Imperial Civilization.

The Romans studied, imitated, and adapted much of Greek and Near Eastern culture.

1. *Economy:* During the late Republic and early Empire, Romans enjoyed extraordinary prosperity. Cities, smaller in the West (except for Rome), were of great importance as centers of commerce, manufacturing, government, and culture. At least 75 percent of the Empire's total product remained agricultural. In Italy, and to a lesser extent elsewhere, the great slave-run estates (latifundia) replaced the small farm. They specialized in the cultivation of vines, olives, fruit, and the raising of livestock, making Italy dependent on imports for grain. Provincial areas started to threaten Italy's economic leadership.

2. *Social Conditions:* The rich led luxurious lives of indulgence, especially compared to the workers and the poor. Yet workers had relatively enviable working conditions, and the poor, who made up some 50 percent of the city's population, were supported at public expense. In general, social mobility became easier within the Empire, and ultimately men from the provinces entered all Roman institutions.

3. *Law:* The development of an evolving, respected legal system was one of Rome's greatest cultural accomplishments. The legal system was divided into laws applying to citizens and laws applying to foreigners. The system was staffed by judges, legal advisors (jurists), and policy-making magistrates. Emperors intervened and modified the laws, above all, by ordering their codification.

4. *Engineering and Architecture:* The Romans were superb engineers and architects. They built long-lasting roads, aqueducts, baths, forums, temples, and public halls throughout the Empire. By using arches on a large scale and by inventing concrete, the Romans were able to build on a scale far beyond that of the Greeks. In sculpting and painting, Romans relied more on Greek models and artists.

5. *Poets:* Poetry was popular in Rome, especially among the educated. The most famous poets Virgil (*Aeneid*), Horace (*Odes*), Ovid (*Ars Amatoria*), and Juvenal often borrowed from Greek models.

6. *Historians:* During the Republic most histories were written by men directly involved in politics. In the early years of the Empire, Livy wrote an ambitious, rhetorical, but questionable history of Rome (*Roman History*). He was succeeded by Tacitus (*Germania, Histories, Annals*), Rome's greatest historian. He focused on customs and character analysis and provided us with one of the only records of the early Germans.

III. Changes in Ancient Society.

A. The Periods of Crisis.

After the death of the Emperor Commodus in 192, emperors were short-lived and controlled by the military (often by murder). Further weakening of the Senate and an unwillingness of talented people to hold public office lowered the quality of the administration. The economy was burdened by high costs (defense, poor relief) and inflation.

B. Slavery.

Slavery in Roman society was extraordinarily widespread and highly organized. Slaves were extensively used in both the rural and urban economies.

C. The Dilemmas of Slavery.

In the long run, slavery reduced incentives to work hard or create labor-saving machinery. Moreover, because of low birth rates and fewer conquests, the number of slaves declined. This led to a declining output and to efforts to provide new incentives, by improving the lot and status of slaves (housed slaves). Finally, increasing domination over the economy by the imperial bureaucracy diminished the market for new slaves.

D. The Plight of the Poor.

Contrasts between rich and poor were extreme. The poor increasingly populated the cities, especially Rome, where they were supported. Large areas of land became depopulated; policy toward the free cultivators (the *coloni*) indicates efforts both to encourage cultivation of abandoned lands and to tax them heavily as a needed source of revenue. At times the poor rose in violent upheavals (*Bagaudae* revolts).

E. The Problem of the Nations.

Rome attempted to retain the loyalty of national groups by guaranteeing peace, protection, justice, and local autonomy. Nevertheless, national resentment grew, as illustrated by the war of the *circumcelliones*.

F. Cultural Disintegration.

At its height, the Greco-Roman tradition offered peace, personal fulfillment, and harmony with nature as spiritual ideals. Yet this was primarily appropriate for the privileged and gifted, and over time, a decline of creativity and a sense of pessimism plagued most thinkers. Both pagans and Christians were psychologically unprepared to propose social reforms.

IV. Christianity.

Christians created a cultural revolution by effectively preaching values opposed to those of classical thoughts.

A. The Mystery Religions.

Like other popular mystery religions of the time, Christianity offered an explanation of the ultimate purposes of human life and of life after death. Christianity also offered rituals, ethics, a historical savior, and an association with Judaism.

B. The Jews in the Roman Empire.

With the exception of one main period (165–63 B.C.), the Jews were directly or indirectly controlled by other states. Despite attempts at repression, Judaism retained its coherence and strength.

1. *The Sects:* The existence of various sects, such as the Sadducees, the Pharisees, and the Essenes, evidences the religious tension and high expectations on the eve of Jesus' career.

C. Origins of Christianity.

The earliest accounts of Jesus date from decades after his death. According to the New Testament, Jesus offered salvation to the deserving and encouraged followers to perform rituals and form a community.

D. Paul and His Mission.

The intellectual Paul converted to Christianity and became its principal architect. He organized Christian churches throughout the Roman world. Though drawing heavily from Jewish tradition, he rejected rigid application of the Mosaic law. Paul's Christian perspective of the universe was organized on two principles: an order of nature established by original creation but faulted by sin; and an order of grace, founded in God's willingness to save mankind, brought to fulfillment with the coming of Jesus.

E. The Church in the Roman Empire.

Between 100 and 300 Christianity grew but remained an illegal minority sect. Its spread was facilitated by the Roman peace, the Jewish Diaspora, and the discontent of the poor.

F. Persecutions.

Christians set themselves apart by refusing to worship Roman gods. Yet persecutions were only occasionally carried out (Nero, 64; Decius, 250; Valerian, 257–260; Diocletian, 303–313), and a relatively small number lost their lives; those who did became venerated martyrs.

G. The Conversion of Constantine.

After the conversion of Constantine in 312, the Church gained legality and privileges, and persecutions were ended.

H. Dogma and Government.

Dissensions within the Church resulted in the formation of dogma and in constitutional development. Gnostics argued that mastery of special knowledge assured salvation, and that Jesus was not a man but a wholly spiritual being. Marcion and his followers rejected a substantial part of the Scriptures. Montanus and his followers raised the issue of who should rule Christian congregations—prophets or priests. Firm responses to these challenges and a gradual development of Church government solidified this historic structure of Christianity. By the third century, the Church was committed to a faith in a historical redeemer, a canon of sacred books, and a hierarchical organization based on bishops.

I. Donatists and Arians.

Other theological controversies mounted in intensity. Donatists, based in North Africa, created a schism by insisting that sacraments administered by "corrupt" priests were not valid. Arians, arguing that Jesus and God were not of the same substance, were condemned at the Nicene Council in 325.

J. The Church and Classical Culture.

Christians found it necessary to learn pagan intellectual skills and turn them to their own purposes, preserving much of classical literature in the process.

K. The Fathers of the Church.

The fathers of the early Church wrote a vast amount of authoritative commentary, persuasion, and teaching. The most important of these were the Greek writers Clement of Alexandria, Origen, and Eusebius of Caesarea and the Latin writers Ambrose, Jerome, and Augustine.

L. Augustine.

Augustine, the best known of the fathers, commented on almost every question of Christian theology, including sexual morality and marriage. In his *Confessions* he revealed his own spiritual progress. As bishop of Hippo he defended the traditional Church against Pelagius, arguing that grace and not just good works is necessary for salvation. He emphasized God's omnipotence and man's helplessness. In his masterpiece, *The City of God,* he described an order in history directed by God and emphasized the distinction between the earthly city (the Empire) and the City of God (for the elect).

V. The Late Roman Empire.

A. Restoration and Reform.

In 284 Diocletian rose to power and brought order to the Empire. He imposed a more authoritarian, bureaucratic rule and reformed taxation. After a period of instability, he was succeeded by another strong emperor, Constantine.

B. Constantine and the Bureaucracy.

Constantine furthered the Diocletian reforms, casting the state into a bureaucratic structure of numerous provincial units. Economic life was rigidified. Members of all trades and professions were frozen in their positions, and tenant farmers were bound to the soil. He exploited his position as patron of the Christian faith. The reforms of Diocletian and Constantine enabled the Western Empire to survive two more centuries and helped the Eastern Empire to become extremely long-lived.

C. Problems of the Western Empire.

Emperors proved unable to hold the Empire together in the 300s, and the Empire was formally divided in half in 395. The western portion of the Empire declined politically. After 395 the Empire was divided into an Eastern and a Western half. In the Western Empire, people became bound to their occupations and commerce declined. Large estates (villas) became more economically and then politically and militarily self-sufficient as Rome declined.

D. The Decline of the Western Empire.

The end of the Roman Empire was a transformation as well as a fall. Above all, it took place in the West, for the Byzantine Empire in the East survived for another thousand years. There are numerous interpretations of the decline of Rome, from barbarian invasions to lead poisoning. It was probably caused by a combination of factors. The West suffered from manpower shortages. It was almost open geographically to invasion by warlike tribes, and it was militarily weakened by decentralization. The rigidity, the repression, and the welfare policies of Rome may have made its people particularly apathetic. Christianity, with its emphasis on equality and a better afterlife, may have weakened Roman society. With the fall of Rome to invaders came an end to the ancient world and the beginning of new civilizations.

SIGNIFICANT INDIVIDUALS

Emperors

Augustus (Octavian) (27 B.C.–A.D. 14)   Constantine (306–337)
Diocletian (284–305)

Writers

Virgil (70–19), Latin poet.
Horace (65–8), Latin poet.
Ovid (43 B.C.–A.D. 17?), Latin love
poet.

Juvenal (A.D. 60?–A.D. 140?), Latin
poet, satirist.
Livy (59 B.C.–A.D. 17), historian.
Cornelius Tacitus (55?–120?), historian.

Religious Leaders

Paul (first century A.D.), Church
founder.
Montanus (ca. 150–200), bishop,
Montanist leader.
Clement of Alexandria (150?–215?),
Greek Church father.
Origen (185?–255?), Greek Church
father.
Eusebius of Caesarea (260?–340?),
Greek Church father.

Ambrose of Milan (340?–397), Latin
Church father.
Jerome (340?–420), Latin Church
father.
Augustine of Hippo (354–430), Latin
Church father.
Pelagius (360?–420?), Irish monk,
theologian.

CHRONOLOGICAL DIAGRAM

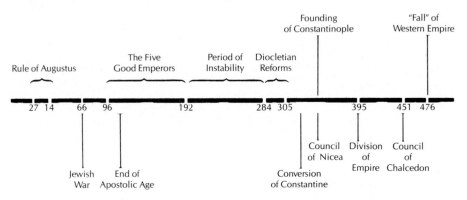

IDENTIFICATION

latifundia
public games
jurists
ius civile
Roman baths
Pompeii
"housed slaves"
coloni
Baugaudae revolt

mystery religions
Essenes
persecutions
conversion of Constantine
Gnostics
Nicene Creed
The City of God
Diocletian reforms

MAP EXERCISE

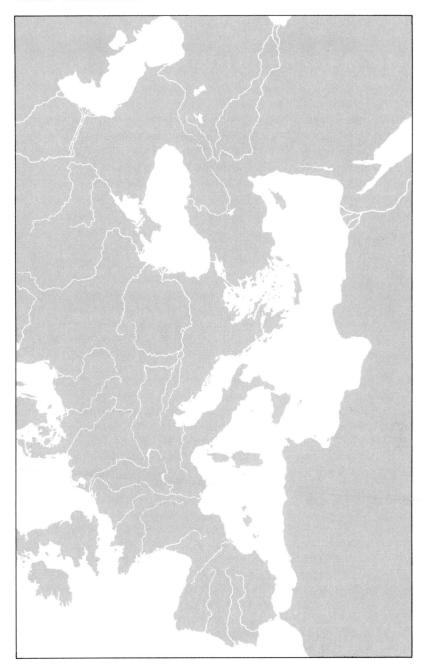

1. Indicate the outlines of the Empire in A.D. 14 and its subsequent maximum expansion.
2. Indicate centers of Christianity around the year 312.

PROBLEMS FOR ANALYSIS

I. The Founding of the Roman Empire.

1. Analyze the ways in which Augustus established the foundations of the Empire.

II. The Empire at Its Height.

1. Analyze the way in which the socioeconomic system of the Empire functioned. What were its economic characteristics? What role did slaves play economically and socially? How sharp were economic and social distinctions between rich and poor?
2. Historians argue that Romans were most skilled in law, engineering, and architecture. Using examples, support this argument.

III. Changes in Ancient Society.

1. While in the short run slavery as an economic system worked well, in the long run it worked to the disadvantage of the Empire. Explain.
2. Analyze the crisis of the third century. How is this reflected in the cultural disintegration of the period?

IV. Christianity.

1. Analyze the similarities and differences of Christianity and other mystery religions. What characteristics of Christianity contributed to its success?
2. How did theological controversies contribute to establishing Christian dogma and order within the Church?

V. The Late Roman Empire.

1. What problems did the reforms of Diocletian and Constantine solve, and what new problems did they create?
2. Considering the variety of interpretations, explain the causes for the decline of the Roman Empire in the West.

DOCUMENTS

The City of God

Augustine (354–430) defended orthodox Christianity as bishop of Hippo (396–430) in North Africa. He became one of the most influential of the early Christian Church fathers. Probably, his most famous work is *The City of God*, from which the following selection is taken. Here, he deals with the relationship between Christian believers and the secular world of his time.

But the families which do not live by faith seek their peace in the earthly advantages of this life; while the families which live by faith look for those eternal blessings which are promised, and use as pilgrims such advantages of time and of earth as do not fascinate and divert them from God, but rather aid them to endure with greater ease, and to keep down the number of those burdens of the corruptible body which weigh upon the soul. Thus the things necessary for this mortal life are used by both kinds of men and families alike, but each has its own peculiar and widely different aim in using them. The earthly city, which does not live by faith, seeks an earthly peace, and the end it proposes, in the well-ordered concord of civic obedience and rule, is the combination of men's wills to attain the things which are helpful to this life. The heavenly city, or rather the part of it which sojourns on earth and lives by faith, makes use of this peace only because it must, until this mortal condition which necessitates it shall pass away. Consequently, so long as it lives like a captive and a stranger in the earthly city, though it has already received the promise of redemption, and the gift of the Spirit as the earnest of it, it makes no scruple to obey the laws of the earthly city, whereby the things necessary for the maintenance of this mortal life are administered; and thus, as this life is common to both cities, so there is a harmony between them in regard to what belongs to it. But, as the earthly city has had some philosophers whose doctrine is condemned by the divine teaching . . . it has come to pass that the two cities could not have common laws of religion, and that the heavenly city has been compelled in this matter to dissent, and to become obnoxious to those who think differently, and to stand the brunt of their anger and hatred and persecutions, except in so far as the minds of their enemies have been alarmed by the multitude of the Christians and quelled by the manifest protection of God accorded to them. This heavenly city, then, while it sojourns on earth, calls citizens out of all nations, and gathers together a society of pilgrims of all languages, not scrupling about diversities in the manners, laws, and institutions whereby earthly peace is secured and maintained, but recognizing that, however various these are, they all tend to one and the same end of earthly peace. It therefore is so far from rescinding and abolishing these diversities, that it even preserves and adopts them, so long only as no hindrance to the worship of the one supreme and true God is thus introduced. Even the heavenly city, therefore, while in its state of pilgrimage, avails itself of the peace of earth, and, so far as it can without injuring faith and godliness, desires and maintains a common agreement among men regarding the acquisition of the necessaries of life, and makes this earthly peace bear upon the peace of heaven; for this alone can be truly called and esteemed the peace of the reasonable creatures, consisting as it does in the perfectly ordered and harmonious enjoyment of God and of one another in God. When we shall have reached that peace, this mortal life shall give place to one that is eternal, and our body shall be no more this animal body which by its corruption weighs down the soul, but a spiritual body feeling no want, and in all its members subjected to the will. In its pilgrim state the heavenly city possesses this peace by faith; and by this faith it lives righteously when it refers to the attainment of that peace by faith; and by this faith it lives righteously when it refers to the attainment of that peace every good action towards God and man; for the life of the city is a social life. [1]

1. According to Augustine, what is the proper relationship between the earthly city and the heavenly city?
2. What is the role of faith in the Christian life and in the secular life?

[1] Augustine, *The City of God, II,* trans. Marcus Dobbs (1871), pp. 326–328.

The Fall of Rome

One of the classic questions for those who study the Roman Empire concerns the causes for its decline and fall. In the following excerpt, M. I. Rostovtzeff analyzes this problem and presents his own highly respected interpretation.

Every reader of a volume devoted to the Roman Empire will expect the author to express his opinion on what is generally, since Gibbon, called the decline and fall of the Roman Empire, or rather of ancient civilization in general. I shall therefore briefly state my own view on this problem, after defining what I take the problem to be. The decline and fall of the Roman Empire, that is to say, of ancient civilization as a whole, has two aspects: the political, social, and economic on the one hand, and the intellectual and spiritual on the other. In the sphere of politics we witness a gradual barbarization of the Empire from within, especially in the West. The foreign, German, elements play the leading part both in the government and in the army, and settling in masses displace the Roman population, which disappears from the fields. A related phenomenon, which indeed was a necessary consequence of this barbarization from within, was the gradual disintegration of the Western Roman Empire; the ruling classes in the former Roman provinces were replaced first by Germans and Sarmatians, and later by Germans alone, either through peaceful penetration or by conquest. In the East we observe a gradual Orientalization of the Byzantine Empire, which leads ultimately to the establishment, on the ruins of the Roman Empire, of strong half-Oriental and purely Oriental states, the Caliphate of Arabia, and the Persian and Turkish empires. From the social and economic point of view, we mean by decline the gradual relapse of the ancient world to very primitive forms of economic life, into an almost pure "house-economy." The cities, which had created and sustained the higher forms of economic life, gradually decayed, and the majority of them practically disappeared from the face of the earth. A few, especially those that had been great centres of commerce and industry, still lingered on. The complicated and refined social system of the ancient Empire follows the same downward path and becomes reduced to its primitive elements: the King, his court and retinue, the big feudal landowners, the clergy, the mass of rural serfs, and small groups of artisans and merchants. Such is the political, social, and economic aspect of the problem.

From the intellectual and spiritual point of view the main phenomenon is the decline of ancient civilization, of the city civilization of the Greco-Roman world. The Oriental civilizations were more stable: blended with some elements of the Greek city civilization, they persisted and even witnessed a brilliant revival in the Caliphate of Arabia and in Persia, not to speak of India and China. Here again there are two aspects of the evolution. The first is the exhaustion of the creative forces of Greek civilization in the domains where its great triumphs had been achieved, in the exact sciences, in technique, in literature and art. The decline began as early as the second century B.C. There followed a temporary revival of creative forces in the cities of Italy, and later in those of the Eastern and Western provinces of the Empire. The progressive movement stopped almost completely in the second century A.D. and, after a period of stagnation, a steady and rapid decline set in again. Parallel to it, we notice a progressive weakening of the assimilative forces of Greco-Roman civilization. The cities no longer absorb—that is to say, no longer Hellenize or Romanize—the masses of the country population. The reverse is the case. The barbarism of the country begins to engulf the city population. Only small islands of civilized life are left, the senatorial aristocracy of the late Empire and the clergy; but both, save for a section of the clergy, are gradually swallowed up by the advancing tide of barbarism. [2]

1. According to Rostovtzeff, why did the Roman Empire decline and fall? Does Rostovtzeff's approach differ from that presented in the text? Explain.

The Power Tactics of Jesus Christ

In the following, highly interpretive selection, Jay Haley approaches the origins of Christianity from an unusual point of view. He trys to analyze the tactics used by Jesus to achieve power, and then he compares those tactics to those used by other messianic or charismatic leaders since Jesus.

Now that Christianity has declined as a force in the world of ideas, we are free to appreciate the skills of Jesus Christ. The innovations of Jesus as an organizer and a leader of men have been overlooked by most Christians and social scientists. Typically the credit for his achievements has been given to the Lord, which seems unfair, or to later followers like Paul, which seems even more unfair. When one abandons the idea that it was the intervention of a God or later leaders which led to the success of Jesus, his ability as an organizer appears incredible. This single individual designed the strategy of an organization which not only took over the Roman Empire but ultimately held absolute power over the populace of the western world for many hundreds of years and was only divested of that power in a violent struggle. No other person has approached such an accomplishment. Until the leaders of communist and other mass movements appeared in this century there was not even a contender.

To understand the messianic revolutionists of today one must appreciate the legacy left by Jesus. . . . The most obvious debt such leaders owe Jesus is his basic innovation: the idea of striking for power by organizing the poor and the powerless. For centuries this idea of Jesus was overlooked and so the poor were not a threat to the establishment; the most that could be expected of them was an occasional sporadic riot. In this century the poor must be taken into account everywhere because there are men who will devote their lives to rousing and organizing them. The ideology of contemporary mass movement leaders differs in certain ways from that of Jesus, but it will be argued here that their basic strategy did not arise spontaneously in our time but was outlined in the New Testament and designed in Galilee by one man.

It would seem evident that the strategies of Jesus have been the model for mass movement leaders, the Messiahs of this century. With the decline of the Christian religion as a philosophy, the organizational tactics of Jesus came into prominence. Contemporary leaders have followed a set of procedures which can be summarized here as they were originated by Jesus.

The basic strategy of leaders of . . . mass movements consists of seeking power outside the establishment by cultivating the people who have been neglected and

---

[2] M. I. Rostovtzeff, "The Decay of Ancient Civilization," in *The Social and Economic History of the Roman Empire,* 2nd edition, revised by P. M. Fraser (Oxford: The Clarendon Press, 1957).

powerless. This populace is the majority in the countries where mass movements have succeeded. The leader defines the poor workers and peasants as more deserving of power than any other class, and he publicly attacks the wealthy and established. If the poor are sufficiently desperate, as at a time of military defeat, the odds increase for the success of the movement.

The leader organizes a cadre he can use as "fishers of men." These disciples are selected from the population to be influenced, and they are expected to be totally devoted to the leader and his movement. They must give up all ambition in the society as it is, cut off all family ties, and abandon all group loyalties except loyalty to the party. Once they have done this, it is difficult for them to defect and abandon the movement; they have sacrificed too much and have no place to go. The leader further ties the cadre to him by emphasizing their persecution by outsiders; and he gives them a sense of mission and purpose in life. Offering practical gains in exchange for their sacrifices, the leader also offers his disciples the status of an elite within the organization and the thrones of power in the kingdom that is to come.

In his public message the leader defines his movement as one that has the benevolent purpose of saving mankind, making it difficult to resist. He also claims the movement will inevitably come to power because it represents the next step in the development of man. When appealing to the masses, the leader promises a paradise in some undefined future if they will only follow him, and he threatens misery if they do not. He puts his hope in the young, who do not yet have an investment in the establishment, and he deliberately incites the young against their elders, to break the family ties that solidify the strength of the establishment.

Defining himself as one who does not seek personal power, the leader says he is fulfilling a mission at great personal sacrifice. He does not say that he should be followed for himself or that he is a great leader but more modestly says that he is merely an interpreter of the great force which will take his following into the bountiful future. However, he also defines himself as the *only* correct interpreter of that force. Willing to live with inconsistency, the leader adapts what he says to the circumstances while at the same time insisting that he is offering a clear and consistent theory as a basis for his actions.

While gathering a following, the leader publicly announces himself as an authority who is equal to the authority of the whole establishment, and he makes audacious comments and attacks on prominent leaders in the opposition. At the same time he uses a flexible strategy, answering attack with attack when this is safe and using non-violent methods within the legal framework if the opposition is too formidable. As the final struggle comes into being, he takes a position of "no compromise" with the governing power. Since his goal is not power within the framework of the establishment, no compromise or bargaining is possible. When such men succeed, their power is unlimited because all other authority has been discredited. What follows is a ruthless elimination of any and all opposition.

One cannot strike for power over masses of people today without using the strategies of Jesus. No other leader has been so publicized or had his sayings and actions become such a part of the thinking of crusading men. Whether Jesus was offering an original religious philosophy or not, he was an extraordinary innovator as a leader of men. Should those who have led great power struggles be enshrined in a hall of fame, the first niche belongs to the Messiah from Galilee. [3]

1. What kind of political leader was Jesus?
2. What tactics did he use to achieve his influential position?
3. What lessons did he provide for future messianic or charismatic leaders?

SPECULATIONS

1. As an early leader of the Christian Church, what policies should you follow to ensure the spread of a single Christian religion? Why?
2. What might Roman emperors have done to prevent the fall of the Empire in the West?
3. Hold a debate between representatives of a pagan classical culture and a Christian culture. Indicate the main points and responses each would make.

TRANSITIONS

In "The Roman Republic," the rise of Rome as a world power was traced. The period ended with the success of Augustus and the fall of the Republic.

In "The Empire and Christianity," the story begins with the establishment of the Empire by Augustus. For two centuries after Augustus the Empire prospered, but during the third century a long series of crises occurred, eventually breaking apart the Empire and leading to its final collapse in the West during the fifth century. Numerous factors, including profound flaws in the slave economy, conflicting values, and changes in all sectors of life, weakened the Empire, causing it to decline. Yet at the same time peoples were laying the basis for a new civilization, above all by building on the legacy of Rome and spreading a new set of religious beliefs—Christianity.

In "The Making of Western Europe," the development of a new civilization in the West between the fifth and tenth centuries will be traced.

[3] Jay Haley, *The Power Tactics of Jesus Christ* (New York: Grossman Publishers, 1969). Copyright © 1969 by Jay Haley. Reprinted by permission of Grossman Publishers.

SECTION SUMMARY
THE ANCIENT WORLD TO A.D. 500
CHAPTERS 1–5

CHRONOLOGICAL DIAGRAMS

Diagram 1
The Ancient Civilizations

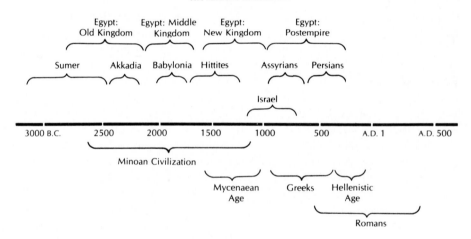

Diagram 2
Greco-Roman Civilization

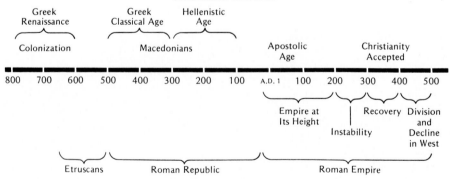

MAP EXERCISE

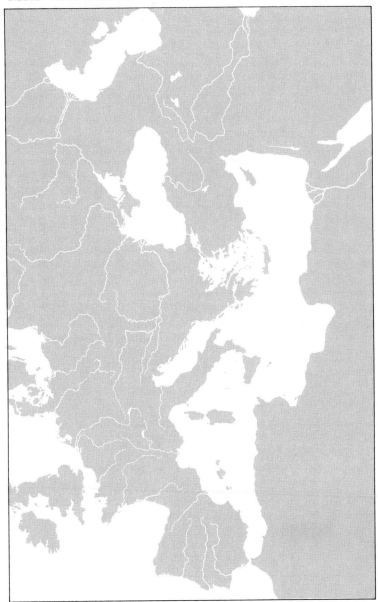

1. Identify the centers and the approximate boundaries of the following civilizations:

   a. Babylonia, 1900 B.C.
   b. Egypt, 1300 B.C.
   c. Israel, 900 B.C.
   d. Persia, 500 B.C.
   e. Minoan and Mycenaean, 1400 B.C.

   f. Greece, 400 B.C.
   g. Hellenistic Kingdoms, 250 B.C.
   h. Rome, 250 B.C.
   i. Rome, 50 B.C.
   j. Rome, A.D. 150

BOX CHART

Reproduce the Box Chart in a larger format in your notebook or on a separate sheet of paper.

Rome	Greece	Egypt	Mesopotamia Near East	
				Chronological Divisions
				Political Institutions and Developments
				Economic System and Characteristics
				Social System and Characteristics
				Religious System and Characteristics
				Cultural Values and Productions
				Problems
				Political Leaders
				Religious Leaders
				Philosophers and Scientists
				Cultural Leaders
				Others
				Turning Points

SIX
THE MAKING
OF WESTERN EUROPE
ca. 500–1000

MAIN THEMES

1. "Barbarian" peoples invaded Roman territories, merging their own institutions and culture with those of the declining Roman civilization.
2. Commerce and industry decreased, and Europe became a peasant society organized around the single-family farm and a central manor.
3. The Christian Church, through the growth of the Roman papacy and monasticism, maintained Roman traditions of social order and classical culture.
4. The Franks and Anglo-Saxons created temporarily effective kingdoms.
5. The Church and scholars of the Carolingian Renaissance helped preserve classical learning.

OUTLINE AND SUMMARY

I. The New Community of Peoples.

The civilization that was the direct ancestor of the modern Western world took shape during the Middle Ages (500–1500) in the west and north of Europe. It was founded upon a new community composed of former Roman subjects and "barbarians."

A. The Great Migrations.

Celtic, Germanic, and Slavic tribes bordered the Roman Empire to the north and east. In the fourth and fifth centuries, Germanic tribes, pressured by population growth and by Huns from the East, successfully invaded Roman territories in great numbers. Visigoths were followed by Vandals, Burgundians, Franks, Ostrogoths, Angles, Saxons, and Jutes. Each took different routes of conquest, establishing themselves from Britain to North Africa with varying amounts of permanence and organization. Most important were the Visigoths, who were the first to decisively defeat the Romans (378) and establish an autonomous kingdom on Roman soil (418); the Ostrogoths, who formally took over Italy from the last Roman emperor (476); and the Franks, who, under Clovis (481–511), unified Gaul, converted to Roman Christianity, and later allied with the papacy. In the fifth and sixth centuries, Slavic tribes penetrated into eastern and southeastern Europe to become ancestors of modern peoples in those areas.

B. Germans and Romans.

Germans constituted a minority of the population within the Roman Empire. They assimilated into Roman culture while also furthering the trend away from urban life toward that of small peasant villages and rural estates. In many ways they were not too different from the less sophisticated majority of Roman subjects.

C. Germanic Society.

1. *The Role of Women:* Women apparently had a higher status in Germanic society than in Roman society, probably because of their valued economic role. Germanic children, although not subject to infanticide as in Roman society, were poorly educated and treated with benign neglect.

2. *Social Structure:* Germanic society was based on individual ownership of land, bonds of blood relationship, and associations of self-help such as the *comitatus* and the guild. Kings rose during the invasions, but they were primarily only military and religious leaders. Many of these German institutions foreshadowed later medieval institutions.

3. *Law and Procedures:* Legal decisions were based on recalled customs rather than written laws. Legal practices included publicly performed symbolic acts, use of witnesses, and use of juries. Councils or assemblies helped chiefs make decisions.

4. *German Culture:* Since most Germans lacked writing skills, they preserved their literature orally. Their poetry typically glorified heroic military values (*Beowulf*). Germanic religion was magical and supernatural. Their most stunning artistic form was their Animal style jewelry. The Germans combined with the masses of nonliterate Roman subjects to nearly eliminate literacy in the West.

II. The New Economy (500–900).

In the Early Middle Ages, Europe became a peasant society built around the single-family farm.

A. Agriculture.

The climate and soil of northern Europe required new methods for successful cultivation. Slowly, these were developed during the Middle Ages through the use of heavier plows, more oxen and horses, improved harnesses, and better crop rotation (the three-field system). As a result, northern Europe was able to support a more dense population.

1. *The Manor:* The manor was a tightly disciplined community of peasants organized under the authority of a lord. It was an almost self-sufficient unit of economic, political, and social organization. The lord was responsible for defense, law and order, and the administration of justice. He collected revenues from various monopolies (milling, brewing, salt) and from taxes, fixed-service obligations from his serfs, and produce from his own lands. Serfs and independent peasants had their own lands and rights to common pasture, which were protected by custom and morals. Though characteristic of only certain areas, the manor offered protection, promoted cooperation, and encouraged agricultural innovation.

B. The Exchange of Wealth.

An "economy of gift and pillage," based on an ethic of reciprocal gift-giving, replaced the market economy of Rome and helped tie together early medieval society. By the seventh century, commerce and industry had almost disappeared in the West, probably due to a lack of skills and interest.

III. The Leadership of the Church.

The Church preserved Roman traditions of social order and classical culture.

A. Origins of the Papacy.

The early bishops of Rome gained a reputation as defenders of orthodoxy. This, the centrality of Rome, and biblical tradition probably combined to make the bishops of Rome the leaders of the Church.

    1. *Growth of Papal Primacy:* Supported by emperors and councils, popes gained authority, but not administrative dominance, in the fifth century.

    2. *Gregory the Great:* Gregory I (589–604), by becoming the most effective leader in Rome, managing Church estates, and mounting effective missionary efforts in England and Spain, widened the authority of the Roman papacy and set a pattern for his successors.

B. Monasticism.

First founded in Egypt in the third century, Christian monasticism became based upon an ascetic community following rules of chastity, poverty, and obedience to a spiritual abbot.

    1. *The Benedictine Rule:* Varieties of monasticism spread in the West, especially among the Irish. St. Benedict (480?–543?) brought order and uniformity to the movement through his example and his rules. These simple, elastic rules granted authority to the abbot, instructed monks in practical and spiritual matters, and required them to do some manual labor.

    2. *The Role of the Monk:* Monks, probably due to their communal organization and asceticism, became extremely important in medieval society. They retained their literacy, preserved Christian and pagan literature, served as teachers and advisors and role models, promoted agriculture, and supported morale in a difficult age.

IV. The New Political Structures.

Early medieval people created two major, though temporary, political structures: the Frankish and Anglo-Saxon kingdoms.

A. The Frankish Empire.

Clovis' Merovingian successors were relatively weak, and thus power gravitated to a line of palace mayors. One of these mayors, Pepin the Short, gained support of aristocrats and Church officials and had himself recognized as king (751). He dignified his monarchy with Christian and Roman influences. Meanwhile, Frankish society was dividing into an aristocracy of warriors who could afford horses (a tremendous military advantage, thanks to the introduction of the stirrup) and of full-time peasants who could not.

   1. *Charlemagne:* Pepin's son, Charlemagne (768–814), conquered vast territories, built up a Frankish Empire, and spread Christianity wherever he went. In 800 Pope Leo III crowned him emperor, symbolically marking the political and cultural autonomy of the West.

   2. *Government:* A grandiose imperial ideology developed around Charlemagne, increasing his dignity. He governed with the help of court officials and local county administrators (counts). He further secured his own authority by traveling extensively, appointing traveling inspectors, and calling yearly general assemblies of notables.

   3. *Decline of the Empire:* Charlemagne's successors were unable to hold the empire together. Central government became less effective, enabling counts and aristocrats to gain hereditary independence.

B. Renewed Invasions.

In the ninth century Charlemagne's empire was invaded by the Saracens from the south, the Magyars from the east, and the Vikings from the north. The Vikings were the most successful, their ships taking them from England and Spain in the West, to Russia and Constantinople in the East. By 1000, however, these new groups became Christianized partners in the association of Western peoples.

C. Anglo-Saxon England.

England was unified religiously during the seventh century by the reforms of the archbishop of Canterbury, who built upon a variety of earlier missionary efforts. Political unity took longer, with various kings acquiring partial or complete authority between the seventh and ninth centuries.

   1. *Alfred the Great:* Alfred (871–899) succeeded against the invading Danes and became England's first effective king. He initiated a cultural revival that included the beginnings of the *Anglo-Saxon Chronicle.* His successors retained power for about a century. There followed a period of instability and rule by Danish kings until the Norman conquest in 1066.

V. Letters and Learning.

Classical learning just barely survived and was used to promote the interests of the Christian religion.

A. The Church and Classical Learning.

The Church was always committed to some learning, for the Bible and other religious texts had to be read and interpreted. In the fifth and sixth centuries, Christian scholars such as Boethius produced textbooks, translations, and compendia of classical learning. In addition, scholars, such as Pope Gregory (*Moralia in Job, Dialogues*) and Gregory of Tours (*History of the Franks*), produced original books. When scholarship on the Continent sank in the seventh century, Irish and English scholars, such as Bede the Venerable (*Ecclesiastical History of the English People*), carried on the Latin tradition. Most of this literature was filled with accounts of miracles, reflecting an assumption that the universe was shaped by miraculous interventions of God.

B. The Carolingian Renaissance.

Pepin, Charlemagne, and their successors energetically promoted learning to encourage religious uniformity and improve the supply of learned officials. Educational reforms were instituted, more efficient handwriting (the Carolingian minuscule) was created, scholarly language was made common (Medieval Latin), and important texts were standardized. These accomplishments revived mastery of correct Latin, led to a freer development of separate but related vernacular languages, and made possible future renaissances in Western thought.

Experiences of Daily Life: Carolingian Families.

In the new peasant economy, with its Christian rules of monogamy and extended incest prohibition, families were fundamentally similar compared to the wide variations in the Classical world.

SIGNIFICANT INDIVIDUALS

Political Leaders

Attila (433?–453), Hun.
Odoacer (476–493), Germanic.
Theodoric (474–526), Ostrogoth.
Clovis (481–511), Frank.
Charles Martel (715–741), Frank.

Pepin the Short (751–768),
    Carolingian.
Charlemagne (768–814), Carolingian.
Alfred (871–899), Saxon.
Canute (1016–1035), Dane.

Religious Leaders

Ulfilas (311?–381), missionary.
Gregory the Great (590–604), pope.

St. Benedict (480?–543?), monastic
    leader.

Cultural Figures

Tacitus (55?–120?), Roman historian.
Einhard (770?–840), Frankish
    biographer.
Boethius (480?–524?), Italian scholar.
Bede the Venerable (673?–735),
    English scholar.

Cassiodorus (490?–585?), Italian
    scholar.
Alcuin of York (735–804), English
    scholar.

CHRONOLOGICAL DIAGRAM

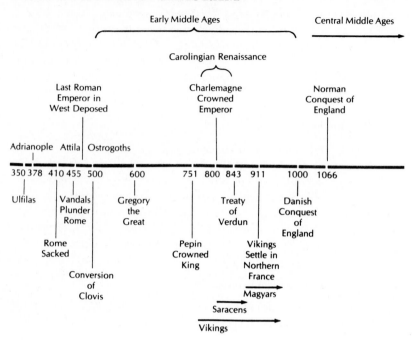

IDENTIFICATION

Celts
Gauls
Franks
Slavs
vulgar culture
Wergeld
the Animal style
heavy plow
three-field system
manor

papal primacy
Benedictine Rule
stirrup
county
Missi Dominici
Danegeld
standardized curriculum
Carolingian minuscule
Medieval Latin

MAP EXERCISE

1. Indicate the areas where the Vandals, Visigoths, Franks, Anglo-Saxons, Burgundians, Alemanni, and Ostrogoths settled.
2. Outline the Frankish Empire under Charlemagne.

PROBLEMS FOR ANALYSIS

I. The New Community of Peoples.

1. Considering the numerous invasions of the Roman Empire by Celtic, Germanic, and Slavic tribes, was there a pattern to their conquests and settlements? Explain.
2. Despite many differences between Germans and Romans, the Germans assimilated into the culture of the Roman Empire. How do you explain this?
3. What legal, political, military, and cultural institutions did the Germans bring with them? Indicate any connections between these and later medieval institutions.

II. The New Economy.

1. In what ways did Europeans make important technological and organizational changes in the economy of the Early Middle Ages?
2. What developments might help explain the decline of commerce and industry during the Early Middle Ages? What explanation makes the most sense to you?

III. The Leadership of the Church.

1. How were the early Roman bishops able to develop themselves into powerful popes? What role did Gregory the Great play in this development?
2. Why was monasticism so important? What were the characteristics of monasticism? Why was the Benedictine Rule so important?

IV. The New Political Structures.

1. How were Carolingian leaders able to acquire power from their Merovingian predecessors and establish an extensive kingdom? Why was this kingdom short-lived?
2. Indicate the similarities and differences between the Anglo-Saxon and Frankish kingdoms. Consider the rise to power of unifying kings and the causes for their decline.

V. Letters and Learning.

1. In what ways was classical culture saved and transformed by the Church? Why was classical culture so important to the Church?
2. What were the principal characteristics of the Carolingian Renaissance? Which of these were most important and why?

DOCUMENTS

Early Feudal Contracts

The following is a form, or formula, for entering into a feudal contract. It is a seventh-century Frankish document whereby one commends oneself into the power and service of a superior in return for guardianship and certain benefits.

> Who commends himself in the power of another:
> To that magnificent lord *so and so,* I, *so and so.* Since it is known familiarly to all how little I have whence to feed and clothe myself, I have therefore petitioned your piety, and your good-will has decreed to me that I should hand myself over to commend myself to your guardianship, which I have thereupon done; that is to say in this way, that you should aid and succor me as well with food as with clothing, according as I shall be able to serve you and deserve it.

And so long as I shall live I ought to provide service and honor to you, suitably to my free condition; and I shall not during the time of my life have the ability to withdraw from your power or guardianship; but must remain during the days of my life under your power or defence. Wherefore it is proper that if either of us shall wish to withdraw himself from these agreements, he shall pay *so many* shillings to the other party (*pari suo*), and this agreement shall remain unbroken. [1]

1. What are the costs and the benefits to each in this sort of contract?
2. Does this differ from a modern contract? Explain.

The following is a provision of a feudal contract between lord and vassal indicating some of the grounds under which vassals would be allowed to leave the relationship.

If any one shall wish to leave his lord (*seniorem*), and is able to prove against him one of these crimes, that is, in the first place, if the lord has wished to reduce him unjustly into servitude; in the second place, if he has taken counsel against his life; in the third place, if the lord has committed adultery with the wife of his vassal; in the fourth place, if he has wilfully attacked him with a drawn sword; in the fifth place, if the lord has been able to bring defence to his vassal after he has commended his hands to him, and has not done so; it is allowed to the vassal to leave him. If the lord has perpetrated anything against the vassal in these five points it is allowed the vassal to leave him. [2]

1. What sorts of problems upset feudal relationships, as illustrated by this document?
2. What does this document imply concerning the strength of central political and legal institutions?

The "Dark Ages"

The older, traditional view of the fall of Rome and the barbarian invasions is that they were unmitigated disasters that ushered in a terrible period in European history: the Dark Ages. The following selection from P. Boissonnade illustrates this view, which remains a point of reference for more recent interpretations.

The material and moral disaster was, indeed, immense, and seemed irreparable. Civilized life, especially in the East, had been thrust back into barbarism. Neither labour nor intelligence was honoured. Force reigned supreme, and the warrior band exploited Western society without pity. A minority of chiefs and fighters lived upon war and pillage, oppressed the wretched population of *coloni* and slaves on its domains, heaped up the fruits of its rapine, filled its harems with girls, its stables with horses, and its kennels with hounds, divided its leisure between banqueting and the chase, dog fights, and violent exercise. The nobility and freemen, shunning the ruined towns, lived in their *villae,* their family dwelling-places, or their hamlets on the edge of the great common forests, like the idle, rude, and brutal conquerors they were. The working

---

[1] E. P. Cheyney, ed., "Documents Illustrative of Feudalism," in *Translations and Reprints from the Original Sources of European History,* IV, No. 3, ed. Department of History of the University of Pennsylvania (Philadelphia, 1898), pp. 3–4.

[2] Ibid., p. 5.

classes, who laboured for them, were exposed to all the risks of an unregulated and anarchical society, whose only rule was violence. The idleness, stupidity, coarseness, ignorance, credulity, and cruelty of the barbarians took the place of the well-regulated activity, the polish, culture, and relative humanity of the Romans. There was no longer any respect for the weak, for peasants and women and children. There was no discipline, no moral code to restrain these invaders, who merely added the vices of civilization to the depravity of barbarism. Far from regenerating the world, they very nearly wiped out civilization for ever. They destroyed the ordered societies of the West, only to replace them by anarchy. Far from bringing freedom in their train, they reestablished slavery. Far from diminishing class distinctions, they reared new barriers between the classes. Far from ameliorating the condition of the lower classes, they made it harder. Far from assisting economic development, they ruined all activity by sowing everywhere pillage, disorder, and destruction. They created nothing, but they destroyed much, and they put a stop to all progress for several centuries. In society and in labour the barbarian settlements produced one of the greatest retrogressions which the world has ever known. Their one useful result was that they gave finer spirits an impetus to energy and to action, and thus, out of sheer reaction, brought about a series of attempts to return to the traditions of Roman government, and roused the Church from its mystic dream, in order that it might save the remnants of civilization from shipwreck. In the East the Roman edifice had weathered the storm, and could serve as a model and framework for the restoration of society and of labour. In the West the spirit and institutions of Rome, adapted to new conditions of environment, were destined to inspire those attempts at economic and social restoration which took place towards the end of the Dark Ages. [3]

1. How much of this interpretation relies on the author's own evaluation of how good or bad the changes were? Do you agree with the author?
2. How does this interpretation compare with that in the text?

Medieval Attitudes

In the following selection, Lynn White, Jr., focuses on the attitudes of the common people during the Early Middle Ages. Note the difference in tone from that of the previous selection.

We are beginning to see that the early Middle Ages in Europe witnessed a profound alteration of attitudes toward nature. This shift in the world view was based partly on the agricultural revolution of that era and partly on the revolution in popular religion which was occurring simultaneously.

In the days of the scratch-plow and squarish fields, land was distributed in units which were thought to be sufficient for the support of one family. The peasant paid rent, which was in effect taxes, to the owning-ruling aristocracy, but the assumption was subsistence farming—man was part of nature. The new heavy plow of northern Europe changed this. Since it demanded a cooperative plow-team, the strips which it plowed were distributed in proportion to a peasant's contribution to the team. Thus the standard of land distribution ceased to be the needs of a family and became the

---

[3] P. Boissonnade, *Life and Work in Medieval Europe, the Evolution of Medieval Economy from the Fifth to the Fifteenth Century,* trans. Eileen Power (London: Routledge & Kegan Paul, Ltd., 1927), p. 31.

ability of a power engine to till the soil. No more fundamental modification in a man's relation to his environment can be imagined: he ceased to be nature's child and became her exploiter. We, who are descended from the peasants who first built such plows, inherit from them that aggressive attitude toward nature which is an essential element in modern culture. We feel so free to use nature for our purposes because we feel abstracted from nature and its processes.[4]

1. What fundamental modification in a person's relation to his or her environment occurred during the Early Middle Ages?
2. Does this interpretation imply that there were some important benefits to the fall of the Roman world and the beginning of the Middle Ages? Explain.

The Coronation of Charlemagne

The following, another traditional interpretation of the Middle Ages, complements that of P. Boissonnade. Here, James Bryce focuses on the coronation of Charlemagne in 800.

The coronation of Charles is not only the central event of the Middle Ages, it is also one of those very few events of which, taking them singly, it may be said that if they had not happened, the history of the world would have been different. In one sense indeed it has scarcely a parallel. The assassins of Julius Caesar thought that they had saved Rome from monarchy, but monarchy became inevitable in the next generation. The conversion of Constantine changed the face of the world, but Christianity was spreading fast, and its ultimate triumph was only a question of time. Had Columbus never spread his sails, the secret of the western sea would yet have been pierced by some later voyager: had Charles V broken his safe-conduct to Luther, the voice silenced at Wittenberg would have been taken up by echoes elsewhere. But if the Roman Empire had not been restored in the West in the person of Charles, it would never have been restored at all, and the inexhaustible train of consequences for good and for evil that followed could not have been. Why this was so may be seen by examining the history of the next two centuries. In that day, as through all the Dark and Middle Ages, two forces were striving for the mastery. The one was the instinct of separation, disorder, anarchy, caused by the ungoverned impulses and barbarous ignorance of the great bulk of mankind; the other was that passionate longing of the better minds for a formal unity of government, which had its historical basis in the memories of the old Roman Empire, and its most constant expression in the devotion to a visible and catholic Church. The former tendency, as everything shows, was, in politics at least, the stronger, but the latter, used and stimulated by an extraordinary genius like Charles, achieved in the year 800 a victory whose results were never to be lost. When the hero was gone, the returning wave of anarchy and barbarism swept up violent as ever, yet it could not wholly obliterate the past: the Empire, maimed and shattered though it was, had struck its roots too deep to be overthrown by force, and when it perished at last, perished from inner decay. It was just because men felt that no one less than Charles could have won such a triumph over the evils of time, by

[4]Lynn White, Jr., "The Life of the Silent Majority," in *Life and Thought in the Early Middle Ages,* ed. Robert S. Hoyt (Minneapolis: University of Minnesota Press, 1967), pp. 99–100. Copyright © 1967 by the University of Minnesota.

framing and establishing a gigantic scheme of government, that the excitement and hope and joy which the coronation evoked were so intense. Their best evidence is perhaps to be found not in the records of that time itself, but in the cries of lamentation that broke forth when the Empire began to dissolve towards the close of the ninth century, in the marvellous legends which attached themselves to the name of Charles the Emperor, a hero of whom any exploit was credible, in the devout admiration wherewith his German successors looked back to, and strove in all things to imitate, their all but super-human prototype. . . . [5]

1. Why does Bryce feel that the coronation of Charlemagne was the central event of the Middle Ages? Compare this view with that presented in the text.
2. As implied in this interpretation, does Bryce feel that great men make history move in certain directions, or that great men are created by powerful, more impersonal historical forces? Explain.

SPECULATIONS

1. Suppose you were a bishop of Rome during the Early Middle Ages. What do you think would be the best way to deal with the decline of the Roman Empire and the barbarian invasions? Why?
2. Do you think it is accurate to consider the Early Middle Ages a "Dark Ages"? If our civilization fell, what would a corresponding "Dark Ages" be like?

TRANSITIONS

In "The Empire and Christianity," the course and transformation of the Roman Empire were analyzed. By the fifth century, the Empire in the West fell and Christianity was established as the dominant religion in the Mediterranean area.

In "The Making of Western Europe," the beginnings of a new Western Civilization are traced. It, like other new civilizations to the East and South which fell heir to the classical tradition, differed most fundamentally from its Roman predecessor by being predominantly peasant and dominated by beliefs in an afterlife and hope of personal salvation. In Western Europe peoples combined "barbarian" and classical inheritances to form distinctive cultures during the Early Middle Ages. Despite a long period of invasions and migrations, these peoples, supported by the settled peasant family and Roman Catholic beliefs, created a relatively poor, rural, vulgar, and unstable civilization, which became the basis for Western Civilization.

In "The Early Medieval East," the three civilizations of Byzantine, Kiev, and Islam will be examined and compared to those of Western Europe during the Early Middle Ages.

[5] James Bryce, *The Holy Roman Empire* (London and New York: The Macmillan Company, 1897), pp. 50–52.

SEVEN
THE EARLY MEDIEVAL EAST
ca. 300–1100

MAIN THEMES

1. The Eastern Roman Empire survived and evolved into the long-lasting Byzantine Empire.
2. The first East Slavic civilization was organized around the Principality of Kiev, a sophisticated but relatively short-lived state.
3. In the seventh century Islam rapidly expanded, conquering and converting vast areas and developing an advanced urban civilization.

OUTLINE AND SUMMARY

I. *The Byzantine Empire.*

The Roman Empire did not fall in the East until 1453.

A. *Early Byzantine Period.*

Byzantine history begins in 324, when Constantine transferred his capital to Byzantium (Constantinople) for military purposes. Soon this city, located at the intersection of commercial routes, became a flourishing Christian center.

    1. *Justinian the Great:* Justinian (527–565) was the most successful of the early emperors who struggled to recover the full empire. From information supplied by Procopius (*On the Wars, On Buildings, Secret History*) we know much of Justinian, his ambitions, his influential wife Theodora, and his capable advisors. After nearly losing power during a rebellion, Justinian turned to ambitious projects. He partially succeeded in restoring western areas to the empire by defeating the Vandals in North Africa, the Ostrogoths in Italy, and the Visigoths in southern Spain. He organized and codified Roman law in the *Corpus Iuris Civilis,* which would form the basis for most Western legal systems. He initiated an extensive rebuilding of his capital, creating many new churches (church of Hagia Sophia), palaces, and public works. Toward the end of his reign Byzantium was faced by war in the east and the west and had to go on the defensive. Justinian proved overly ambitious for his resources, and his successors were unable to hold on to most of his territorial acquisitions.

B. Middle Byzantine Period.

Emperor Heraclius (610–641) gave Byzantium its Eastern orientation. He succeeded against the aggressive Persians and followed a policy of granting land to
soldiers and encouraging them to settle there (system of themes), making them
more effective workers and fighters. After 632 Muslims overran most of the empire
and held it until Leo III (717–741) began a reconquest of Asia Minor. In the following centuries warrior emperors recovered areas in the East, the Balkan peninsula, southern Italy, and the Caucasus. A temporary policy forbidding veneration
of images (726–784, 813–843) further split Western and Eastern churches.

C. Byzantine Civilization.

Byzantines expanded Hellenistic ideas of natural law into a religious belief in
one empire and one faith. The empire thus united its many peoples religiously
and politically. The emperor was a holy figure who held political and religious
authority, though the extent of his religious authority has been questioned, since
he was not a priest.

1. *The Eastern Church:* A comparison of the Eastern and Western churches
clarifies other contrasts between the two peoples. The Eastern Church developed
and functioned under secular supervision, while the Western Church freed itself
from secular control and often assumed secular powers itself. Both considered
themselves universal and orthodox. The two Churches maintained nearly identi-
cal beliefs, with some differences concerning the nature of the Holy Spirit, the
existence of purgatory, and the legitimacy of divorce. The Eastern Church tolerated the use of vernacular languages, leading to an earlier development of vernacular literature than in the West, which tolerated only Latin. The Eastern
Church was much more decentralized and dependent upon secular authority; in
turn, the state in the East made use of the great wealth and spiritual power of the
Church. The lack of friction between Church and state encouraged submissive-
ness and withdrawal by the Eastern Church in deference to the state.

2. *Byzantine Society:* Urban life survived, and some of the greatest cities of the
age (Trebizond, Constantinople) were located within the empire. Rural society was
largely made up of free peasants who participated in a highly developed village
government. Economically, the empire was relatively wealthy, thanks to its commerce and its productive guilds (making mostly luxury items). The state retained
some monopolies, particularly over silk products. Government was centralized
under the emperor and his elaborate civil service. The government remained
much more efficient and professional than in the West, with such refinements as
an effective fiscal system, a state post, a secret police, and a corps of trained dip-
lomats. Preference for eunuchs in governmental service, especially in palace
administration, led to a gradual seclusion of women within the household.

3. *Byzantine Culture:* Byzantine wealth supported a tradition of learning among
the clergy and some laymen. Scholars used Greek and preserved almost all we
know of classical Greek literature. Architects created impressive structures, the
greatest of all being the Hagia Sophia. Although marred by the iconoclastic movement, the Byzantines excelled in creating colorful but relatively static mosaics.

D. Decline of the Empire.

As the system of themes began to weaken in the tenth century, the free peasants were transformed into serfs. Power slipped from the central government into the hands of strong local landlords. With a weakened navy, emperors became more dependent on the Venetian navy.

1. *The Seljuks:* In the eleventh century most of Asia Minor was conquered by the Seljuk Turks, ending the Byzantine Empire as a great power in the East.

2. *Schism with the West:* In 1054 rivalry, disputes, and snobbery led to a formal schism between the Eastern and Western churches.

E. The Western Debt to Byzantine Civilization.

The Byzantine Empire helped protect the West and provided an example of advanced civilized life when the West was at a low point. Byzantine scholars preserved classical Greek literature.

II. The Principality of Kiev.

The East Slavs (the Rus) founded a civilization based on the values of Eastern Christianity during the Early Middle Ages.

A. The Foundations of Kiev Rus.

According to the *Primary Chronicle,* in the ninth century East Slavs, under the leadership of Vikings, became unified in the territory between Novgorod and Kiev. Oleg (873?–913) and his successors founded the Rus state. In 989 Vladimir converted to Eastern Christianity and brought the East Slavs into the Church and the Eastern cultural world.

1. *Yaroslav the Wise:* Under Yaroslav (1015–1054), the Principality of Kiev reached its height. He expanded his territorial control, gained independence for the Rus Church, codified laws, built cathedrals, promoted learning, and developed contacts with the West.

B. Kievan Civilization.

Kievan economy was primarily agricultural, but there was considerable trade with surrounding peoples and civilizations, particularly the Byzantines. Peasants were generally free, though there were some serfs and slaves. Kiev was considered one of the great cities of the age. Kievan government was a balance of monarchical, aristocratic, and popular elements, the prince relying on advice from his nobles (boyars) and his assemblies. Popular courts handled legal matters. Eastern Christianity brought the influence of Byzantine education, literature (*Primary Chronicle, Song of Igor's Campaign*), art (icons), and architecture (the onion domes). The East Slavs came to view their country as Holy Rus, alone against a sea of pagan barbarians.

C. Decline of the Principality.

Political quarrels weakened Kiev internally. Steppe nomads cut off contact with the Black Sea, and thus, trade with the Byzantine Empire. By the twelfth century, Kiev had been sacked and the center of Rus life moved north around Moscow.

III. Islam.

Followers of Muhammad exploded out of Mecca in the seventh century, conquering and partially converting territories larger than the Roman Empire.

A. The Arabs.

The Arabs, molded by the harsh environment of the Arabian peninsula, were proud animal herders and warriors. Their land was a focus of territorial and religious rivalry when Muhammad arrived.

B. Muhammad.

Muhammad rose from humble origins in Mecca. He experienced revelations after 610, and in 622 he fled from Mecca to Yathrib (Medina), where he became a political leader. He combined his concern for law, administration, and government with religious conversion: through enthusiastic proselytizing and war his teachings spread rapidly.

C. The Religion of Islam.

The prophecies of Allah ("the God") were passed from the angel Gabriel to Muhammad, and then to his followers, who collected them in the Koran. The Muslim religion emphasizes the power and concern of Allah; followers are to submit to the will of Allah and follow an ethically and legally upright life. Muslims have no clergy; there is but one sacred community of Allah, created by Allah through Muhammad and the Koran.

1. *Expansion of Islam:* Islam had great appeal to Arabs. It was relatively simple; it combined familiar features of Christianity, Judaism, paganism, and perhaps Zoroastrianism; and it depended on the Arabic language. The Arabs' policy of encouraging conquest while tolerating Christians and Jews aided in the rapid spread of the religion and of Islamic rule. There was a sudden expansion under the first four caliphs (632–661) and continued expansion under the Omayyad caliphs (661–750). In the eighth and ninth centuries internal religious and political rivalries combined with overexpansion to break Islam apart into independent caliphates. Islam's extension into Europe was finally halted by Charles Martel at Tours in 732.

D. Islamic Civilization.

Islamic civilization reached its peak in the ninth and tenth centuries. Its expanse made it a varied civilization, though its common religion and language brought some unity. Commerce was particularly important, the merchant being a highly esteemed figure. A cosmopolitan urban life in the great cities (Baghdad, Cairo, Cordoba, Damascus) flourished. Spain and Baghdad became strong centers of this civilization. Males dominated women to an unusual degree, particularly among the upper classes. The caliph was, in theory, the supreme religious and civil authority; but, in practice, he was primarily a military chief and a judge. Many existing governmental institutions were retained in the territories conquered by the Muslims. Islamic scholars preserved works of the Greeks and added their own contributions in astronomy, astrology, mathematics, medicine, and optics. Their development of the zero, arabic numerals, and algebra was particularly important. Scholars, such as Averroes, wrote philosophical and theological treatises that exerted a profound influence on both Christian and Islamic philosophy.

E. Decline of Medieval Islam.

During the eleventh century, Christians went on the offensive in the West and the Mediterranean, breaking Islamic control and commerce in various areas. Meanwhile, in the East, Turks gained supremacy. Internally, commerce declined and an aristocracy of rural warriors grew, bringing a new rigidity into society.

F. The Western Debt to Islamic Civilization.

The West borrowed many specific accomplishments of Islam, such as their cultivation of new crops, their system of numbers, and their scholarship, but these influences were not fundamental. The two civilizations were perhaps too threatening to each other to accept each other's cultural influence in basic ways.

Experiences of Daily Life: Byzantine Sport.

Byzantium sponsored big athletic spectacles such as the chariot races in the Hippodrome.

SIGNIFICANT INDIVIDUALS

Political Leaders

Justinian (527–565), Byzantine
  Emperor.
Heraclius (610–641), Byzantine
  Emperor.
Oleg (873?–913), founder, Rus state.

Theodora (527–548), Byzantine
  Empress.
Vladimir (980–1015), Rus ruler.
Yaroslav (1015–1054), Rus ruler.

Cultural Leaders

Procopius (6th century), Byzantine
  historian.
Al-Mumun (813–833), caliph and
  patron of philosophy.

ibn-Rushd (Averroes) (1126?–1198),
  Islamic philosopher.

Religious Leaders

Muhammad (570–632), founder of
Islam.

CHRONOLOGICAL DIAGRAM

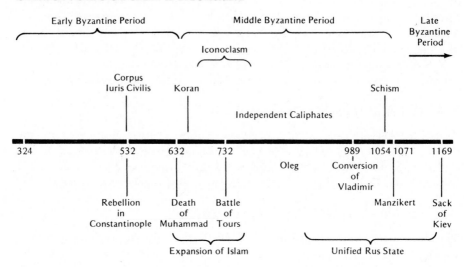

IDENTIFICATION

Constantinople
Hagia Sophia
iconoclasm
"caesaropapism"
filioque dispute
Byzantine mosaics
Seljuk Turks

East Slavs
rota system
Koran
Omayyad caliphs
independent caliphates
Mecca
zero

MAP EXERCISES

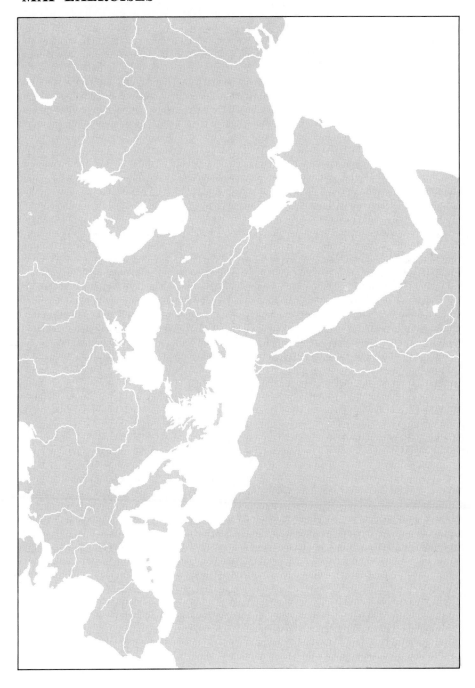

1. Indicate the areas of Islamic and Byzantine control during the ninth and tenth centuries.

1. Outline the boundaries of Kiev in the eleventh century. Indicate the locations of Novgorod, Moscow, and the city of Kiev.

PROBLEMS FOR ANALYSIS

I. The Byzantine Empire.

1. Justinian was both successful and unsuccessful in carrying out his ambitious plans. Compare his accomplishments with his ambitions. Do you think he would be considered a Roman or a Byzantine emperor? Why?

2. Compare the Eastern and the Western churches. How did their connections to secular authority differ?

3. Develop a well-supported argument that the Byzantine Empire, in its cities, its economy, its government, and its culture, became the center of the civilized world around the Mediterranean after the fall of Rome.

4. Explain the decline of the Byzantine Empire.

II. *The Principality of Kiev.*

1. Should the Principality of Kiev be considered one of the most advanced civilizations of its time? Why?

2. Should the Principality of Kiev be thought of as the foundation of modern Russia? Why?

III. *Islam.*

1. How do you explain the extremely rapid spread of Islam in the seventh century? Was it mainly due to the nature of the religion? What role did the characteristics and environment of the Arabs play in this? Was it simply a function of conquest?

2. Compare the cosmopolitan Islamic civilization with the civilization of Western Europe during the Early Middle Ages. How did they differ politically and culturally?

3. In some ways Islam significantly influenced the West, yet some historians argue that the two civilizations were fundamentally separate. Do you agree? Why?

DOCUMENTS

The Justinian Code

The following is a selection from *The Institutes*, part of Emperor Justinian's major codification of Roman law during the sixth century.

PREAMBLE

In the Name of Our Lord Jesus Christ

The Emperor Caesar Flavius Justinianus, Vanquisher of the Alamani, Goths, Francs, Germans,

. . . Triumphant Conqueror, Ever August, to the Youth Desirous of Studying the Law. Greetings.

The Imperial majesty should be not only made glorious by arms, but also strengthened by laws, that, alike in time of peace and in time of war, the state may be well governed, and that the emperor may not only be victorious in the field of battle, but also may by every legal means repel the iniquities of men who abuse the laws, and may at once religiously uphold justice and triumph over his conquered enemies.

1. By our incessant labours and great care, with the blessing of God, we have attained this double end. The barbarian nations reduced under our yoke know our efforts in war; to which also Africa and very many other provinces bear witness, which,

after so long an interval, have been restored to the dominion of Rome and our empire, by our victories gained through the favour of heaven. All nations moreover are governed by laws which we have either promulgated or arranged.

2.   When we had arranged and brought into perfect harmony the hitherto confused mass of imperial constitutions, we then extended our care to the endless volumes of ancient law; and, sailing as it were across the mid-ocean, have now completed, through the favour of heaven, a work we once despaired of.

3.   When by the blessing of God this task was accomplished, we summoned the most eminent Tribonian, master and ex-quaestor of our palace, together with the illustrious Theophilus and Dorotheus, professors of law, all of whom have on many occasions proved to us their ability, legal knowledge and obedience to our orders; and we specially charge them to compose, under our authority and advice, Institutes, so that you may no more learn the first elements of law from old and erroneous sources, but apprehend them by the clear light of imperial wisdom; and that your minds and ears may receive nothing that is useless or misplaced, but only what obtains in actual practice. So that whereas, formerly, the foremost among you could scarcely, after four years' study, read the imperial constitutions, you may now commence your studies by reading them, you who have been thought worthy of an honour and a happiness so great as that the first and last lessons in the knowledge of the law should issue for you from the mouth of the emperor.

4.   When therefore, by the assistance of the same eminent person Tribonian and that of other illustrious and learned men, we had compiled the fifty books, called Digests or Pandects, in which is collected the whole ancient law, we directed that these Institutes should be divided into four books, which might serve as the first elements of the whole science of law.

5.   In these books a brief exposition is given of the ancient laws, and of those also, which, overshadowed by disuse, have been again brought to light by our imperial authority.

6.   These four books of Institutes thus compiled, from all the Institutes left us by the ancients, and chiefly from the commentaries of our Gaius, both from his institutes, and his Journal, and also from many other commentaries, were presented to us by the three learned men we have above named. We read and examined them, and have accorded to them all the force of our constitutions.

7.   Receive, therefore, with eagerness, and study with cheerful diligence, these our laws, and show yourselves persons of such learning that you may conceive the flattering hope of yourselves being able, when your course of legal study is completed, to govern our empire in the different portions that may be entrusted to your care.

Given at Constantinople on the eleventh day of the calends of December, in the third consulate of the Emperor Justinian, ever August.

BOOK ONE

Justice is the constant and perpetual wish to render every one his due.

Jurisprudence is the knowledge of things divine and human; the science of the just and the unjust.

Having explained these general terms, we think we shall commence our exposition of the law of the Roman people most advantageously, if we pursue at first a plain and easy path, and then proceed to explain particular details with the utmost care and exactness. For, if at the outset we overload the mind of the student, while yet new to the subject and unable to bear much, with a multitude and variety of topics, one of two things will happen—we shall either cause him wholly to abandon his studies, or, after great toil, and often after great distrust of himself (the most frequent stumbling-block in the way of youth), we shall at last conduct him to the point, to which, if he had been led by an easier road, he might, without great labour, and without any distrust of his own powers, have been sooner conducted.

The maxims of law are these: to live honestly, to hurt no one, to give every one his due.

The study of law is divided into two branches; that of public and that of private law. Public law regards the government of the Roman Empire; private law, the interest of individuals. We are now to treat of the latter, which is composed of three elements, and consists of precepts belonging to natural law, to the law of nations, and to the civil law. . . .[1]

1. What, apparently, was the purpose of writing these *Institutes*?
2. In what ways does this support the interpretation that one of Rome's greatest legacies is its legal system? Explain.

The Koran

The following is an excerpt taken from the *Koran,* a collection of prophecies written during the seventh century.

Praise be to God, Maker of the Heavens and of the Earth! Who employeth the ANGELS as envoys, having two and three and four pairs of wings: He addeth to his creature what He will! Truly God hath power over all things.

The Mercy which God layeth open for man no one can withhold; and what He withholdeth, none can afterwards send forth. And He is the Mighty, the Wise.

O men! bear in mind the favour of God towards you. Is there a creator other than God who nourisheth you out of heaven and earth? There is no God but He! How then are ye turned aside from Him?

If they treat thee as an impostor, then before thee have apostles been treated as impostors—But to God shall all things return.

O men! verily the promise of God is true: let not then the present life deceive you with vain hopes: and let not the Deceiver deceive you as to God.

Yes, Satan is your foe. For a foe then hold him. He summoneth his followers only to become inmates of the flame.

The unbelievers,—for them a terrible punishment!—

But believers and doers of good works, for them is mercy, and a great reward!

Shall he, the evil of whose deeds are so tricked out to him that he deemeth them good, be treated like him who seeth things aright? Verily God misleadeth whom He will, and guideth whom He will. Spend not thy soul in sights for them: verily God knoweth their doings.

It is God who sendeth forth the winds which raise the clouds aloft; then drive We them on to some land dead from drought, and give life thereby to the earth after its death. So shall be the Resurrection.

If any one desireth greatness, greatness is wholly with God. The good word riseth up to Him, and the righteous deed doth He exalt. But a severe punishment awaiteth the plotters of evil things; and the plots of such will be in vain.

---

[1] *The Institutes of Justinian,* trans. Thomas C. Sandars (London: Longmans, Green, 1874), pp. 1–7.

Moreover God created you of dust—then of the germs of life—then made you two sexes and no female conceiveth or bringeth forth without his knowledge; and the aged ageth not, nor is aught minished from man's age, but in accordance with the Book. An easy thing truly is this to God.

Nor are the two seas alike: the one is fresh, sweet, pleasant for drink, and the other salt, bitter; yet from both ye eat fresh fish, and take forth for yourselves ornaments to wear; and thou seest the ships cleaving the waters that ye may go in quest of his bounties; and haply ye will be thankful.

He causeth the night to enter in upon the day, and the day to enter in upon the night; and He hath given laws to the sun and to the moon, so that each journeyeth to its appointed goal: This is God your Lord: All power is his: But the gods whom ye call on beside Him have no power over the husk of a date-stone! [2]

1. In mood, style, or content, compare this with any Christian writings. What are the similarities? What are the differences?
2. What distinctions are made between believers and unbelievers, and between men and women?

Byzantium and Islam

In the following selection, Speros Vryonis, Jr., focuses on the conflict in the East between Byzantium and the rising power of Islam during the seventh century.

The critical phase of the struggle between Byzantium and the new Islamic giant took place in the reign of Constantine IV (668–85), when the ambitious caliph Muawiyya set out to take Constantinople. He sent his armies repeatedly into Asia Minor and, in a phenomenal display of adaptation, created an Arab naval power which soon occupied Cyprus, Rhodes, Chios and Cyzicus. His forces first besieged Constantinople in 669, but the major effort of the Arabs came in the five-year period 674–78. The Arab fleet based at Cyzicus and the armies which marched across Anatolia tried to storm the powerful bastion, but in vain, and both the Arab fleet and army suffered a humiliating disaster in which the dreaded Greek fire invented by a Greek from Syria made its debut. Constantine IV had providentially equipped his fleet with siphons for propelling the secret weapon, and Greek fire became one of the most dreaded weapons of the imperial fleets. This Byzantine victory was crucial for the history of both Christendom and Islam, far more so than the victory of Charles Martel at Poitiers (732). The empire was able to overcome the greatest military effort of Islam and thus to preserve the Christian character of European civilization. The defeat of Muawiyya turned the Arab power back to the Middle East whence it had come, and though the Arabs succeeded in taking Spain, Islamic civilization was eventually confined to non-European areas. [3]

1. Why was this Byzantine victory so crucial for the history of both Christendom and Islam?

---

[2] *The Koran,* trans. J. M. Rodwell.

[3] Speros Vryonis, Jr., *Byzantium and Europe* (London: Thames and Hudson Ltd., 1967), pp. 63–64.

Islam and Western Europe

Some fifty years ago Henri Pirenne presented a new interpretation of the Early Middle Ages and the significance of Islam for its development. Although more recent interpretations question Pirenne's view, it has proven to be extraordinarily influential and provocative.

> The tremendous effect the invasion of Islam had upon Western Europe has not, perhaps, been fully appreciated.
>
> Out of it arose a new and unparalleled situation, unlike anything that had gone before. Through the Phoenicians, the Greeks, and finally the Romans, Western Europe had always received the cultural stamp of the East. It had lived, as it were, by virtue of the Mediterranean; now for the first time it was forced to live by its own resources. The center of gravity, heretofore on the shore of the Mediterranean, was shifted to the north. As a result the Frankish Empire, which had so far been playing only a minor role in the history of Europe, was to become the arbiter of Europe's destinies.
>
> There is obviously more than mere coincidence in the simultaneity of the closing of the Mediterranean by Islam and the entry of the Carolingians on the scene. There is the distinct relation of cause and effect between the two. The Frankish Empire was fated to lay the foundations of the Europe of the Middle Ages. But the mission which it fulfilled had as an essential prior condition the overthrow of the traditional world-order. The Carolingians would never have been called upon to play the part they did if historical evolution had not been turned aside from its course and, so to speak, "de-Saxoned" by the Moslem invasion. Without Islam, the Frankish Empire would probably never have existed and Charlemagne, without Mahomet, would be inconceivable. [4]

1. According to Pirenne, what were the main consequences of the invasion of the Mediterranean and Europe by Islam?

SPECULATIONS

1. If you were transported back in time as the chief advisor to Justinian, what would you recommend? Why?
2. Suppose the Western Roman Empire survived in a shrunken form — confined to Italy and areas bordering the Mediterranean in France, Spain, and north-western Africa. Speculate on how this might have changed the course of European and Islamic history.

TRANSITIONS

In "The Making of Western Europe," the development of a new civilization in the West from a mixture of "barbarian" and Roman peoples during the Early Middle Ages was examined.

---

[4] Henri Pirenne, *Medieval Cities: Their Origins and the Revival of Trade,* trans. Frank D. Halsey (Princeton: Princeton University Press © 1925, 1952; Princeton Paperback, 1969), pp. 26-27. Reprinted by permission of Princeton University Press.

In "The Early Medieval East," the focus is shifted to three Eastern civilizations that arose during this same period: Byzantine, Kiev, and Islam. Byzantium developed directly from the old Roman Empire, evolving into a distinct civilization but retaining a strong continuity with the past. Kiev was heavily influenced by contact with Byzantium. Islam influenced the West, but remained fundamentally unique and apart. These civilizations enjoyed a clear superiority over those in Western Europe, thanks to the preservation of Roman institutions; the Hellenistic, Semitic, and Persian cultural heritages; the survival of cities; and the creation of an authentic urban life. Western Europe would benefit from the security against invasions from Asia, enlarged access to the classical heritage, and new learnings offered by the presence of these Eastern civilizations.

In "Two Centuries of Creativity," we will return to the West, where striking changes led to a more firmly established civilization after the year 1000.

EIGHT
TWO CENTURIES OF CREATIVITY
ca. 1000–1200

MAIN THEMES

1. After 1000, the European population expanded, commerce increased, and cities grew.
2. European society stabilized through the spread of feudal institutions and the rule of more effective kings.
3. The clergy and papacy gained in strength and influence through reform of the Church.
4. The period was one of high cultural creativity marked by increased schooling, new interest in the humanities, and greater construction of Romanesque churches.

OUTLINE AND SUMMARY

I. The Economic and Social Changes.

After 1000, Europe entered a new period of change and growth.

A. The Beginnings of Expansion.

Europeans began spreading out from impacted settlements after the year 1000. They cleared land, established new villages, and extended frontiers. Historians are not certain why this occurred, but factors such as fewer invasions, improved climate, and encouragement from landlords were probably involved. A sustained population growth resulted.

   1. *Frontiers:* Within Western Europe, peasants leveled forests and drained marshes. Other pioneers pushed outside frontiers to the east and north. Christian Europeans began reconquering Spain, Italy, and the western Mediterranean.

B. Social Changes.

Expansion and economic revival led to improved conditions for peasants. Increasingly, they were able to free themselves from serfdom until it nearly disappeared throughout Western Europe by the thirteenth century. Local commerce and cottage industries grew in importance. Nevertheless, life for peasants, and particularly women, remained relatively harsh. Landlords became less tied to their land, relying on rents, which freed them to travel and share in courtly society. Rural churches grew as did the importance of the literate local priest.

C. Commerce.

There was a major rebirth of long-distance trade during the Central Middle Ages. In the Mediterranean, Venice, Pisa, and Genoa led in developing trade between Europe, North Africa, and the East. Trade in the north grew between major ports around the Baltic. Between the two zones, overland trade developed, particularly at the great fairs of Champagne in France.

D. The Rebirth of Urban Life.

Towns grew, though still at a relatively slow pace. They expanded from simple administrative centers and fortified enclosures to permanent centers of commerce, and later, industry (especially woolen cloth). Urban populations, especially the wealthy in northern Italy and Flanders, organized into communes and gained considerable liberties from their bishops or lords. Social movement between urban aristocrats (patricians), small merchants (now forming into guilds), and others was relatively fluid; talent was rewarded in this dynamic environment. Increased demand for skill in calculations and literacy characterized the developing culture of medieval towns.

II. Feudalism and the Search for Political Order.

To differing degrees, European communities sought social stability through the institutions of the feudal system.

A. Feudal Institutions.

Feudalism is an extraordinarily difficult term to define. To Marxist historians it means an economic system based upon serfdom. To most non-Marxist scholars, it refers to the social and political institutions established by contract between a lord and his vassal. In a broader sense it refers to the society and government in which powerful men define their rights and obligations through individual contracts. Feudal practices developed spontaneously during the first feudal age (about 500–1050) and more self-consciously in the second (1050–1300).

    1. *The Feudal Milieu:* Feudalism first grew in the region between the Loire and Rhine rivers, where alternatives for defense, such as familial (in Celtic and South Slavic areas) or communal (in northern Italy) associations were lacking. It was then exported to other areas. Initially the bond was mainly ethical and emotional (quasi-familial), but later it became more juridical.

    2. *Vassalage:* Vassalage refers to the bond between a lord and his vassal (inferior). It imposed upon both parties obligations of military support, financial aid, legal counsel, and moral support, the balance depending on the agreement and the relative power of the parties. Much of the lord's obligation was increasingly satisfied by a grant of land (fief). Over time, complications developed. Various courts claimed conflicting jurisdiction over vassals, and multiple vassalage created conflicting loyalties. Both developments signified a moral weakening of vassalage and an opportunity for monarchs to strengthen their authority.

3. *The Fief:* Theoretically, the fief granted by the lord to the vassal was conditional, temporary, and nonhereditary. In practice, however, the fief became inheritable and transferable upon the payment of a fee and the acquisition of the lord's permission. The spread of this form of land tenure between the ninth and twelfth centuries helped stabilize property and political relationships in Europe.

4. *Private Justice:* Lords and vassals within the feudal pyramid could tax, judge, and punish their dependents. During the second feudal age an exertion of royal prerogatives slowly diminished private justice.

5. *Stages of Feudal Development:* In the ninth and tenth centuries, Carolingian administration disintegrated into local hands, especially holders of castles (castellans). During the next two centuries these fortresses proliferated. After 1050 a slow process of feudal centralization began under counts, dukes, and some kings.

B. Norman and Angevin England.

England offers the best example of feudal concepts in the service of princes.

1. *The Norman Conquest:* The energetic Duke William of Normandy (1027–1087) conquered the English army at the Battle of Hastings in 1066. He decisively added to changes already taking place, making his vassals more directly tied to the monarchy and spreading feudal institutions, such as the great council, from the Continent. Feudal obligations were clarified by a comprehensive survey of English lands (the *Domesday Book*).

2. *Angevin Kingship:* Henry II, a descendent of William, was the first of the "Angevin" kings, and one of England's best. Through inheritances and his marriage to Eleanor of Aquitaine, he ruled over England and western France. He developed a more effective system of justice, relying on authoritative itinerant judges who impounded "good men" of a locale to investigate crime and settle civil disputes. Decisions became precedents for similar cases, and over time, a body of "common" law of England was developed that served as the basis for the English and other future legal systems. Justices also investigated local sheriffs. Henry strengthened royal administration, especially for fiscal matters (the Exchequer).

3. *Thomas à Becket:* Henry II and the archbishop of Canterbury, Thomas à Becket, struggled over the authority of Church (canonical) courts. The murder of Thomas led to the defeat of Henry on this issue.

C. Capetian France.

After the age of Charlemagne, central government almost disappeared in France. After 1050 French kings followed a policy of developing lord-vassal relations with rulers of important principalities (such as Normandy, Flanders, and Champagne), slowly building some authority.

1. *The Capetians:* Hugh Capet was elected king in 987, and his descendents held the throne until 1792. Initially the French kings held only limited, but strategically located, territory around Paris. They consolidated their power, and eventually, under Louis VI (1108–1137) and Philip II, extended royal territories north and south.

2. *Administration:* By improving financial and judicial administration, respecting the governments of fiefs, and insisting on the loyal service of great dukes and counts, French kings built upon feudal practices to strengthen central authority and political order.

D. The German Empire.

In the tenth and eleventh centuries German political power became concentrated in comparatively large blocks under dukes who, facing the eastern frontiers, considered themselves champions of the Christian faith.

1. *Otto I, the Great:* Otto I (936–973) was the first of the Saxon kings to restore the German Empire. He enjoyed military successes and promoted German missionaries in the East. He invaded Italy and was crowned Roman emperor by Pope John XII. This newly acquired prestige, combined with access to Church resources (control of office and lands), increased his power in German and Italian lands.

2. *Frederick I, Barbarossa:* Under the powerful Frederick I of Hohenstaufen (1152–1190) the German Empire came to be known as the Holy Roman Empire. He was somewhat successful in consolidating his power in Germany, using his feudal powers to subdue the duke of Saxony. He attempted to establish effective control as heir to the Caesars, but a coalition of Italian towns (the Lombard League), supported by the papacy, defeated him at Legnano in 1176. This was the first time an army of townsmen had defeated an established army under noble leadership. His successors were unable to establish an effective government over his far-flung lands.

III. The Reform of the Western Church.

In the eleventh and twelfth centuries the Church experienced fundamental and long-lasting transformations.

A. Moral Crisis.

The Church suffered from a failure of its clergy to remain celibate, the sale of Church offices and services (simony), and lay dominion over Church offices and lands.

B. Early Attempts at Reform.

Some bishops and German emperors attempted reforms, but with only limited success. The spread of Cluniac monasticism was more successful. The monastery of Cluny and its daughter houses throughout Europe were placed directly under the pope and the Abbot of Cluny. Radical reformers started to turn to the long-degraded office of the pope for reform leadership.

C. Papal Reform.

In the eleventh century reforming popes (Leo IX, Nicholas II) strengthened supervision of the Church, freed the papacy from military dependence on the German Empire, and succeeded in transferring the power to elect popes from the emperor to the College of Cardinals.

1. *Gregory VII:* Pope Gregory VII (1073–1085) made greater claims than ever for papal power, asserting authority over kings in at least spiritual matters.

2. *The Investiture Controversy:* Popes and Holy Roman Emperors struggled over the claims of laymen to dispose of ecclesiastical offices and revenues by their own authority and in their own interests. The most famous confrontation came between Gregory VII and Emperor Henry IV in 1077. Gregory VII was symbolic victor over the penitent emperor at Canossa, but in reality, Henry came out ahead. In 1122 the controversy was settled by compromise, through the Concordat of Worms: Church appointments were to be made by the Church after consultation and compromise with the emperor.

3. *The Consolidation of Reform:* Popes consolidated their powers by encouraging the development of ecclesiastical law (the *Decretum*) and courts. They also tightened control over the canonization of saints, election of bishops, and collection of finances (tithes).

D. The Reform and Medieval Society.

Long-lasting consequences flowed from Church reforms. The clergy was more separated than ever from the laity. Intellectual and Scholastic life was revived, including the establishment of schools and universities for the clergy. Above all, the psychology of Gregorian reform—humans have the power to face an evil world and improve it—fed into dynamic cultural attitudes that would characterize Westerners in centuries to come.

IV. The Cultural Revival.

The period was marked by high cultural creativity.

A. The Rise of Universities.

Between 1050 and 1200 the predecessor of universities, the cathedral (bishop's) school, assumed intellectual leadership in Europe. For both teachers and students, these schools were relatively fluid. A tradition of student life and wandering scholars developed. Slowly, discipline was imposed by the establishment of certification (the ancestor of modern academic degrees) and unification of masters and students into guilds. From these grew medieval universities, the first forming in Paris between 1200 and 1231. Italian schools followed a similar development but were built upon surviving professional schools and there was a greater control by students over professors. From these institutions, organized for the pursuit of the preservation of learning, arose a class of people professionally committed to the life of thought.

B. Scholasticism.

Most broadly, Scholasticism refers to medieval teaching in general. More specifically, it refers to medieval theology, especially the art of analyzing logical relationships among propositions in a dialogue or discourse (dialectic). St. Anselm applied the dialectic to connect the existence of God with his perfection (ontological argument). Abelard (*Sic et Non*) forcefully illustrated the power of Scholastic argumentation. Two other related trends developed: a growing interest in humanistic studies and a revival of Aristotelian philosophy. The reconciliation of Aristotelian reason and Christian beliefs became the central philosophical problem of the thirteenth century.

C. Vernacular Literature.

There are three principal genres of vernacular literature that grew during the period. The heroic epic (*Song of Roland*) glorified masculine values. Troubadour lyric poetry, written for courts often dominated by women, celebrated women and love. The courtly romance (Chrétien de Troyes) combined the two in tales of love and adventure.

D. Romanesque Art.

The architectural and artistic style of the period is called Romanesque, a uniquely European combination of original and borrowed forms. It was most characterized by churches utilizing the groin vault to support stoned windowed roofs. Walls of these churches were decorated with antirealistic stone sculpture teeming with movement, reflecting the mystical spirit of the times. Religious needs stimulated metalwork, glass making, and vestment weaving, as well as the development of polyphonic music (part-singing).

Experiences of Daily Life: Nobles.

After Carolingian times, a hereditary nobility appeared in medieval society. This new patrilineal elite family was superimposed upon the older family based on bilateral kinship, creating new social patterns and tensions.

SIGNIFICANT INDIVIDUALS

Political Leaders

William of Normandy (1027–1087), king of England.

Harold Godwin (1066), king of England.

Henry II of Anjou (1154–1189), king of England.

Eleanor of Aquitaine (1137–1189), queen of France, England.

Hugh Capet (987–996), king of France.

Louis VI (1108–1137), king of France.

Philip II Augustus (1180–1223), king of France.

John (1199–1216), king of England.

Otto I (936–973), Saxon king, emperor.

Frederick I, Barbarossa (1152–1190), German emperor.

Religious Leaders

Thomas à Becket (1118?–1170), archbishop of Canterbury.

Innocent III (1198–1216), pope.

Leo IX (1049–1054), reforming pope.

Gregory VII (1073–1085), reforming pope.

Cultural Figures

St. Anselm of Canterbury (1033–1109), Scholastic.

Peter Abelard (1079–1142), Scholastic.

Chrétien de Troyes (12th century), French poet.

CHRONOLOGICAL DIAGRAM

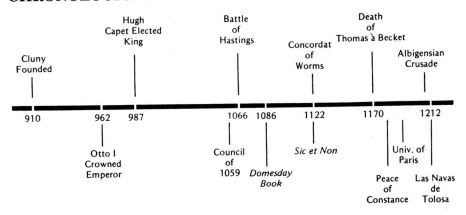

IDENTIFICATION

the mansi

Reconquista

"spices"

fairs of Champagne

commune

vassal

fief

private justice

castellans

Curia Regis (great council)

justices in eyre

the bailli

"Stem" duchies

simony

Cluniac monasticism

investiture controversy

Gregorian ideals

tithes

Scholasticism

Romanesque style

PROBLEMS FOR ANALYSIS

I. The Economic and Social Changes.

1. Explain the causes and significance of the population changes that occurred during the eleventh and twelfth centuries.
2. In what ways was there a revival of commerce and social life during this period? Who benefited from this?

II. Feudalism and the Search for Political Order.

1. Why was feudalism effective in promoting social order in Europe during the eleventh and twelfth centuries? What was the cement that held feudal relations together?
2. Compare the development of feudalism in any two countries. Explain the similarities and differences. Did feudalism function to strengthen or weaken the authority of the king?

III. The Reform of the Western Church.

1. What conditions created a need for reform within the Western Church?
2. What roles did popes and Cluniac monasticism play in the reform of the Church? What was so "reforming" about their activities?
3. What was the significance of the reform of the Western Church? Was it a movement that only affected the Church internally, or were there broader consequences? Explain.

IV. The Cultural Revival.

1. Compare the universities and student life in the twelfth century with those of today. What was so important about the development of universities at this early date?
2. Did religious concerns completely dominate cultural life during the eleventh and twelfth centuries? Support your argument.

DOCUMENTS

Feudal Relations

The following is an example of feudal relations between a king and his vassals. In this thirteenth-century document, King Louis IX of France deals with military service owed by his vassals.

The baron and all vassals of the king are bound to appear before him when he shall summon them, and to serve him at their own expense for forty days and fory nights, with as many knights as each one owes; and he is able to exact from them these services when he wishes and when he has need of them. And if the king wishes to keep them more than forty days at their own expense, they are not bound to remain if they do not wish it. And if the king wishes to keep them at his expense for the defence of the realm, they are bound to remain. And if the king wishes to lead them outside of the kingdom, they need not go unless they wish to, for they have already served their forty days and forty nights. [1]

1. What did King Louis IX expect from his vassals militarily?
2. What does this indicate about the balance of power between a monarch and his vassals during the thirteenth century?

Papal Powers

During the eleventh century Gregory VII (1073–1085) asserted papal powers against powers claimed by the medieval monarchy, principally the emperors of the Holy Roman Empire.

1. That the Roman church was established by God alone.
2. That the Roman pontiff alone is rightly called universal.
3. That he alone has the power to depose and reinstate bishops.
4. That his legate, even if he be of lower ecclesiastical rank, presides over bishops in council, and has the power to give sentence of deposition against them.

. . .

7. That he alone has the right, according to the necessity of the occasion, to make new laws, to create new bishoprics, to make a monastery of a chapter of canons, and *vice versa,* and either to divide a rich bishopric or to unite several poor ones.
8. That he alone may use the imperial insignia.
9. That all princes shall kiss the foot of the pope alone.

. . .

11. That the name applied to him [pope] belongs to him alone.
12. That he has the power to depose emperors.
13. That he has the right to transfer bishops from one see to another when it becomes necessary.
14. That he has the right to ordain as a cleric anyone from any part of the church whatsoever.

. . .

16. That no general synod may be called without his order.
17. That no action of a synod and no book shall be regarded as canonical without his authority.
18. That his decree can be annulled by no one, and that he can annul the decrees of anyone.
19. That he can be judged by no one.

. . .

21. That the important cases of any church whatsoever shall be referred to the Roman church [that is, to the pope].
22. That the Roman church has never erred and will never err to all eternity, according to the testimony of the holy scriptures.

[1] King Louis IX, *University of Pennsylvania Translations and Reprints,* trans. E. P. Cheyney, IV, No. 3 (1897).

23. That the Roman pontiff who has been canonically ordained is made holy by the merits of St. Peter.
24. That by his command or permission subjects may accuse their rulers.
25. That he can depose and reinstate bishops without the calling of a synod.
26. That no one can be regarded as catholic who does not agree with the Roman church.
27. That he has the power to absolve subjects from their oath of fidelity to wicked rulers. [2]

1. How does this illustrate the conflict between religious and secular authority? Does this document indicate that the lines between religious and secular authority were clear?

2. How would a monarch, such as Emperor Henry IV (1056–1106), respond to these claims?

Scholastic Thought

Peter Abelard (1079–1142) was one of the most influential Scholastic thinkers and teachers. The following is a selection from his most famous book, *Sic et Non*. Note how relatively modern some of his views are.

There are many seeming contradictions and even obscurities in the innumerable writings of the church fathers. Our respect for their authority should not stand in the way of an effort on our part to come at the truth. The obscurity and contradictions in ancient writings may be explained upon many grounds, and may be discussed without impugning the good faith and insight of the fathers. A writer may use different terms to mean the same thing, in order to avoid a monotonous repetition of the same word. Common, vague words may be employed in order that the common people may understand; and sometimes a writer sacrifices perfect accuracy in the interest of a clear general statement. Poetical, figurative language is often obscure and vague.

Not infrequently, apocryphal works are attributed to the saints. Then, even the best authors often introduce the erroneous views of others and leave the reader to distinguish between the true and the false. Sometimes, as Augustine confesses in his own case, the fathers ventured to rely upon the opinions of others.

Doubtless the fathers might err; even Peter, the prince of the apostles, fell into error; what wonder that the saints do not always show themselves inspired? The fathers did not themselves believe that they, or their companions, were always right. Augustine found himself mistaken in some cases and did not hesitate to retract his errors. He warns his admirers not to look upon his letters as they would upon the Scriptures, but accept only those things which, upon examination, they find to be true.

All writings belonging to this class are to be read with full freedom to criticize, and with no obligation to accept unquestioningly; otherwise the way would be blocked to all discussion, and posterity be deprived of the excellent intellectual exercise of debating difficult questions of language and presentation. But an explicit exception must be made in the case of the Old and New Testaments. In the Scriptures, when anything strikes us as absurd, we may not say that the writer erred, but that the scribe made a

[2] Brian Pullan, ed., *Sources for the History of Medieval Europe from the Mid-Eighth to the Mid-Thirteenth Century* (Oxford: Blackwell, 1966), pp. 136–138.

blunder in copying the manuscripts, or that there is an error in interpretation, or that the passage is not understood. The fathers make a very careful distinction between the Scriptures and later works. They advocate a discriminating, not to say suspicious, use of the writings of their own contemporaries.

In view of these considerations, I have ventured to bring together various dicta of the holy fathers, as they came to mind, and to formulate certain questions which were suggested by the seeming contradictions in the statements. These questions ought to serve to excite tender readers to a zealous inquiry into truth and so sharpen their wits. The master key of knowledge is, indeed, a persistent and frequent questioning. Aristotle, the most clear-sighted of all the philosophers, was desirous above all things else to arouse this questioning spirit, for in his *Categories* he exhorts a student as follows: "It may well be difficult to reach a positive conclusion in these matters unless they be frequently discussed. It is by no means fruitless to be doubtful on particular points." By doubting we come to examine, and by examining we reach the truth. [3]

1. What is Abelard's purpose here? Is he challenging the Church?
2. Characterize this document as an example of Scholastic thought.

Religion and Violence in Medieval Culture

In the following selection, Crane Brinton deals with two topics: the role of religion in people's lives during the Middle Ages and the reality of violence.

First of all, there is the immediacy, the commonsense acceptance, of the supernatural, which we have of course already encountered. There are millions of men and women in the twentieth century who as good Christians believe in Christianity. Many of them would be gravely offended were we to suggest that their belief is one whit less strong than that of their medieval ancestors. But even for believers today the boundaries of the supernatural have been pushed back, and whole regions of their conscious life made subject to the regularities we think of as natural. They may pray for rain; but they also read the weather reports drawn up by meteorologists who, whatever their religion, do not believe that God interferes directly with cold fronts. Moreover, there are today millions of men and women—no one knows quite how many—who do not believe in the immortality of the human soul, and for whom, therefore, the notion of heaven and hell is meaningless, or actually offensive. There are a great many more for whom heaven and hell have become very vague concepts indeed; they believe in immortality, heaven, and hell, but as rather remote things, closer acquaintance with which can be indefinitely postponed. Hell, particularly, has for many moderns lost its bite; it has become for them a place for distinguished sinners only, much like the Greek hell.

Not so for the men of the Middle Ages. God, as we have pointed out, was as real, as present for them, as the weather is for us, heaven or hell for each man as certain as sunshine or rain. Medieval intellectuals for the most part held that God made things happen on this earth in accordance with certain regularities basically directed for man's good—that is, that the universe was basically moral and therefore that much

[3] Peter Abelard, "Sic et Non," in James Harvey Robinson, ed., *Readings in European History*, Vol. I (Boston: Ginn, 1904), pp. 450–451.

was known and predictable. Their God was a reliable God in something of the same sense that modern scientists think nature reliable. Some of this sense of regularity, if only in the form of what we like to call common sense, undoubtedly was shared by the masses, or they could hardly have gone about their daily living. None the less, there is widespread among the medieval masses, and even among the intellectuals, a feeling of the irrationality, the uncertainty, the unexpectedness of life on this earth. At one most obvious level, this comes out in the prevalence of what we now call superstition in the Middle Ages. The slightest dip into medieval writing brings up an example—that eggs laid on Good Friday are good to put out fires, that elves sour milk, that the king's touch can cure scrofula, and many, many more. True, many of these superstitions are still alive, and we have added some of our own. But the range and depth of medieval superstition puts ours in the shade. . . .

A third note of medieval culture, less pleasing to its modern admirers, is the frequence of violence. Murder and sudden death were not as unusual to medieval man as to modern man. We must be careful here, as always with big generalizations. The lover of the Middle Ages may well reply that modern warfare kills far more effectively than did the medieval, that nothing in medieval annals is worse than what went on in the concentration camps of the last war. He is right, of course, but he must be reminded of our modern successes in medicine and in provisioning large populations.

For all our terrible wars, we have up to the moment maintained a larger population in the West than ever before. But the real point is the absence in the Middle Ages, in spite of the Christian tradition, of a feeling for the relative permanence of human life. Men simply did not expect life to be without hazard. Indeed, they saw the hand of God in the decision of violence. One of the best known of medieval institutions is that of trial by combat, a procedure limited to conflicts among the knightly class. As a last resort, a dispute could be settled by combat between the disputants or between their champions, and the decision was seen as the direct intervention of God who gave victory to the right. Gradually through the Middle Ages this procedure was supplanted by legal processes that became the foundations of our own.

We need not labor the point. The upper classes, heirs of the rough fighter of the Dark Ages, carried on well into the more advanced culture of the Middle Ages the tradition of violence in which their fathers had been bred. We have seen how this tradition was gradually formalized into the mock violence of late chivalry. The Church and the growing territorial states both had a part in the gradual substitution of orderly processes of law for this appeal to force. Growing trade brought with it growing protection of industry and commerce, until the robber baron was tamed. Even so, the grave social conflicts of the later Middle Ages brought renewed violence of another kind, and terrible plagues, like the Black Death of the fourteenth century, added their toll. Later medieval literature and art . . . came to be obsessed with death. . . .

Finally, and most important, if hardest for us to understand, the security of medieval life was a very different thing from what we in the mid-twentieth century understand by security. The medieval man did not count on the kind of life on earth we accept as something given. He did not expect our physical comforts and luxuries, did not expect to avoid smallpox by vaccination, did not expect good roads, did not, in short, expect a thousand things we take for granted. He was used to a hard life (in our terms), used to violence and uncertainty. Nothing in his philosophy—and we use the word philosophy advisedly, even of the common man—led him to expect that his life on earth could actually be very different from what it had always been. Such beliefs do not mean that the medieval man expected nothing, that he was never discontented. A shrewish wife, for instance, was as unpleasant to live with in the thirteenth as in the twentieth century.

But—and we are getting toward the heart of the matter—in no class of society would the thirteenth-century husband dream of trying to divorce his wife for "mental cruelty," or indeed for any other reason. Marriage was for him made in heaven, even if it were not well made. God had made marriage indissoluble. So too with many other aspects of human life, which we tend to regard as arrangements a man can make or unmake on his own initiative, and on his own responsibility. For the medieval man, much of his life was out of his own hands, in the hands of God working through society. We come back to the inescapable fact of the penetration of medieval life by the Christian attitude—not the Christian attitude at its perfection of spiritual striving, though the Middle Ages made a more natural place for this than our own—but the Christian attitude in its acceptance of the world as a place of probation, of toil and sorrow for the human soul. It is no accident that one of the best-known passages of Dante is

> E'en la sua volontate è nostra pace;
> Ella è quel mare al qual tutto si move
> Ciò ch'ella crea, e che natura face.

"And in his will is our peace: that will is the ocean to which moves everything that it creates or that nature makes."

The Christian promise of salvation in an afterlife for the man or woman who lives on earth according to the precepts of the Church no doubt helps explain the Christian hold over the medieval mind. But the notion of religion as an opiate is a product of the modern mind, which thinks—or hopes—that suffering is not in the order of things. Christianity for the medieval man not merely gave promise of a better life in the next world; it gave to this uncertain life of violence, striving, imperfection, and want on earth meaning, limits, and purpose that came near to closing, for most men, the gap between what they had and what they wanted. Medieval man was more nearly than we *resigned* to a world he could not greatly change. He felt secure in the midst of what we should regard as insecurity—violence, physical want, hardship, even fears bred of ignorance of what we regard as natural phenomena. He felt this security precisely because he was keenly aware of his own weakness. He was neither ashamed of nor disturbed by this weakness; it was not his fault, nor was it, humanly speaking, anyone's fault—certainly one could not be impious enough to attribute the fault to God. The medieval man *felt* as truth what in a later philosopher, Leibnitz, was no more than a rather insincere intellectual formula—that this is the best of all possible worlds. Not a happy, not a contented world, for in such a world men would usurp the place of God. It was, quite simply, God's world. [4]

1. Did Christianity eliminate superstition for most people? Was there a conflict between superstition and Christianity?

[4] Crane Brinton, *Ideas and Men: The Story of Western Thought,* 2nd edition (Englewood Cliffs, N.J.: Prentice-Hall, 1963), pp. 192-193, 196, 200. Reprinted by permission of Prentice-Hall, Inc.

2. Is it fair to argue that violence was more accepted as part of everyday life during the Middle Ages than it is today? Was the violence expected then different from that experienced by people today?
3. How does Brinton interpret the Christian attitude toward life during the Middle Ages?

SPECULATIONS

1. Do you think there is something special about the year 1000? Explain.
2. What policies would you recommend to an eleventh-century king to maximize his power? Why?
3. Should we consider the Church special, or is it just an institution with problems like the government or any other institution? Can you support your view historically?

TRANSITIONS

In "The Early Medieval East," the development of three civilizations on the borders of the West was traced and compared to the new civilization in the West, which was just emerging during the Early Middle Ages.

In "Two Centuries of Creativity," focus is again on the West. The eleventh and twelfth centuries mark a new vigorous period of growth in Europe. So striking is the creativity at almost every level of life that some scholars believe this to be a medieval renaissance legitimately part of "traditional Europe," lasting until the eighteenth and nineteenth centuries.

In "The Summer of the Middle Ages ca. 1200–1350," the civilization of the Middle Ages is at its peak and faces new problems.

NINE
THE SUMMER
OF THE MIDDLE AGES
ca. 1200–1350

MAIN THEMES

1. Agriculture, commerce, and industry expanded greatly in the thirteenth century.
2. In the various states of Europe, representative assemblies gained power, and constitutional stability improved.
3. The papacy greatly unified Europe spiritually, but it left a disturbing legacy of political and ecclesiastical problems.
4. In its Scholasticism, its Gothic style, and its culture, the thirteenth century was a period of intellectual synthesis.

OUTLINE AND SUMMARY

I. Economic Expansion.

A. The Countryside.

Agricultural production was stimulated by strong demand and regional specialization; rents increased and wages fell.

B. The Cities.

Commerce and industry developed dramatically. Medieval manufacturing did not rely on power and took place mostly in the home rather than the factory. Great entrepreneurs controlled the capital, provided the raw materials, and often supplied the tools for manufacturing. The manufacture of woolen cloth was the largest town industry, supporting many workers. The cloth was created in a series of steps (sorting, spinning, weaving, fulling, dyeing) performed by specialized workers.

C. The Guilds.

Commercial classes promoted their interests by forming professional associations (guilds). By the twelfth century there were numerous specialized guilds of artisans and merchants. Guilds met regularly, set standards, provided for members' welfare, and undertook civic activities. They also developed the apprentice system, which provided for lay education and an ordered method for supplying skilled labor.

D. Business Institutions.

Sophisticated commercial and banking institutions were developed. Since Christian ethics condemned interest payments on a loan (usury), alternatives, such as the bill of exchange, were developed. Capital was also recruited through temporary partnerships and business associations.

E. The Companies.

In some Italian towns more permanent partnerships, or companies, were formed, some becoming extremely large. They performed important commercial and banking services, in some cases supporting kings and popes.

F. Medieval Views of Economic Life.

Traditional Christian views were not positive toward property and wealth, accepting them as necessary evils. This changed somewhat in the thirteenth century. Thomas Aquinas gave property and wealth a basis in natural law and increased their dignity; merchants were not condemned as before. Yet there continued to be strong moral obligations to use property for the common good.

II. The States of Europe.

During the thirteenth century governments gained constitutional stability and increasingly utilized representative assemblies.

A. England.

The effective functioning of the English government, despite the almost perpetual absence of its warrior king, Richard the Lion-Hearted, and the humiliations of his successor John, is evidence for its fundamental strength.

1. *Magna Carta:* When John made apparently excessive financial demands on his barons, they, with the support of the Church, took up arms and forced him to grant the "Great Charter" of liberties (Magna Carta). In fact, it was a relatively undemocratic document, mainly specifying legal feudal relationships. In it the king promised not to disturb the customary liberties of the upper classes, to follow known legal procedures, and not to impose new taxes without consent from the upper classes (the realm). It was, however, a step toward constitutional government and a symbol of traditional balance between authority and liberty.

2. *Provisions of Oxford:* Under Henry III (1216–1272), the king and his barons struggled again over appointments to royal offices and the imposition of taxes. Henry temporarily submitted to the barons in 1258 by accepting the Provisions of Oxford. Continued discord led to a baronial revolt led by Simon de Montfort, which though temporarily successful ultimately succumbed to King Edward in 1265.

3. *Legal Reforms:* Edward I (1272–1307) became one of England's greatest medieval kings. His most important accomplishment was the developing and clarifying of English law, especially real estate law.

4. *Parliamentary Origins:* During the thirteenth century meetings of the traditional great council became more frequent. They were first called parliaments under Henry III. At some point Parliament was split into separate houses of Lords and Commons, with the Commons benefiting from the participation of the lower aristocracy and the eventual unwillingness of the upper clergy to serve in the House of Lords.

5. *Parliamentary Functions:* Parliament gave advice to the king, supported his decisions, facilitated the collection of taxes, passed on new taxes, and served as England's highest court.

B. France.

The thirteenth century was also an age of constitutional consolidation in France. Louis VIII helped expand French territories and solidify a monarchy based on inheritance.

1. *St. Louis:* The pious Louis IX was recognized as a saint during his lifetime. He acted strongly to improve justice, gain peace with his neighbors, and make war against the Muslims.

2. *Legal Reforms:* Louis' fairness and concern in legal matters gave great prestige to royal justice. The legal system was further strengthened by his codifying the laws (*Establishments of St. Louis*), creating royal inspectors, and confirming the Parlement of Paris as France's highest court.

3. *Peace and War:* Louis made a long-lasting peace with the Spanish kings of Aragon (Treaty of Corbeil, 1258). At the Treaty of Paris (1259) Louis made a more difficult peace with King Henry III of England. In 1248 and 1270 Louis unsuccessfully led the last major Western crusades against the Muslims.

4. *Philip IV:* Philip was probably most important for bringing an increased lay authority to the monarchy. He warred unsuccessfully against the English and attempted to replenish his treasury by persecuting Jews, extorting money from foreign merchants, and arresting the wealthy Knights Templars within France. Philip struggled with Pope Boniface VIII over the right to tax the clergy. This led to a wider conflict over sovereignty.

5. *Philip's Heritage:* Philip was overly ambitious in his efforts to achieve an absolute monarchy, leaving a deeply disturbed France.

C. The Iberian Kingdoms.

After the nearly complete success of the Christian *Reconquista* (1236), Spain was left in a disunified state. Even within the three major Christian kingdoms of Portugal, Castile, and Aragon, there were self-governing groups (Jews and Muslims) and towns (Barcelona, Valencia, Toledo, Seville). The military aristocracy was unusually independent, as were religious orders of knights (Calatrava, Santiago, and Alcántara). To bolster their power, Iberian kings used representative assemblies (Cortes), systematized laws and customs (*Siete Partidas*), and gained powers over the Church. Having achieved stability, these kingdoms expanded into the Mediterranean, Sicily, Sardinia, and Athens.

D. The Holy Roman Empire.

Facing geographic, cultural, and political obstructions to unity, the Holy Roman Empire disintegrated into a large number of small and virtually autonomous principalities.

1. *Frederick II Hohenstaufen:* Frederick II was an unusual personality. He had renaissance interests in learning. His political and diplomatic style was similar to more modern rulers. He reinforced political fragmentation in Germany by granting virtual sovereignty to ecclesiastical princes and lay nobles within their own territories. In southern Italy he built what some have called the first modern state.

III. The Church.

In the thirteenth century the papacy came close to building a unified Christian commonwealth in Europe based on peace, faith, and obedience.

A. The Growth of Heresy.

Starting in the eleventh century, heresies began appearing in Europe. The causes were complex: reaction to abuses in the Church; social dislocations caused by population growth (especially in towns); envy of Church wealth by nobles; discontent with Church and society by many women; and spiritual tension, leading many to try and break the monastic monopoly over the religious experience.

B. The Waldensians and Albigensians.

The Waldensians of southern France attacked moral laxness in the Church and followed a life of poverty. Though they were declared heretical in 1215, the Church never completely suppressed the movement. The Albigensians also attacked the Church and emphasized the struggle between good and evil. This became a strong movement but did not survive the Middle Ages.

C. The Suppression of Heresy.

The new Dominican order attempted to reconvert the Albigensians. Pope Innocent III initiated a crusade against them in the early 1200s. In 1231 Pope Gregory IX instituted a special papal court to investigate and punish heresy (the papal Inquisition). A suspect, facing an assumption of guilt, secret denunciations, and torture, had little chance of proving innocence. The Inquisition eventually eroded the Church's prestige.

D. The Franciscans.

The Franciscans, led by St. Francis of Assisi (1182?–1226), initiated spiritual regeneration in the thirteenth century. St. Francis combined piety, orthodoxy, and mystical insights. He quickly attracted followers, especially among laymen in the growing towns, and his order grew to become the largest in the Church.

E. Papal Government.

Pope Innocent III (1198–1216) best illustrates the aspirations and problems of the medieval Church. He tried to unify Christendom by eliminating heresy and bringing the Eastern Church under him, with mixed results. He struggled with European princes (John of England, Emperor Frederick II, Philip II of France, and others) for authority, with similarly mixed results. He tried to clarify Christian discipline and beliefs.

F. The Fourth Lateran Council.

In 1215 Innocent summoned the Lateran Council, which clarified such matters as the importance of the sacraments, transubstantiation, and priestly discipline.

G. The Papacy in the Thirteenth Century.

The papacy grew administratively and financially during the thirteenth century, but popes were becoming dependent on exploiting spiritual powers for financial profit.

H. Boniface VIII.

Boniface VIII became entangled in struggles with secular rulers, leading to his temporary capture, and in 1309, to the election of the first in a series of French-supported popes in Avignon. The thirteenth-century papacy, though powerful at the top, weakened the ability of bishops to maintain discipline at the local level.

IV. The Summer of Medieval Culture.

This was an age of intellectual synthesis.

A. The Medieval Synthesis.

The principal intellectual effort of the time was to reconcile Aristotelian philosophy, based on the power of human reason, and Christian attitudes, based on the necessity of divine revelation and grace. This effort at synthesis can be seen in the Scholasticism of Thomas Aquinas, the Gothic cathedral, and the *Comedy* of Dante Alighieri.

    1. *Thomas Aquinas:* St. Thomas Aquinas (1225?–1274) was the greatest Christian theologian since Augustine. In his *Summa Theologica* he argued that both faith and reason lead to a single truth, and that while the universe was made up of individual objects, all objects were bound into a fundamental hierarchy under God.

2. *John Duns Scotus:* Duns Scotus criticized Thomas, arguing that faith preceded reason. He began a new period of analysis in fourteenth-century theology.

3. *The Gothic Cathedral:* In the thirteenth century the Gothic style spread through Europe. The most stunning examples are the great urban churches. Gothic style is characterized by the broken arch, ribbed vaulting, flying buttresses, higher walls, large stained windows, and realistic statues.

4. *The Gothic Spirit:* The architectural style, the use of light, and the performance of the sacred liturgy with polyphonic music combined in these churches to convey a sense of order in a universe governed by a wise, loving, present God.

5. *Dante:* Dante's *Comedy* best summarizes the culture of the age. His works were greatly influenced by two experiences: his early love for a young girl named Beatrice and his exile from Florence.

6. *The* Comedy: This poem tells how Dante, an aging man, is led through hell and purgatory by Virgil, who represents human reason, and to heaven by Beatrice, who represents supernatural revelation and grace. He thus dealt with his own life as well as the issues of his age, by exploring the relation between optimistic, classical rationalism and Christian faith in divine will.

Experiences of Daily Life: Baruch the Jew.

Increasingly in the fourteenth century, Jews suffered from popular outbursts of illegal antisemitism.

SIGNIFICANT INDIVIDUALS

Political Leaders

Richard I, the Lion-Hearted (1189–1199), king of England.

Henry III (1216–1272), king of England.

Simon de Montfort (1208?–1265), English statesman and soldier.

Edward I (1272–1307), king of England.

St. Louis IX (1226–1270), king of France.

Philip IV, the Fair (1285–1314), king of France.

Frederick II Hohenstaufen (1194–1250), Holy Roman Emperor.

Religious Leaders

Peter Waldo (12th century), founder of Waldensians.

Conrad of Marsburg (12th century), inquisitor.

St. Francis of Assisi (1182?–1226), founder of the Franciscans.

Bernard Gui (12th century), inquisitor.

Innocent III (1198–1216), pope.

Boniface VIII (1294–1303), pope.

Clement V (1305–1314), pope at Avignon.

Cultural Figures

Thomas Aquinas (1225?–1274), Scholastic.

John Duns Scotus (1265?–1308), theologian.

Dante (1265–1321), Florentine poet.

CHRONOLOGICAL DIAGRAM

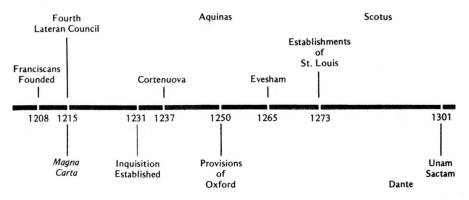

IDENTIFICATION

putting-out system
guilds
apprenticeship system
usury
bill of exchange
the companies
Parliament
Parlement of Paris
Templars

Cortes
Waldensians
Albigensians
Inquisition
Body of Canon Law
Summa Theologica
realism
Gothic

MAP EXERCISE

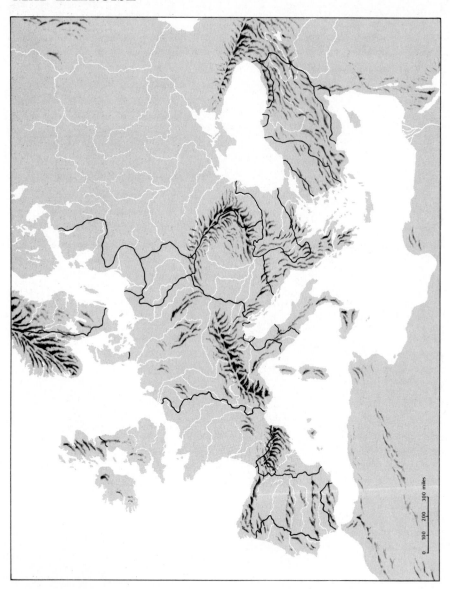

1. Label the main political divisions of Europe around 1250.

PROBLEMS FOR ANALYSIS

I. Economic Expansion.

1. It can be argued that industry and commerce acquired many modern charac-
    teristics by the thirteenth century. Considering methods of manufacturing,
    the guilds, business institutions, and views toward economic life, do you
    agree? Why?

II. The States of Europe.

1. The Magna Carta is sometimes thought of as a democratic document. In
    light of the political developments in England during the thirteenth century,
    do you agree? Why?
2. Compare constitutional consolidation in France with the disintegration of the
    Holy Roman Empire. How do you explain the differences?
3. Considering institutions, such as Parliament, the Parlement of Paris, and the
    Cortes, should the thirteenth century be considered politically as a period of
    representative assemblies? Why?

III. The Church.

1. Does the growth of heresy, and its suppression, indicate that the Church was
    effectively unified during the thirteenth century? Why?
2. Compare the factors that evidenced the growing strength of the Church with
    those that evidenced future problems for the Church.

IV. The Summer of Medieval Culture.

1. Compare the ideas of Aquinas and Duns Scotus. How does the analysis of
    Duns Scotus signify a change from the synthesis of Aquinas?
2. In what ways does Dante's *Comedy* summarize the culture of this age? Com-
    pare the *Comedy* of Dante with the *Summa Theologica* of Aquinas.

DOCUMENTS

Ecclesiastical Life

Eudes, archbishop of Rouen from 1242 to 1267, was a concerned administrator
who spent a considerable amount of time traveling through the territories he was
responsible for, checking up on his clergy. The following is an excerpt from his
register for two days in 1249.

> *June 30.* We visited the deanery of Meulan at Chars. We found that the priest at Cour-
> dimanche has occasionally celebrated Mass though he is under suspension and that he
> has kept a concubine; he rides horseback dressed in a short mantle, and he runs about

too much. Item, the priest at Courcelles does not keep residence well nor is he in the habit of wearing his gown. Item, the priest at Hérouville only rarely wears a gown. Item, the priest at Valmondois sells his services; he is noted for having money, is contentious, and is given to drinking. Item, the priest at Vaux is a trader and had, and still has, a certain vineyard which he holds as security from a certain wastrel to whom he has loaned his too precious coins; he does not say his Hours well and sometimes he comes to Mass straight from his bed. Item, the priest at Chars is ill famed of a certain widow; he runs about too much. Item, the priest at Courcelles does not keep residence well, nor does he wear a gown. Item, the priest at Longuesse is ill famed of Eugénie, his parishioner, and has had children by her; he promised us that if he should be ill famed of these matters again he would regard his church as resigned.

We spent the night at Sérans, at our own expense.

. . .

October 24. We visited the abbey of St-Étienne-de-Caen, where there are sixty-three monks. All but three are priests. In one of the priories there are rabbit dogs; we forbade the monks who are staying there to become hunters. There are some who do not confess every month; we enjoined them to correct this. It used to be their practice that all those ministering [to the celebrants] at all Masses, save those [Masses] for the dead, received Communion, but this practice, through negligence, has gradually been abandoned; we enjoined the abbot and prior to have this custom more fully observed by all. The cloister is badly kept; we enjoined them to correct this. Traveling monks do not observe the fasts of the Rule; we enjoined them to correct this. In the priories they do not observe the fasts of the Rule and they eat meat freely; we enjoined them to correct this. They owe fifteen hundred pounds, but about as much is owed to them; they have an income of four thousand pounds. Total for procuration: seven pounds, ten shillings, ten pence. [1]

1. What were the archbishop's main concerns?
2. What does this document reveal about ecclesiastical life during the thirteenth century?

The Magna Carta

In 1215 King John of England was forced to agree to the "Great Charter" (Magna Carta) by a group of barons, with their forces behind them. The following are excerpts from that document.

1. In the first place, we have granted to God, and by this our present charter confirmed, for us and for our heirs forever, that the English church shall be free, and shall hold its right entire and its liberties uninjured; and we will that it be thus observed; which is shown by this, that the freedom of elections, which is considered to be most important and especially necessary to the English church, we, of our pure and spontaneous will, granted, and by our charter confirmed before the contest between us and our barons had arisen; and obtained a confirmation of it by the lord Pope Innocent III.; which we shall observe and which we will, shall be observed in good faith by our heirs forever.

[1] J. F. O'Sullivan, ed., *The Register of Eudes of Rouen,* trans. S. M. Brown (New York: Columbia University Press, 1964), pp. 43, 292.

We have granted moreover to all free men of our kingdom for us and our heirs forever all the liberties written below, to be had and holden by themselves and their heirs from us and our heirs.

2.   If any of our earls or barons, or other holding from us in chief by military service shall have died, and when he has died his heir shall be of full age and owe relief, he shall have his inheritance by the ancient relief.

. . .

8.   No widow shall be compelled to marry so long as she prefers to live without a husband, provided she gives security that she will not marry without our consent, if she holds from us, or without the consent of her lord from whom she holds, if she holds from another.

. . .

12.   No scutage or aid shall be imposed in our kingdom except by the common council of our kingdom, except for the ransoming of our body, for the making of our oldest son a knight, and for once marrying our oldest daughter, and for these purposes it shall be only a reasonable aid; in the same way it shall be done concerning the aids of the city of London.

13.   And the city of London shall have all its ancient liberties and free customs, as well by land as by water. Moreover, we will and grant that all other cities and boroughs and villages and ports shall have all their liberties and free customs.

. . .

16.   No one shall be compelled to perform any greater [military] service for a knight's fee or for any other free tenement than is owed from it.

. . .

20.   A free man shall not be fined for a small offense, except in proportion to the measure of the offense; and for a great offense, saving his freehold; and a merchant in the same way, saving his merchandise; and the villein shall be fined in the same way, saving his wainage [harvested crops for seed and estate needs], if he shall be at our mercy; and none of the above fines shall be imposed except by the oaths of honest men of the neighborhood.

21.   Earls and barons shall be fined only by their peers, and only in proportion to their offense.

. . .

23.   No manor or man shall be compelled to make bridges over the rivers except those which ought to do it of old and rightfully.

. . .

28.   No constable or other bailiff of ours shall take anyone's grain or other chattels, without immediately paying for them in money, unless he is able to obtain a postponement at the good will of the seller.

. . .

30.   No sheriff or bailiff of ours or anyone else shall take horses or wagons of any free man for carrying purposes except on the permission of that free man.

. . .

35.   There shall be one measure of wine throughout our whole kingdom, and one measure of ale, and one measure of grain.

. . .

39.   No free man shall be taken or imprisoned or dispossessed, or outlawed, or banished, or in any way destroyed, nor will we go upon him, nor send upon him, except by the legal judgment of his peers or by the law of the land.

. . .

41. All merchants shall be safe and secure in going from England and coming into England and in remaining and going through England, as well by land as by water, for buying and selling, free from all evil tolls, by the ancient and rightful customs, except in time of war, and if they are of a land at war with us.

. . .

45. We will not make justiciars, constables, sheriffs, or bailiffs, except of such as know the law of the realm and are well inclined to observe it.

. . .

60. Moreover, all those customs and franchises mentioned above which we have conceded in our kingdom, and which are to be fulfilled, as far as pertains to us, in respect to our men; all men of our kingdom as well clergy as laymen, shall observe as far as pertains to them, in respect to their men. [2]

1. How democratic is this document?
2. In what ways does it reflect the institutions and practices of feudalism?

Crime and Punishment

In the following selection, the noted historian John Huizinga discusses crime and punishment during the Middle Ages.

> The Middle Ages knew nothing of all those ideas which have rendered our sentiment of justice timid and hesitating: doubts as to the criminal's responsibility; the conviction that society is, to a certain extent, the accomplice of the individual; the desire to reform instead of inflicting pain; and, we may even add, the fear of judicial errors. Or rather these ideas were implied, unconsciously, in the very strong and direct feeling of pity and of forgiveness which alternated with extreme severity. Instead of lenient penalties, inflicted with hesitation, the Middle Ages knew but the two extremes: the fulness of cruel punishment, and mercy. When the condemned criminal is pardoned, the question whether he deserves it for any special reasons is hardly asked; for mercy has to be gratuitous, like the mercy of God. In practice, it was not always pure pity which determined the question of pardon. The princes of the eleventh century were very liberal of "lettres derémission" for misdeeds of all sorts and contemporaries thought it quite natural that they were obtained by the intercession of quite natural relatives. The majority of these documents, however, concern poor common people. [3]

1. How do ideas of justice differ between modern times and the Middle Ages, according to Huizinga? How do these differences reflect the different environment of the society of the Middle Ages?

Family Life

The following selection discusses family life and child care in a thirteenth-century baron's household.

---

[2] Edward P. Cheyney, ed., "English Constitutional Documents of the Middle Ages," in *Translations and Reprints from the Original Sources of European History*, I, No. 6, ed. the Department of History of the University of Pennsylvania (Philadelphia, 1897), pp. 6–17.

[3] John Huizinga, *The Waning of the Middle Ages* (New York: St. Martin's Press, Inc., 1954), pp. 23–24.

Indeed the medieval magnates had surprisingly little to do with their children. Almost immediately after birth, they were handed over to the care of a nurse whose duties, as described by Bartholomew the Englishman, included not only the physical care of the child, but also the display of affection which is now considered essentially maternal. According to Bartholomew the nurse's duties were very extensive. She was ordained to nourish and feed the child, to give it suck, to kiss it if it fell, and comfort it if it wept, and to wash it when it was dirty. The nurse was also to teach the child to speak by sounding out the words for him, to dose him with medicines when necessary, and even to chew the toothless child's meat so that he could swallow it. The mother must have been a rather remote figure. Discipline was always considered the father's primary duty. Bartholomew specifically insisted that the father must treat his child with harshness and severity. He should teach him with scoldings and beatings, put him under wardens and tutors, and, above all, show "no glad cheer lest the child wax proud." The old adage of "spare the rod and spoil the child" was firmly entrenched in all medieval treatises on the proper upbringing of children. [4]

1. What were the proper roles of the father, mother, and nurse in childrearing?

The Thirteenth Century

In the following excerpt, James J. Walsh argues that the thirteenth century was the greatest of all centuries.

It cannot but seem a paradox to say that the Thirteenth was the greatest of centuries. To most people the idea will appear at once so preposterous that they may not even care to consider it. A certain number, of course, will have their curiosity piqued by the thought that anyone should evolve so curious a notion. Either of these attitudes of mind will yield at once to a more properly receptive mood if it is recalled that the Thirteenth is the century of the Gothic cathedrals, of the foundation of the university, of the signing of Magna Charta, and of the origin of representative government with something like constitutional guarantees throughout the west of Europe. The cathedrals represent a development in the arts that has probably never been equaled either before or since. The university was a definite creation of these generations that has lived and maintained its usefulness practically in the same form in which it was then cast for the seven centuries ever since. The foundation stones of modern liberties are to be found in the documents which for the first time declared the rights of man during this precious period.

In taking up the thesis, The Thirteenth the Greatest of Centuries, it seems absolutely necessary to define just what is meant by the term great, in its application to a period. An historical epoch, most people would concede at once, is really great just in proportion to the happiness which it provides for the largest possible number of humanity. That period is greatest that has done most to make men happy. Happiness consists in the opportunity to express whatever is best in us, and above all to find utterance for whatever is individual. An essential element in it is the opportunity to develop and apply the intellectual faculties, whether this be of purely artistic or of thoroughly practical character. For such happiness the opportunity to rise above one's original station is one of the necessary requisites. Out of these opportunities there comes

[4] Margaret Labarge, *A Baronial Household of the Thirteenth Century* (London: Eyre & Spottiswoode, 1965), pp. 42–48.

such contentment as is possible to man in the imperfect existence that is his under present conditions.

Almost as important a quality in any epoch that is to be considered supremely great, is the difference between the condition of men at the beginning of it and at its conclusion. The period that represents most progress, even though at the end uplift should not have reached a degree equal to subsequent periods, must be considered as having best accomplished its duty to the race. For purposes of comparison it is the amount of ground actually covered in a definite time, rather than the comparative position at the end of it, that deserves to be taken into account. This would seem to be a sort of hedging, as if the terms of the comparison of the Thirteenth with other centuries were to be made more favorable by the establishment of different standards. There is, however, no need of any such makeshift in order to establish the actual supremacy of the Thirteenth Century, since it can well afford to be estimated on its own merits alone, and without any allowances because of the stage of cultural development at which it occurred.

Is it any wonder, then, that we should call the generations that gave us the cathedrals, the universities, the great technical schools that were organized by the trades guilds, the great national literatures that lie at the basis of all our modern literature, the beginnings of sculpture and of art carried to such heights that artistic principles were revealed for all time, and, finally, the great men and women of this century — for more than any other it glories in names that were born not to die — is it at all surprising that we should claim for the period which, in addition to all this, saw the foundation of modern law and liberty, the right to be hailed — the greatest of human history? [5]

1. What is the basis for Walsh's argument? Do you agree?
2. If you were to argue this interpretation, what would you say?

SPECULATIONS

1. If you could select any century between 400 and 1400 to live in, would you select the thirteenth century? What would the advantages and disavantages be?
2. If you were a pope during the thirteenth century, what policies would you follow to promote the best interests of the Church?
3. Would you recommend to thirteenth-century kings that they support representative assemblies or fight against them? Why?

TRANSITIONS

In "Two Centuries of Creativity ca. 1000–1200," the quickening pace of development in the West was traced.

---

[5] James J. Walsh, *The Thirteenth, Greatest of Centuries,* 12th edition (New York: Fordham University Press, 1952), pp. 1–17. Copyright 1907 by James J. Walsh.

In "The Summer of the Middle Ages ca. 1200–1350," the period between 1200 and 1348 is examined. During most of this time Europe enjoyed relative prosperity, peace, institutional stability, and intellectual synthesis. Yet overpopulation, misery among the poor, the specter of war, and intellectual and religious dissent also characterize the period. The relative successes of the thirteenth century would not survive the disasters and changes of the fourteenth and fifteenth centuries.

In "The Crusades and Eastern Europe ca. 1100–1550," focus will shift to the East and to the growing connections between the two areas.

TEN
THE CRUSADES
AND EASTERN EUROPE
ca. 1100–1550

MAIN THEMES

1. The crusades, initiated for a variety of reasons, led to an expansion of Europeans into the East.
2. After the eleventh century, the Byzantine Empire declined until it was finally overwhelmed by the expanding Ottoman Empire in 1453.
3. Princes of Moscow succeeded in dealing with the powerful Mongols and founded the modern Russian state in the fifteenth century.

OUTLINE AND SUMMARY

I. The Crusades.

In the eleventh century Western peoples launched a series of armed expeditions, known as the crusades, to the East in an effort to free the Holy Land from Islamic rule. While interpretations of the crusades differ, it is certain that they initiated a long-term expansion of Europe.

A. Origins.

Two circumstances led to the first crusades: a conflict between increasing numbers of pilgrims traveling to Palestine and the Seljuk Turks, who controlled the area; and an appeal by Byzantium to Pope Urban II to help defend Constantinople against that same Islamic power.

B. The Motives of the Crusaders.

For participants, the crusades were acts of assertive religious devotion. But social and economic motivations were important. The crusades served as an outlet for a growing population, especially knights, who had few other opportunities for advancement in a stabilizing Europe. Moreover, many crusaders came from the violent fringes of society; the crusades provided them appropriate outlets.

C. The First Crusade.

The first crusade (1096–1099) was initiated by Pope Urban II's call to arms in 1095. There were two sorts of responses: one made up of peasants and the poor, who were roused to action by preachers (the Popular Crusade); and one that was more organized and led by various nobles. The first group was completely defeated by the Turks. The second was more successful, thanks to some help from Byzantium, daring military victories (Dorylaeum, Edessa, Antioch), and the Turkish inability to present a united front.

D. The Kingdom of Jerusalem.

The crusaders established shaky but surprisingly long-lasting control over Near Eastern lands around Jerusalem, Tripoli, Antioch, and Edessa, and they applied feudal concepts and institutions there. They remained, however, a precarious foreign aristocracy in a hostile land.

E. The Later Crusades.

Europeans conducted further crusades in the twelfth century, the last (1189–1192) constituting a great effort by Emperor Frederick Barbarossa, Philip II of France, and Richard I of England. Yet none of these enjoyed success, as the Turks slowly recaptured lands. The last Christian outpost on mainland Asia (Acre) was lost in 1291. By then the crusading spirit had long since diminished.

F. Results of the Crusades.

For a century crusaders managed to hold Jerusalem, and they retained other outposts in Palestine for an additional century. In the longer run, the crusades slowed the Turkish advance in the Mediterranean and Europe. There were other more, indirect consequences. Castle construction was improved, military skills were copied on both sides, new taxing methods to support the crusades were developed, and the sale of indulgences to support the crusades was allowed.

G. Military-Religious Orders.

Military-religious orders of knights (Templar, Hospitalers, and Teutonic Knights) were organized successfully to supply the East and to defend safe passage to the East. The Templars created a great banking institution, the Hospitalers became the long-lasting Knights of Malta, and the Teutonic Knights conquered extensive domains around the Baltic Sea.

H. Economy.

The crusades increased the circulation of money and treasure, enlivened trade with the East, and created demands for Eastern commodities, which led Europeans to explore new ways to import sugar, spices, and similar products.

I. Religion and Learning.

With the exception of an increased geographic knowledge, the crusades had no great religious or intellectual consequences for either Christian or Islamic society.

II. Byzantium and the Ascendancy of the Ottoman Empire.

After 1071 the Byzantine Empire's control was limited to the area around Constantinople.

A. The Passing of East Rome.

Crusaders stormed Constantinople in 1204 and divided the Byzantine Empire among themselves; Venetians gained the most. Elements of the old Byzantine Empire remained, but they were unable to prevent independent kingdoms of Bulgarians and Serbs from forming in the thirteenth and fourteenth centuries.

B. The Fall of Constantinople.

Seljuk Turks, Mongols, and Ottoman Turks, in turn, dominated the Middle East between the eleventh and fourteenth centuries. Constantinople finally fell to the Ottomans in 1453. The fall shocked the Christian world and stimulated efforts to find new trade routes to the East. It also symbolizes, for many historians, the end of the Middle Ages.

C. Expansion of the Ottoman Empire.

In the fifteenth century the Ottomans entered upon a century of expansion. Mohammad II made the Ottomans a major land and sea power, especially in southeastern Europe. Other rulers led conquests in Arab lands in the early sixteenth century. Suleiman II (1520–1566) led the empire to its height of power, extending borders in the west to the gates of Vienna and Algeria, and in the east to Arabia and Persia. He became a diplomatic ally of France against Charles V, the Holy Roman Emperor, leading to commercial ties with France.

    1. *Ottoman Institutions:* Ottomans took advantage of their geographic position, internal political and religious feuds among Christians, and strong military traditions to create their empire. They organized conquered territories well, followed tolerant policies that allowed religious, social, economic, and cultural practices of conquered peoples to continue, and developed effective military and administrative institutions. Ottoman sultans ruled through a council of advisors (the divan) presided over by an administrative officer (the grand vizier). Religious affairs were administered by a class of judges. The army was made up of unpaid holders of fiefs granted by the sultan in exchange for military service, and of paid soldiers, who were technically considered slaves. Janissaries, an elite corps of professional soldiers, became the backbone of Ottoman victories. Local government was usually left to self-governing communities of Christians and Jews and to the holders of fiefs. A new system of recruitment for palace administration and the corps of Janissaries, based on the early selection of boys for intense training, was developed in the fifteenth century and became a fundamental institution of the empire.

    2. *The Sultan:* The sultan retained supreme civil, military, and religious au-

thority. Power was transferred to successors by the law of fratricide, which provided that a designated son would take office and his brothers were put to death.

3. *The Limits of Ottoman Power:* After Suleiman the Magnificent, there were no further expansions. Newly developing trade routes decreased the commercial importance of the Ottoman Empire, and succeeding sultans lacked the dynamism of earlier rulers. The Ottomans were slowly left behind by the advancing, energetic Europeans.

III. The Birth of Modern Russia.

Pressured by raiding nomads in the south and east, the Rus colonized and built new civilizations in the forests to the north and west.

A. The Mongols.

Between the thirteenth and fifteenth centuries, a division of the Mongol Empire (the Golden Horde) was the supreme power over most of Russia. Mongols exacted recognition (*yarlik*) and tribute from the East Slavs, allowing them to maintain their local control, their language, and their culture. Mongol pressure forced the Rus north and west into three areas: Galicia, Novgorod, and Russian Mesopotamia (between the upper Volga and the Oka rivers). The latter area became the nucleus of a new Russian state. From the twelfth to the fifteenth centuries there was no central government; local princes held the power. The economy was almost completely agricultural, and society was made up primarily of free peasants. Culturally, Russia's wooden churches and icon painting (Andrei Rublev) stand out.

B. The Rise of Moscow.

A central location and the talent of its early princes made Moscow the leader of Russia. Its princes added territory through war, marriage, and purchase, and made Moscow a symbol of national unity in the face of Mongols and Western Christians. Ivan I (1328–1341) added territories, obtained a privileged position with the Mongols, and courted the Russian Church. Dimitri successfully led Russians to their first victory over the Mongols in 1380. Ivan the Great (1462–1505) and his successor Basil III completed the process of gathering Russian land, freeing Russia from the power of the Golden Horde, and founding modern Russia.

C. Institutional and Social Change.

Ivan III founded the modern Russian state by depicting himself as the successor of Byzantine emperors, promulgating a new code of laws (*Sudebnik*), creating a new class of serving gentry, and unifying Russia to face the outside world. He passed on to his successors a centralized, autocratic government.

Experiences of Daily Life: Wood and Russian Culture.

People in the new center of Russian civilization lived within a material culture dominated by wood.

SIGNIFICANT INDIVIDUALS

Political Leaders

Baldwin (1058–1118), crusader.
Constantine XIII (1448–1453), last Byzantine emperor.
Mohammad II, the Conqueror (1451–1481), Ottoman sultan.
Osman (1288–1326), founder of the Ottoman dynasty.
Suleiman II, the Magnificent (1520–1566), Ottoman sultan.

Genghis Khan (1206–1227), khan of Mongols.
Ivan I (1328–1341), Muscovite prince.
Ivan III, the Great (1462–1505), tsar of Russia.
Basil III (1505–1533), tsar of Russia.

Cultural Figure

Andrei Rublev (1370?–1430?), Russian religious painter.

CHRONOLOGICAL DIAGRAM

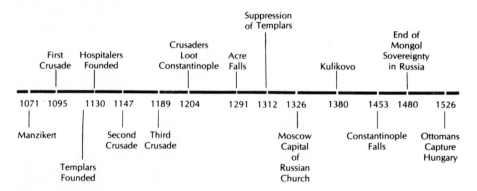

IDENTIFICATION

Saladin tithe
Hospitalers
Teutonic Knights
yarlik
Golden Horde

vizier
Janissaries
law of fratricide
Russian Mesopotamia
ax and icon

MAP EXERCISE

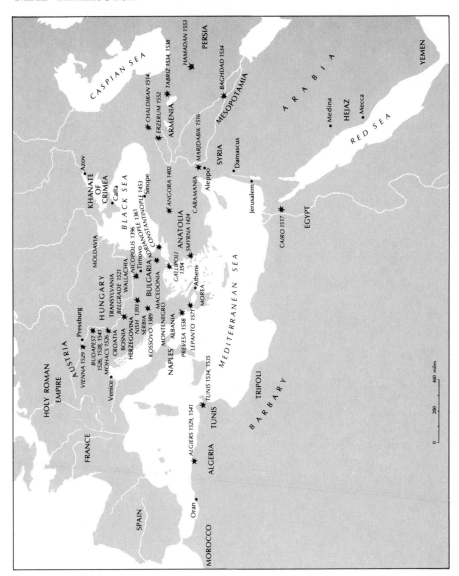

1. Indicate the expansion of the Ottoman Empire between 1300 and 1566.
2. Indicate the location of the Crusader kingdoms.

PROBLEMS FOR ANALYSIS

I. The Crusades.

1. What circumstances led to the first crusades? What balance of religious, economic, and social motives do you think led people to participate in these crusades?
2. Considering the effort involved and the results of the crusades, were they a success or a failure? Why?
3. What were the most important consequences of the crusades? Is it fair to argue that the crusades proved to be of greater economic than religious significance for Europe? Why?

II. Byzantium and the Ascendancy of the Ottoman Empire.

1. In what ways did the decline of Byzantium lead to important changes in the Mediterranean and the West?
2. How did the various Ottoman institutions contribute to the successful rise and expansion of this powerful empire? What role did the sultan and the Janissaries play?

III. The Birth of Modern Russia.

1. Why did Moscow become the center of the Russian state? What role did the relations between the Mongols and the prince of Moscow play in this?
2. On what basis should Ivan III be considered the founder of the modern Russian state? What policies did he pursue to this end?

DOCUMENTS

The First Crusade

In 1095, Emperor Comnenus of the Byzantine Empire requested military aid to help fight Turkish forces. Pope Urban II (1088–1099) quickly made the following plea at the Council of Clermont, which led to the First Crusade.

In 1095 a great council was held in Auvergne, in the city of Clermont. Pope Urban II, accompanied by cardinals and bishops, presided over it. It was made famous by the presence of many bishops and princes from France and Germany. After the council had attended to ecclesiastical matters, the pope went out into a public square, because no house was able to hold the people, and addressed them in a very persuasive speech, as follows: "O race of the Franks, O people who live beyond the mountains [that is, reckoned from Rome], O people loved and chosen of God, as is clear from your many deeds, distinguished over all other nations by the situation of your land, your catholic faith, and your regard for the holy church, we have a special message and exhortation for you. For we wish you to know what a grave matter has brought us to your country. The sad news has come from Jerusalem and Constantinople that the people of Persia, an accursed and foreign race, enemies of God, 'a generation that set not their heart aright, and whose spirit was not steadfast with God' [Psalms 78:8], have invaded the lands of those Christians and devastated them with the sword, rapine, and fire. Some of the Christians they have carried away as slaves, others they have put to death. The churches they have either destroyed or turned into mosques. They desecrate and overthrow the altars. They circumcise the Christians and pour the blood from the circumcision on the altars or in the baptismal fonts. Some they kill in a horrible way by cutting open the abdomen, taking out a part of the entrails and tying them to a stake; they then beat them and compel them to walk until all their entrails are drawn out and they fall to the ground. Some they use as targets for their arrows. They compel some to stretch out their necks and then they try to see whether they can cut off their heads with one stroke of the sword. It is better to say nothing of their horrible treatment of the women. They have taken from the Greek empire a tract of land so large that it takes more than two months to walk through it. Whose duty is it to avenge this and recover that land, if not yours? For to you more than to other nations the Lord has given the military spirits, courage, agile bodies, and the bravery to strike down those who resist you. Let your minds be stirred to bravery by the deeds of your forefathers, and by the efficiency and greatness of Karl the Great, and of Ludwig his son, and of the other kings who have destroyed Turkish kingdoms, and established Christianity in their lands. You should be moved especially by the holy grave of our Lord and Saviour which is now held by unclean peoples, and by the holy places which are treated with dishonor and irreverently befouled with their uncleanness.

"O bravest of knights, descendants of unconquered ancestors, do not be weaker than they, but remember their courage. If you are kept back by your love for your children, relatives, and wives, remember what the Lord says in the Gospel: 'He that loveth father or mother more than me is not worthy of me' [Matthew 10:37]; 'and everyone that hath forsaken houses, or brothers, or sisters, or father, or mother, or wife, or children, or lands for my name's sake, shall receive a hundredfold and shall inherit everlasting life' [Matthew 19:29]. Let no possessions keep you back, no solicitude for your property. Your land is shut in on all sides by the sea and mountains, and is too thickly populated. There is not much wealth here, and the soil scarcely yields enough to support you. On this account you kill and devour each other, and carry on war and mutually destroy each other. Let your hatred and quarrels cease, your civil wars come to an end, and all your dissensions stop. Set out on the road to the holy sepulchre, take the land from that wicked people, and make it your own. That land which, as the Scripture says, is flowing with milk and honey, God gave to the children of Israel. Jerusalem is the best of all lands, more fruitful than all others, as it were a second Paradise of delights. This land our Saviour made illustrious by his birth, beautiful with his life, and sacred with his suffering; he redeemed it with his death and glorified it with his tomb. This royal city is now held captive by her enemies, and made pagan by those who know not God. She asks and longs to be liberated and does not cease to beg you to come to her aid. She asks aid especially from you because, as I have said, God has given more of the military spirit to you than to other nations. Set out on this journey and you will obtain the remission of your sins and be sure of the incorruptible glory of the kingdom of heaven."

When Pope Urban had said this and much more of the same sort, all who were present were moved to cry out with one accord, "It is the will of God, it is the will of God." When the pope heard this he raised his eyes to heaven and gave thanks to God, and, commanding silence with a gesture of his hand, he said: "My dear brethren, today there is fulfilled in you that which the Lord says in the Gospel, 'Where two or three are gathered together in my name, there am I in the midst' [Matthew 18:20]. For unless the Lord God had been in your minds you would not all have said the same thing. For although you spoke with many voices, nevertheless it was one and the same thing that made you speak. So I say unto you, God, who put those words into your hearts, has caused you to utter them. Therefore let these words be your battle cry, because God caused you to speak them. Whenever you meet the enemy in battle, you shall all cry out, 'It is the will of God, it is the will of God.' And we do not command the old or weak to go, or those who cannot bear arms. No women shall go without their husbands, or brothers, or proper companions, for such would be a hindrance rather than a help, a burden rather than an advantage. Let the rich aid the poor and equip them for fighting and take them with them. Clergymen shall not go without the consent of their bishop, for otherwise the journey would be of no value to them. Nor will this pilgrimage be of any benefit to a layman if he goes without the blessing of his priest. Whoever therefore shall determine to make this journey and shall make a vow to God and shall offer himself as a living sacrifice, holy, acceptable to God [Romans 12:1], shall wear a cross on his brow or on his breast. And when he returns after having fulfilled his vow he shall wear the cross on his back. In this way he will obey the command of the Lord, 'Whosoever doth not bear his cross and come after me is not worthy of me.' " [Luke 14:27]. When these things had been done, while all prostrated themselves on the earth and beat their breasts, one of the cardinals, named Gregory, made confession for them, and they were given absolution for all their sins. After the absolution, they received the benediction and the permission to go home. [1]

1. What kinds of arguments did Urban use?
2. Should this speech be understood as revealing the primary motivations for the First Crusade? How does this compare with the analysis in the text?
3. Why might Urban be so interested in helping the emperor of Byzantium?

Byzantium

In the following selection, Speros Vryonis, Jr., summarizes the significance of Byzantium, which was declining in the latter part of the Middle Ages and finally fell in 1453 to the Turks.

Pitiful as was its end, the history of Byzantium nevertheless reads like a great epic. The Byzantines carried the torch of civilization unextinguished at a time when the barbarous Germanic and Slav tribes had reduced much of Europe to near chaos: and they maintained this high degree of civilization until western Europe gradually emerged and began to take form. It is no exaggeration to credit the empire with the preservation of European civilization from Islam in the seventh and eighth centuries. Had the empire fallen before the Arab attacks, Islam would have spread to much of Europe, with unforeseeable consequences, while it was still in an amorphous state. The Slavonic east would doubtless have received the Islamic faith, as would much of central Europe. Italy, isolated between Muslim Spain and an Islam established in the Balkans and central Europe, would have been seriously threatened, and so would the

---

[1] Oliver J. Thatcher and Edgar H. McNeal, eds., *A Source Book for Mediaeval History* (New York: Charles Scribner's Sons, 1905), pp. 518–521.

papacy. Indeed, invasions from Arab-held Sicily might well have established the sway of Islam in the Italian peninsula.

The empire developed a great and original art which was decisive in much of the Slav world, and the influence of which is to be discerned in Venetian and Ottoman architecture as well as in some of the earlier schools of painting in Italy. Its civilization played an important rôle in the evolution of such widely divergent phenomena as religious music, monasticism and humanism in the west. Certainly one of its greatest services was the preservation of so much of the classical Greek literary heritage, an inheritance which is at the very basis of western humanism. And finally, it created Christian theology, the most impressive intellectual monument of the Middle Ages. [2]

1. According to Vryonis, why was Byzantium so important to the history of Europe?

SPECULATIONS

1. At times, it appeared that either the Mongols or the Turks might sweep through Europe. Suppose that happened. How do you think it might have changed the development of Europe?
2. Considering your knowledge of the crusades, what sort of cause might lead you to join a "crusade"? What would your motives be?
3. Do you think Pope Urban II was justified in calling for the First Crusade?

TRANSITIONS

In "The Summer of the Middle Ages ca. 1200–1350," the civilization of the Middle Ages in the West at its peak was examined, a civilization that benefited from two previous centuries of creative development.

In "The Crusades and Eastern Europe ca. 1100–1550," focus is shifted eastward. After 1000 the Byzantine, Arab, and Kievan civilizations were all in decline. The Seljuks and then the Ottomans gained as the Byzantine and Arab states weakened, and a new Russian state centered at Moscow grew. Religious, commercial, and military contacts between the East and West grew, above all through the crusades and commercial expansion of Western Europe.

In "The West in Transition: Economy and Institutions 1300–1500," we will see a shift to more troubled times in the West during the fourteenth and fifteenth centuries.

---

[2] Speros Vryonis, Jr., *Byzantium and Europe* (London: Thames and Hudson, Ltd., 1967), p. 193.

SECTION SUMMARY
THE MIDDLE AGES AND
THE MEDIEVAL EAST
500–1300
CHAPTERS 6–10

CHRONOLOGICAL DIAGRAM

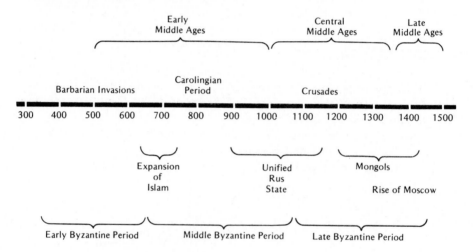

MAP EXERCISES

1. Indicate the following:
   a. Areas controlled by the Byzantine Empire during the early period, the middle period, and the late period. Indicate the approximate dates for each.
   b. Areas controlled by Islam at its maximum point of westward expansion. Indicate the approximate date.
   c. Areas controlled by the early Rus state (Kiev). Indicate the approximate date.
   d. Areas controlled by Charlemagne. Indicate the approximate date.

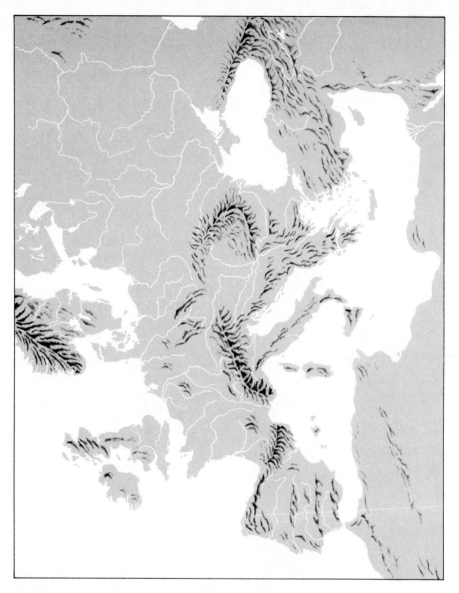

1. Indicate the crusader kingdoms and their approximate dates.
2. Indicate the political division of Europe around 1250.
3. Indicate the Russian state around 1500.
4. Indicate the areas controlled by the Ottoman Turks around 1550.

BOX CHARTS

Reproduce the Box Charts in a larger format in your notebook or on separate sheets of paper.

Chart 1

	Cultural Values and Productions	Religious System and Characteristics	Social System and Characteristics	Economic System and Characteristics	Political Institutions and Developments
Byzantium to ca. 1000					
Rus. to ca. 1200					
Islam to ca. 1100					
Europe to ca. 1000					

Chart 2

Europe: Characteristics, Developments, Turning Points

1000 ———————————————→ 1300

		Regional Differences
Political Institutions and Developments		
Economic System and Characteristics		
Social System and Characteristics		
Religious System and Characteristics		
Cultural Values and Productions		

Chart 3

	Europe 1300 → 1559	Turning Points	Problems
Political Institutions and Developments			
Economic System and Characteristics			
Social System and Characteristics			
Religious System and Characteristics			
Cultural Values and Productions			

ELEVEN
THE WEST IN TRANSITION:
ECONOMY AND INSTITUTIONS
1300–1500

MAIN THEMES

1. Europeans suffered economic depressions and demographic disasters in the fourteenth and fifteenth centuries.
2. Economic, psychological, and social factors led the lower classes in rural and urban areas to revolt, adding to the upheaval of the period.
3. Wars, weakening central authority, and questions about royal succession reflected the considerable political instability of the period.
4. The papacy suffered a major schism and growing unpopularity, which seriously weakened its authority.

OUTLINE AND SUMMARY

I. Economic Depression and Recovery.

In the fourteenth and fifteenth centuries, plagues, famines, and depressions struck Europe.

A. Demographic Catastrophe.

Europe suffered a rapid decline of population between 1300 and 1450, losing more than one-half of its thirteenth-century population.

    1. *Pestilence:* The great plague of the fourteenth century, a pandemic called the Black Death, was carried to Europe from the East in 1347. Cities were struck repeatedly during the century, often losing more than half their populations. The Black Death was probably a pneumonic plague rather than the bubonic plague, but the high death rate is difficult to explain.

    2. *Hunger:* Due probably to an overexpansion of population between 1000 and 1300, Europe suffered from a series of famines in the fourteenth century. This contributed to a population loss, which had both negative and positive consequences: pessimism discouraged economic effort, but the resulting shortage of labor encouraged the development of more efficient routines and of capital investment.

B. Economic Effects of the Decline in Population.

The loss of population was economically disruptive.

    1. *Agriculture:* Prices are indicative of economic forces. After the Black Death

prices rose and remained high until the end of the fourteenth century, indicating falling production. In the fifteenth century, prices declined, wages rose, and diets improved. Sheep raising grew at a particularly rapid rate, encouraging English landlords to increase their land holdings, switch from crop raising, and expel peasants who lived on the land (enclosure). By the middle of the fifteenth century prices stabilized and agriculture had attained a new, more diversified stability.

2. *Industry and Trade:* Entrepreneurs faced rapidly increasing wages. Efforts to secure effective governmental intervention to control wages and prices (the Statute of Laborers) failed. To control competition, entrepreneurs and cities restricted markets and established monopolies by limiting imports and forming guilds and monopolistic trade associations (Hanseatic League).

C. The Forces of Recovery.

Hard times and labor shortages inspired technical advances.

1. *Metallurgy:* After 1460 there were a series of important inventions in mining, smelting, working, and casting of metals. Silver and iron production expanded dramatically, especially in Central Europe.

2. *Firearms:* Firearms, such as cannons, came into use during the fourteenth century, another example of substituting capital for labor.

3. *Printing:* The replacement of parchments by paper and the invention of printing with movable metal type by Johannes Gutenberg (the Gutenberg Bible, 1455) multiplied the output and cut the price of books. Reading would no longer be a monopoly of the rich and the clergy, and ideas could be spread with unprecedented speed.

4. *Navigation:* Larger ships and a variety of technical developments, such as the stern rudder, the Alfonsine Tables, the compass, and the portolani (port descriptions) gave European mariners a mastery of Atlantic coastal waters.

5. *Business Institutions:* Mercantile houses, such as the Medici bank of Florence (1397–1498), became more flexible through a system of interlocked partnerships. Banking was modernized by book transfers (an ancestor of the modern check) and double-entry bookkeeping (especially in Italy). Maritime insurance became common, encouraging investments in shipping.

6. *The Economy in the Late Fifteenth Century:* Europe, though a much smaller community, was more productive and richer than ever, thanks to increased diversification, capitalization, and rationalization in economic matters.

II. Popular Unrest.

During the fourteenth and fifteenth centuries peasants and artisans revolted against the propertied classes many times.

A. Rural Revolts.

The most prominent fourteenth-century rural uprising was the English Peasants' War of 1381. Angered by efforts of the government to limit wages and increase taxes, and by attempts of landlords to revive feudal dues, peasants, supported by urban workers, marched on London. After gaining apparent concessions from King Richard II, they were violently suppressed by the great landlords. Other revolts occurred throughout Europe into the sixteenth century.

B. Urban Revolts.

For similar reasons, poor people revolted in cities throughout Europe. The temporarily successful Ciompi uprising at Florence (1378) revealed urban class tensions that would disturb capitalistic society in future centuries.

C. The Seeds of Discontent.

The discontent that led to revolts did not come from people living in desperate poverty, but rather from people who were making economic gains and were thus in a stronger bargaining position. Moreover, psychological tensions accompanying plagues, famines, and wars gave people the emotional energy to take extreme actions. By 1450 a new stability was emerging. Most workers enjoyed higher wages, cheaper bread, and a better standard of living than before, as reflected in renewed population growth.

III. The Governments of Europe.

Protracted violence during the period reflected a weakening of governmental systems.

A. Crisis and the Feudal Equilibrium.

The balance of shared responsibilities that characterized governments was broken in the fourteenth century and had to be rebuilt.
   1. *Dynastic Instability:* Dynasties in France, England, and elsewhere failed to perpetuate themselves, leading to wars (the Hundred Years' War, the English War of the Roses) between competing successors to the crown.
   2. *Fiscal Pressures:* The costs of war went up, thanks to the increasing use of firearms and to mercenaries, while traditional revenues sank. Kings imposed new national taxes (on salt, hearths, individuals, windows), which led to conflicts of authority with assemblies, such as the Parliament in England and the Estates General in France.
   3. *Factional Conflicts:* Many nobles suffered from the economic dislocations of the times. Attempting to improve their positions, they tended to coalesce into factions, disputing with each other over control of the government or distribution of its favors. This factional warfare throughout Europe constantly disturbed the peace.

B. England, France, and the Hundred Years' War.

The greatest struggle of the epoch, the Hundred Years' War between France and England, was apparently fought over succession to the French throne. Yet more important was the clash of French and English interests in the cloth-making county of Flanders and the friction over competing claims to Aquitaine and Ponthieu. This war between Edward III of England and Philip of France was rooted in a breakdown of France's medieval feudal constitution.

1. *The Tides of Battle:* In this confused struggle, England was initially victorious (1338–1360); France enjoyed a resurgence, and then there was a stalemate from 1367 to 1415; England then rallied, and under Henry V was on the verge of complete victory over the Dauphin (the future Charles VII) at Orléans.

2. *Joan of Arc:* A mystically inspired peasant girl, Joan of Arc, saved the French Capetian dynasty by turning the tide at Orléans and ensuring the coronation of the Dauphin at Reims. A growing loyalty to the king led to a series of French successes following the execution of Joan in 1431, eliminating England as a Continental power by 1453.

3. *The Effects of the Hundred Years' War:* The war confirmed the supremacy of the infantry over mounted knights. In England, the need for new taxes strengthened Parliament at the expense of royal power. In France, new taxes (the gabelle, or salt tax) helped establish royal domination over the fiscal system. Both countries suffered from factional struggles. In England, the Lancastrians and Yorkists warred with each other for thirty-five years (The War of the Roses), until Henry VII (Tudor) defeated the Yorkists in 1485. In France, the struggle between Armagnacs and Burgundians finally ended under Charles VII, thanks, in part, to the creation of Europe's first standing professional army since Rome. For a while, Burgundy threatened to establish a strong "middle kingdom" between France and the Holy Roman Empire, but the death of its last duke in 1477 ended it. England had thus stabilized and consolidated itself, while France's king gained power and prestige.

C. The Holy Roman Empire.

The Holy Roman Empire was no longer a major European power. The emperors were generally more concerned with the interests of their Hapsburg dynasty. They were subject to the Golden Bull (1356), which provided for the election of the emperor by seven powerful German electors. Late in the thirteenth century, governments of Swiss cantons (districts) confederated to form an exception to the trend toward centralized governments.

D. The States of Italy.

In the north and in the center of Italy, self-governing city-states dominated political life at the beginning of the fourteenth century. Factional rivalries, economic contraction, and rising military costs combined to weaken these smaller governments. Strong, sometimes despotic governments and regional states replaced them. Gian Galeazzo Visconti (1378–1402), who expanded Milan into a major regional power, is a good example of a powerful despotic ruler. Venice, under a kind of corporative despot (the Council of Ten), similarly expanded its territories. The banker Cosimo de' Medici rose to power in Florence; under his rule and that of his grandson, Lorenzo the Magnificent (1478–1492), Florence, with its festivals, social life, buildings, and cultural community, set the style for Italy, and eventually, for Europe.

1. *The Papal States and the Kingdom of Naples:* In the fourteenth and fifteenth centuries, popes had great difficulty in asserting effective control over their papal states in central Italy. Political chaos also reigned in the Kingdom of Naples and Sicily until 1435, when the king of Aragon, Alfonso V, unified them.

2. *Foreign Relations:* By 1450 Italy was divided among the Duchy of Milan, the republics of Venice and Florence, the Papal States, and the Kingdom of Naples. Thanks to new diplomatic methods and to the Peace of Lodi (1454), the Italian states developed an effective balance-of-power system, which maintained peace for the next forty years.

IV. The Papacy.

Powerful forces beset the papacy, weakening its authority and influence.

A. The Avignon Exile.

From 1308 to 1377 popes resided in Avignon, a French-speaking independent state in southern France.

B. Fiscal Crisis.

Lacking sufficient territorial resources for financial requirements, popes used their powers to make appointments, grant dispensations, collect tithes, and grant indulgences to raise funds. Though successful in raising funds, the practices were unpopular and helped create chaos in many parts of the Western Church.

C. The Great Schism.

Political struggles between the French and Italian factions led to the election of two, and later, three popes (the Great Schism, 1378–1417). Europe split its support between the popes, each collecting his own taxes and excommunicating everyone on the other side.

D. The Conciliar Movement.

Theologians and jurists argued that the Church should be governed by a general council, thereby reducing the pope's role. Their ideas turned into a movement during the schism, and at the Council of Constance (1414–1418) the views of the conciliarists prevailed. But the schism was ended at that council, and the princes of Europe favored papal over conciliar power. The movement proved to be impractical, as revealed at the Council of Basel (1431–1443). It ended in 1449, with the election of Nicholas V. Meanwhile, monarchs throughout Europe exerted greater control over their territorial churches, evidencing a deterioration of papal control over the international Christian community.

E. The Popes as Patrons of the Arts.

The popes of the fifteenth and early sixteenth centuries strongly supported the arts. The Vatican Library was formed, the Sistine Chapel was constructed, artists such as Botticelli, Perugino, and Michelangelo were commissioned, and the new St. Peter's Church was started. In retrospect, these popes acted more like great Renaissance princes than leaders of a troubled Church.

Experiences of Daily Life: Women and Sanctity.

In the late Middle Ages, women gained prominence in religious life, particularly as mystical, visionary, or charismatic saints and as extraordinarily pious people.

SIGNIFICANT INDIVIDUALS

Political Leaders

Wat Tyler (14th century), English peasant leader.

Jack Straw (14th century), English peasant leader.

John Ball (14th century), English peasant leader.

Henry VII (1458–1509), king of England.

Philip the Bold (1363–1414), Duke of Burgundy.

Gian Galeazzo Visconti (1378–1402), ruler of Milan.

Cosimo de' Medici (1389–1464), banker, ruler of Florence.

Lorenzo the Magnificent (1478–1492), Medici ruler of Florence.

Alfonso V (1416–1458), king of Aragon.

Religious Leaders

Martin V (1417–1431), pope.

Nicholas V (1447–1455), pope.

Julius II (1503–1513), pope.

Cultural Figures

Johannes Gutenberg (1400?–1468), German inventor.

Aldus Manutius (1450–1515), Venetian printer.

CHRONOLOGICAL DIAGRAM

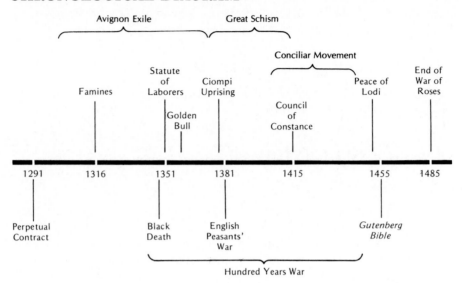

IDENTIFICATION

Black Death

enclosure

Statute of Laborers

Hanseatic League

Alfonsine Tables

Golden Bull

Peace of Lodi

Great Schism

double-entry bookkeeping

English Peasants' War

Ciompi uprising

War of the Roses

the gabelle

Conciliar Movement

Council of Constance

MAP EXERCISE

1. MARCH OF MONTFERRAT
2. MARCH OF MANTUA
3. DUCHY OF MODENA
4. REPUBLIC OF LUCCA
5. COUNTY OF ASTI

1. Label the five major states of Italy in 1454.

PROBLEMS FOR ANALYSIS

I. *Economic Depression and Recovery.*

1. What were the main developments that characterized the economic and demographic disasters of the fourteenth and fifteenth centuries? How can these developments best be explained?

2. Considering the loss of population, the technical advances, and the innovations in business institutions, was the long-term effect of the depression and demographic decline economically beneficial? Why?

II. Popular Unrest.

1. Analyze the governmental policies, the economic circumstances, and the psychological tensions that led to the rural and urban revolts of the fourteenth century. Was desperate poverty a primary cause?

III. The Governments of Europe.

1. In what ways was the feudal equilibrium in government broken in the fourteenth century? How is this illustrated by the Hundred Years' War?
2. Compare political development in the Holy Roman Empire with that in France or England.
3. In what ways were the states of Italy able to gain relative stability during the fifteenth century?

IV. The Papacy.

1. Explain how the Avignon Exile, the Great Schism, and the Conciliar Movement contributed to the weakening of the Church, and especially, papal authority. How did the papacy's secular concerns contribute to this?

DOCUMENTS

The Great Schism

When Pope Urban VI (1378–1389) decided to remain in Rome rather than return to Avignon, French cardinals declared him deposed and elected Clement VII (1378–1394), who returned to Avignon. Thus, the Great Schism began. The following manifesto was issued by French cardinals to justify their actions.

> . . . After the apostolic seat was made vacant by the death of our lord, pope Gregory XI, who died in March, we assembled in conclave for the election of a pope, as is the law and custom, in the papal palace, in which Gregory had died. . . . Officials of the city with a great multitude of the people, for the most part armed and called together for this purpose by the ringing of bells, surrounded the palace in a threatening manner and even entered it and almost filled it. To the terror caused by their presence they added threats that unless we should at once elect a Roman or an Italian they would kill us. They gave us no time to deliberate but compelled us unwillingly, through violence and fear, to elect an Italian without delay. In order to escape the danger which threatened us from such a mob, we elected Bartholomew, archbishop of Bari, thinking that he would have enough conscience not to accept the election, since every one knew that it was made under such wicked threats. But he was unmindful of his own salvation and burning with ambition, and so, to the great scandal of the clergy and of the

Christian people, and contrary to the laws of the church, he accepted this election which was offered him, although not all the cardinals were present at the election, and it was extorted from us by the threats and demands of the officials and people of the city. And although such an election is null and void, and the danger from the people still threatened us, he was enthroned and crowned, and called himself pope and apostolic. But according to the holy fathers and to the law of the church, he should be called apostate, anathema, Antichrist, and the mocker and destroyer of Christianity. . . . [1]

1. What legalistic justification do the cardinals use here?
2. What do they feel is their ultimate moral or religious sanction?

The Conciliar Movement

The schism was terminated at the Council of Constance (1414–1418), but the council in turn threatened papal authority by asserting its own authority within the Church.

In the name of the Holy and indivisible Trinity; of the Father, Son, and Holy Ghost. Amen.

This holy synod of Constance, forming a general council for the extirpation of the present schism and the union and reformation, in head and members, of the Church of God, legitimately assembled in the Holy Ghost, to the praise of Omnipotent God, in order that it may the more easily, safely, effectively and freely bring about the union and reformation of the church of God, hereby determines, decrees, ordains and declares what follows: —

It first declares that this same council, legitimately assembled in the Holy Ghost, forming a general council and representing the Catholic Church militant, has its power immediately from Christ, and every one, whatever his state or position, even if it be the Papal dignity itself, is bound to obey it in all those things which pertain to the faith and the healing of the said schism, and to the general reformation of the Church of God, in head and members.

It further declares that any one, whatever his condition, station or rank, even if it be the Papal, who shall contumaciously refuse to obey the mandates, decrees, ordinances or instructions which have been, or shall be issued by this holy council, or by any other general council, legitimately summoned, which concern, or in any way relate to the above mentioned objects, shall, unless he repudiate his conduct, be subject to condign penance and be suitably punished, having recourse, if necessary, to the other resources of the law. [2]

1. Without the schism that preceded the council, would this general Church council have been able to assert these claims?
2. Is the justification for the assertion of authority different in this document from that in the previous document issued by the French cardinals?

---

[1] Baluzius, "Vitae Paparum Avenionensium," in Oliver J. Thatcher and Edgar H. McNeal, eds., *A Source Book for Mediaeval History* (New York: Charles Scribner's Sons, 1905), 325–326.

[2] Von der Hardt, "Magnum Constantiense Concilium," in James Harvey Robinson, ed., *Translations and Reprints from the Original Sources of European History,* Vol. III, No. 6 (Philadelphia: University of Pennsylvania, 1902), pp. 31–32.

Medieval Heresy

In the following selection, Gordon Leff analyzes heresy in the latter part of the Middle Ages.

In these conditions heresy was endemic, since to step outside the accepted framework was to be opposed to authority. But heresy was far from an automatic process in which error was inseparable from excommunication and burning. In the first place, as we shall have ample occasion to see, error was of various degrees, and far from uniformly heretical. Moreover, it often took generations to define, as in the disputes over the poverty of Christ within the Franciscan order. In the second place, heresy was not just a matter of doctrine but also one of discipline — pertinacious error. The heretic was one who persisted in his mistake, refusing correction after his fault had been shown to him. It was for obduracy that he was finally punished after all efforts to make him abjure had failed. Consequently the test of heresy was a moral and practical one — willingness to submit; and conviction for it was an admission of defeat. It meant failure to save a soul from certain damnation: in consigning a man to the flames he was being consigned to the devil. Hence the great — often tireless — efforts to gain a recantation; what was at stake was a man's eternal life and obedience to God's saving will on earth. The church, as the medium for both, was, in asserting its authority, affirming God's law. Only if this is grasped can the zeal with which heresy was combated be understood: the misconception that belief can be enforced, and the undoubted injustices and cruelties which accompanied efforts to do so, must not blind us to the very genuine concern to save souls and the conviction that it was done in the service of God. Even Hus's judges, certain though they were of his guilt, tried to the end to persuade him to abjure.

There was a wide range of punishments: perpetual imprisonment, either solitary and in irons and on diet of bread and water (*murus strictus*), or a less restricted confinement (*murus largus*); the wearing of crosses as a sign of infamy; the performance of major or minor pilgrimages, lasting up to three or four months; fines, which were supposed to defray the expense of the tribunal and be used for good works; confiscation of goods, total for those abandoned to the lay power, even if they afterwards repented and were imprisoned: in the case of France, the proceeds went to the king; elsewhere, in Italy and in Germany, they were shared, usually between the locality, the inquisition and the papal court. Finally houses in which heretics had sheltered were to be destroyed and the inquisitor could employ their materials on building new edifices such as hospitals. Heretics were deprived of all civil rights.

The extraordinary jurisdiction exercised by inquisitors also extended to remission and commutation; by their right of grace they could exempt anyone from the worst penalties if he should come forward and confess his own errors or reveal those of others within a prescribed period, usually a month. This so-called 'time of grace' was frequently used; nor, as Bernard Gui pointed out, was it unprofitable since it usually led to the capture of more heretics.

The arbitrary nature of these procedures need hardly be stressed. Inevitably they led to cruelties and abuses; but they should not be exaggerated. It has been calculated that of a total of 930 condemnations by Bernard Gui the inquisitor for Toulouse from 1307 to 1324, 307 were imprisoned, and 139 relaxed to the secular arm — a comparatively small number for nearly a generation of one of the most intensive phases of inquisitorial activity in the middle ages. No total estimate for the whole period is possible; but it is unlikely to have exceeded thousands. It is not however quantitatively that the importance of medieval heresy can be properly assessed. For this we must look to its significance for contemporaries. The fact that a whole elaborate machinery was created and extended to most parts of western Christendom is the best proof of it. From the time of Innocent III onwards heresy became one of the central preoccupations of church and secular power alike. It grew with the middle ages, just as heresy increasingly merged with criticism of the church and spiritual life. [3]

1. Why was heresy combated with such zeal?
2. Characterize the legal procedures and the punishments used when dealing with heretics.

Medieval Warfare

The reality of war is often disregarded. In the following selection, H. J. Hewitt examines medieval warfare and strategy.

> The men who landed in France were shortly to spend much of their time and energy in the destruction of property, in the forcible seizure of food and forage, and in plundering. These three operations were of course illegal in their own country. They were, however, normal and purposeful accompaniments of war; they were diametrically opposed to the lives and interests of the people of the invaded regions; and they could be carried to lengths which exceeded military necessity, military advantage or even good sense. At times, therefore, it would fall to a commander to set limits to his soldiers' activities and enforce his orders—if he had sufficient control over the men to do so. Before dealing with these activities in detail, it is appropriate to consider briefly the background to the discipline of the armies.
>
> The broad conclusions are that the troops were unaccustomed to restraint imposed by authority; that they were often acting—as we shall see—under circumstances in which restraint would be very unnatural; that while the army was on the march, punishment short of death could not readily be imposed; that discipline could be, and probably often was, strong enough to prevent attacks on church property; that some destruction by burning may have resulted from mischance rather than design. But on very many occasions, no orders for restraint appear to have been given and the terrible work of war proceeded in the customary way. That the French, the Scots and the Flemings, when occasion offered, spread the work by the same means is evident to any student of the chronicles.
>
> We proceed to the army's typical activities. Having brought an armed force to the Anglo-Scottish border, or having landed on the coast of France, or led an army from Sluys or Bordeaux to the French frontier, what was the commander's aim?
>
> It was not, as might have been supposed, to seek out the enemy and bring him to decisive combat. Notwithstanding the ideals of chivalry, the Orders of the Garter and of the Star, the romance of the Round Table, the Fight of the Thirty; notwithstanding the laudable desire of young knights to display prowess, the king, the prince and Henry of Lancaster were not—or not usually—bent on that critical conflict of arms, nor did they refer to such an aim in their reports, nor did adulatory chroniclers attribute that aim to them.

[3] Gordon Leff, *Heresy in the Later Middle Ages*, Vol. I (Manchester: Manchester University Press, 1967), pp. 1–2, 46–47.

The commander's purpose was to work havoc, to inflict damage or loss or ruin or destruction on the enemy and his subjects by devastation.

Exerting pressure by devastation is, however, only one of the army's activities. It has to live on the country, that is to say it has to gather from the invaded region enough food and forage to sustain man and horse. It has also to move forward at quite short intervals. It will often be more profitable to seize cattle, poultry and bags of corn than to destroy them. It will also be more congenial to the soldier to seize certain goods than to destroy them. These circumstances do not alter the fundamental aim of working havoc; but they complicate the procedure for, although the army may often find villages from which the inhabitants have fled in terror, it will also arrive at towns where the people offer furious resistance not only to the soldiers' entry to the town, but also to every act of appropriation or destruction. Victualling, looting and destroying, though routine activities in principle, are not invariably carried out with quiet efficiency by well disciplined troops. On the contrary, between hungry, thirsty, weary or drunken soldiers on the one side and desperate "civilians" on the other, there will be scenes of high drama and great violence.

For medieval war did not consist wholly or mainly in battles and sieges with the marches necessary to effect encounters. It consisted very largely in the exertion of pressure on the civil population, and this pressure took the form of destruction, of working havoc. The ends sought in twentieth-century warfare by blockade and aerial bombardment had to be sought in the fourteenth century by operations on the ground. That in recent periods civilians suffered in mind, body and estate and were intended to suffer, is universally allowed. The circumstances of the fourteenth century, though not wholly parallel, are sufficiently similar to enable us to infer the purpose and the effect of the devastation carried out in that period. [4]

1. What were the principal military strategies used, according to this interpretation?
2. Does this document indicate that ideals of chivalry are simply romantic myths? Explain.

SPECULATIONS

1. Suppose you were one of the popes during the Great Schism. How would you explain the Great Schism, and what policies would you follow? Why?
2. If England had been more successful militarily in the Hundred Years' War, do you think it might have maintained control over much of France for a long time? Why?
3. If a series of plagues and famines struck this country today, how do you think the people would react? What would the consequences be? Do you think there would be an experience parallel to that in fourteenth-century Europe? Why?

[4] H. J. Hewitt, *The Organization of War Under Edward III* (Manchester: Manchester University Press, 1966), pp. 93–118.

TRANSITIONS

In "The Crusades and Eastern Europe ca. 1100–1550," connections between the West and East were examined in light of the decline of Byzantium, the rise of the Ottomans, and the formation of modern Russia.

In "The West in Transition: Economy and Institutions 1300–1500," it was seen that Europe suffered a temporary decline. Compared to the thirteenth century, population decreased, political instability spread, wars proliferated, and papal authority disintegrated. Yet Europe would recover and gain new dynamism by the second half of the fifteenth century. The period between the middle of the fourteenth and fifteenth centuries should be considered both an autumn and a renaissance for Europe.

In "The West in Transition: Society and Culture 1300–1500," the culture, values, and society of that same period will be examined.

TWELVE
THE WEST IN TRANSITION: SOCIETY AND CULTURE
1300–1500

MAIN THEMES

1. The culture of the Renaissance was produced within the dynamic society of Italian cities. Humanism was at the core of this culture.

2. Northern culture remained more medieval and centered upon the court, the chivalric knight, and the theme of decay.

3. An analytical and pietistic approach characterized religious developments in the North.

4. The fine arts, supported by laymen, advanced magnificently in the fourteenth and fifteenth centuries.

5. Foundations for the later scientific revolution were formed during this period.

OUTLINE AND SUMMARY

I. Society and Culture in Italy.

In the fourteenth and fifteenth centuries Italian society produced a cultural Renaissance.

A. Cities.

Italy was more highly urbanized than other areas of Europe. Its urban population was unusually well educated and active in economic and political affairs.

B. Families.

Italian families were distinctively small (fewer than four persons per household); males were usually much older than their brides. This demographic pattern led to a surplus of unmarried women and a low birth rate, which in turn attracted ambitious immigrants to the cities. Women dominated family life, and children became of extraordinary concern. Within Italian cities, these social developments facilitated economic specialization among men, an unusual cultural sensitivity, and an extraordinarily cosmopolitan outlook.

C. Leadership of the Young.

Mortality levels were high during the fourteenth and fifteenth centuries. Life expectancy averaged 30 years, except during the Black Death, when it dropped to 18. This increased opportunities for youths to rise in society and influence the style of the times.

D. Learning and Literature.

Scholastic education was inappropriate for laymen interested in business, politics, and practical ethics.

1. *Humanism:* By the late thirteenth century an intellectual movement, Humanism, was founded in Italian cities. Humanism stressed moral philosophy and eloquence, Latin and classical writings, and human perfection through new learning and traditional religious piety.

2. *Petrarch:* Petrarch became the leading humanist of the fourteenth century. In his search for classical manuscripts, his support of education and scholarship, and his writing, he created an influential model of the Italian humanist.

3. *Boccaccio:* Boccaccio wrote *The Decameron* between 1348 and 1351, the first prose masterpiece written in Italian, which would become a model for clear and lively narration.

4. *The Civic Humanists:* This group of Florentine scholars, led by Coluccio Salutati, instituted a movement to recover antiquity—particularly through the command of the Greek language. They argued for training in the classics, participation in public affairs, and support of Florentine republican institutions.

5. *Humanism in the Fifteenth Century:* Humanism spread from Florence to other Italian cities. The movement is characterized by the historical criticism of Lorenzo Valla (proved the forgery of the Donation of Constantine), the educational ideas of Guarino da Verona, and the institution of humanistic educational ideas by Vittorino da Feltre in his model school, Happy House. By the late fifteenth century, the success of Humanism led to its declining vitality in Italy. Philosophers became the new leaders of Italian intellectual life.

6. *The Florentine Neoplatonists:* A group of influential Florentine philosophers, most notably Marsilio Ficino and Pico della Mirandola, attempted to reconcile Platonic philosophy and Christian belief. They argued that a person should strive for personal perfection and contemplate the beautiful.

7. *The Heritage of Humanism:* Italian humanists utilized the past, through linguistic skills, historical criticism, and philosophical speculation, to better guide people in the present. They addressed themselves, through their writings and their schools, to lay society. Their work profoundly influenced Western culture.

II. The Culture of the North.

In the North, more distant from the monuments of antiquity in Italy and less urbanized, the court and the knight dominated culture for most of the later fourteenth and fifteenth centuries.

A. Chivalry.

A lingering of medieval civilization and an emotional distortion of reality, which characterized northern culture, are reflected in the idealization of the knight, with his inflated notions of battle and romance.

B. The Cult of Decay.

The North was a psychologically disturbed and religiously unsettled world at this time. Themes of death, decay, and demonology dominated its culture.

C. Contemporary Views of Northern Society.

Observers of northern society included Jean Froissart, who depicted chivalric society; William Langland, who in *Visions of Piers Plowman* commented more broadly on medieval society; and Geoffrey Chaucer, who summed up the moral and social ills of his times in *Canterbury Tales*.

III. Religious Thought and Piety.

Thinkers of the fourteenth and fifteenth centuries were much more concerned with analytical thought and piety than thirteenth-century Scholastics.

    1. *The "Modern Way":* William of Ockham was the most prominent of a group of philosophers who believed in nominalism. Ockham argued that the most simple explanation, based on direct experience, is the best way to understand reality. This comparatively pessimistic but popular philosophy came to be known as the *via moderna* ("modern way").

    2. *Social Thought:* Marsilius of Padua (*Defender of Peace*) and others influenced by nominalism criticized the papal and clerical domination of Western political life by formulating radical ideas about political sovereignty.

A. Styles of Piety.

The consolations of mystical piety, formerly restricted to monastic orders, spread through literature and religious guilds to laymen.

    1. *The Rhenish Mystics:* A number of figures in the Rhine Valley, such as Meister Eckhart, Gerhard Groote, and Thomas à Kempis (*The Imitation of Christ*), stressed emotional communion with God and simple humility in everyday life. Their teachings, known as *devotio moderna* ("modern devotion"), spread through a religious congregation (the Brethren of the Common Life) and its schools. This lay piety was a striking contrast to the formal ritualism and Scholasticism of the thirteenth century.

    2. *Heresies:* Heresies, reflecting problems within the Church, arose in the fourteenth and fifteenth centuries. Heretics, such as John Wycliffe (Lollards) and John Huss (Hussites), revolted against the Church and some of its doctrines, anticipating the concerns of later Protestantism, such as predestination.

IV. The Fine Arts.

This was a brilliant period for the fine arts.

A. Patrons and Values.

In the fourteenth and fifteenth centuries, laymen joined the Church as great patrons of the arts. While much art remained religious, it was more concrete and emotional in character. At the same time, nonliturgical art spread to residences in the form of tapestries, paintings, statuary, finely made furniture, and windows of tinted glass. Music and painting became more popularized and concerned with beauty. An increasing demand enabled many to become professional artists and musicians with heightened social status.

B. Techniques and Models.

New methods of musical notation and a variety of musical instruments were invented and employed. Artists, such as Giotto and Masaccio, achieved depth and realism in their naturalistic works. Flemish artists used oils and perfected portrait painting. Classical values, such as idealized beauty, simplicity, and balance, were integrated into Italian art, as in the sculpting of Donatello. Later, Italian architects, such as Andrea Palladio, would develop a pure classical style in their buildings.

C. The Great Masters.

Italy and the Low Countries were the major centers of Western art in the fifteenth century.

1. *The North:* Jan van Eyck (*The Virgin and Child in the Church*) exemplified the realism and detail of Flemish painting. Rogier van der Weyden (*Descent From the Cross*) emphasized another characteristic of Flemish art: dramatic composition and emotional intensity. Masters, musicians, and composers, such as Guillaume Dufay and Josquin des Pres, developed and popularized polyphonic music.

2. *Italy:* High Renaissance Italian art is best represented by Leonardo da Vinci, Raphael Santi, and Michelangelo Buonarroti. Although he was imaginative in technology and science, da Vinci was most accomplished as a psychologically perceptive painter (*Last Supper, Mona Lisa*). Raphael was a superbly versatile painter revealing Renaissance admiration for harmony, serenity, pure beauty, and pure form. Michelangelo was a genius in architecture, sculpture, and painting. His work was extraordinarily dynamic, combining psychological awareness with a neoplatonic vision of how things ought to be.

V. Science and the Renaissance.

Some of the early foundations for the scientific revolution were laid during the fourteenth and fifteenth centuries.

A. The Reception of Ancient Science.

Naturalistic science, primarily Aristotelian, was mastered by the thirteenth century. In the fourteenth century nominalists, such as Jean Buridan, questioned Aristotle and established a basis for Galileo's theories and the later emphasis upon measurement. The humanistic tradition of criticism, care, and precision contributed to later scientific developments. Increasing concern with practical matters, such as navigation and warfare, and the growing ability of artists to

accurately depict human anatomy, maps, or astronomical charts, would pro-
vice support for the scientific revolution of the sixteenth and the seventeenth
centuries.

Experiences of Daily Life: The Worker in the Venice Arsenal.

Venice's shipbuilding and arms manufacturing facility was the largest industrial
enterprise in Europe and provided employment for thousands.

SIGNIFICANT INDIVIDUALS

Italian Humanists

Francesco Petrarch (1304–1373), writer.
Giovanni Boccaccio (1313–1375),
    writer.
Coluccio Salutati (14th century),
    civic humanist.

Lorenzo Valla (1407–1457), writer.
Vittorino de Feltre (1378–1446),
    educator.

Scholars and Philosophers

Marsilio Ficino (1433–1499),
    Florentine neoplatonist.
Pico della Mirandola (1463–1494),
    Florentine neoplatonist.

William of Ockham (1300?–1349?),
    English nominalist.
Marsilius of Padua (1290?–1343),
    Italian.

Religious Reformers

Meister Eckhart (1260?–1327),
    Rhenish preacher.
Gerhard Groote (1340–1383),
    Rhenish reformer.
Thomas à Kempis (1380–1471),
    German religious writer.

John Wycliffe (1320?–1384), English
    heretic.
John Huss (1369–1415), Czech
    heretic.

Painters

Giotto (1276?–1337), Florentine.
Masaccio (1401–1428), Florentine.
Jan van Eyck (1385–1440), Flemish.
Rogier van der Weyden (1399?–
    1464), Flemish.
Raphael Santi (1483–1520), Italian.

Leonardo da Vinci (1452–1520),
    Italian.
Michelangelo Buonarroti (1475–
    1564), Italian painter, sculptor,
    architect.

CHRONOLOGICAL DIAGRAM

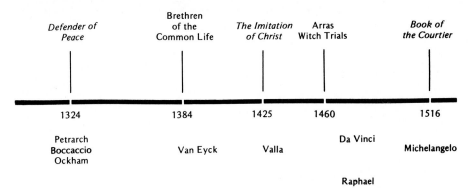

IDENTIFICATION

civic Humanism
Casa Giocosa (Happy House)
Neoplatonism
chivalry
Knights of the Garter
the "Modern Way"

Ockham's razor
nominalism
confraternities
lay piety
Lollards
Hussites

PROBLEMS FOR ANALYSIS

I. Society and Culture in Italy.

1. What role did demographic patterns, and in particular family life, play in the development of the Renaissance in Italian cities?
2. What are the main characteristics of Italian Humanism? How do these compare with earlier medieval Scholasticism? Why were Italian humanists so interested in the past?

II. The Culture of the North.

1. What social and historical factors help explain the difference between the culture of the north and the culture of Italy?
2. Is it fair to argue that the culture of the North was one of pessimism and decay, a holdover from the Middle Ages? Why?

III. Religious Thought and Piety.

1. Compare the analytical religious thought of nominalists, such as William of Ockham, with the synthetic Scholasticism of Thomas Aquinas.

2. Was mystical piety a rejection of the teachings of the medieval Church? Should Rhenish mystics be distinguished from heretics, such as John Wycliffe and John Huss? Why?

IV. *The Fine Arts.*

1. How accurate is it to say that the fine arts were secularized by Renaissance artists? Explain.
2. Compare Italian and northern art.

V. *Science and the Renaissance.*

1. In what ways was a foundation for the scientific revolution created in the fourteenth and fifteenth centuries?

DOCUMENTS

Petrarch

The following is a selection from the letters of Petrarch (1304–1374), the first great Italian humanist.

> You ask me finally to lend you the copy of Homer that was on sale at Padua, if, as you suppose, I have purchased it; since, you say, I have for a long time possessed another copy; so that our friend Leo may translate it from Greek into Latin for your benefit and for the benefit of our other studious compatriots. I saw this book, but neglected the opportunity of acquiring it, because it seemed inferior to my own. It can easily be had with the aid of the person to whom I owe my friendship with Leo; a letter from that source would be all-powerful in the matter, and I will myself write him.
>
> If by chance the book escape us, which seems to me very unlikely, I will let you have mine. I have been always fond of this particular translation and of Greek literature in general, and if fortune had not frowned upon my beginnings, in the sad death of my excellent master, I should be perhaps today something more than a Greek still at his alphabet. I approve with all my heart and strength your enterprise, for I regret and am indignant that an ancient translation, presumably the work of Cicero, the commencement of which Horace inserted in his *Ars Poetica,* should have been lost to the Latin world, together with many other works. It angers me to see so much solicitude for the bad and so much neglect of the good. . . .
>
> As for me, I wish the work to be done, whether well or ill. I am so famished for literature that just as he who is ravenously hungry is not inclined to quarrel with the cook's art, so I await with lively impatience whatever dishes are to be set before my soul. And in truth, the morsel in which the same Leo, translating into Latin prose the beginning of Homer, has given me a foretaste of the whole work, although it confirms the sentiment of St. Jerome, does not displease me. It possesses, in fact, a secret charm, as certain viands, which have failed to take a moulded shape, although they are lacking in form, nevertheless preserve their taste and odor. May he continue with the aid of Heaven, and may he give us Homer, who has been lost to us!

In asking of me the volume of Plato which I have with me, and which escaped the fire at my trans-Alpine country house, you give me proof of your ardor, and I shall hold this book at your disposal, whenever the time shall come. I wish to aid with all my power such noble enterprises. But beware lest it should be unbecoming to unite in one bundle these two great princes of Greece, lest the weight of these two spirits should overwhelm mortal shoulders. Let your messenger undertake, with God's aid, one of the two, and first him who has written many centuries before the other. Farewell. [1]

1. In what ways does this letter point up the concerns of Italian Humanism?
2. Does this letter evidence any conflict between the concern for pagan literature and Christianity?

Leonardo da Vinci

Leonardo da Vinci (1452–1520) is perhaps best known as an artist, but he was also a true "Renaissance man," with talents in many fields. In the following selection, Leonardo offers his services as a producer of war materials, and almost as an afterthought, as a sculptor.

Having now sufficiently seen and considered the proofs of all those who count themselves masters and inventors of instruments of war, and finding that their invention and use of the said instruments does not differ in any respect from those in common practice, I am emboldened without prejudice to anyone else to put myself in communication with Your Excellency, in order to acquaint you with my secrets, thereafter offering myself at your pleasure effectually to demonstrate at any convenient time all those matters which are in part briefly recorded below.

1. I have plans for bridges, very light and strong and suitable for carrying very easily, with which to pursue and at times defeat the enemy; and others solid and indestructible by fire or assault, easy and convenient to carry away and place in position. And plans for burning and destroying those of the enemy.

2. When a place is besieged I know how to cut off water from the trenches, and how to construct an infinite number of bridges, mantlets, scaling ladders, and other instruments which have to do with the same enterprise.

3. Also if a place cannot be reduced by the method of bombardment, either through the height of its glacis or the strength of its position, I have plans for destroying every fortress or other stronghold unless it has been founded upon rock.

4. I have also plans for making cannon, very convenient and easy of transport, with which to hurl small stones in the manner almost of hail, causing great terror to the enemy from their smoke, and great loss and confusion.

5. Also I have ways of arriving at a certain fixed spot by caverns and secret winding passages, made without any noise, even though it may be necessary to pass underneath trenches or a river.

6. Also I can make armored cars, safe and unassailable, which will enter the serried ranks of the enemy with their artillery, and there is no company of men at arms so great that they will not break it. And behind these the infantry will be able to follow quite unharmed and without any opposition.

[1] Petrarch, "Epistolae," in *A Literary Source Book of the Renaissance*, trans. M. Whitcomb (1900), pp. 13–15.

7. Also, if need shall arise, I can make cannon, mortars, and light ordnance, of very beautiful and useful shapes, quite different from those in common use.

8. Where it is not possible to employ cannon, I can supply catapults, mangonels, *trabocchi* [old war engines: trébuchets], and other engines of wonderful efficacy not in general use. In short, as the variety of circumstances shall necessitate, I can supply an infinite number of different engines of attack and defense.

9. And if it should happen that the engagement is at sea, I have plans for constructing many engines most suitable either for attack or defense, and ships which can resist the fire of all the heaviest cannon, and powder and smoke.

10. In time of peace I believe that I can give you as complete satisfaction as anyone else in architecture in the construction of buildings both public and private, and in conducting water from one place to another.

Also I can execute sculpture in marble, bronze, or clay, and also painting, in which my work will stand comparison with that of anyone else, whoever he may be.

Moreover, I would undertake the work of the bronze horse, which shall perpetuate with immortal glory and eternal honor the auspicious memory of the Prince your father and of the illustrious house of Sforza.

And if any of the aforesaid things should seem impossible or impracticable to anyone, I offer myself as ready to make trial of them in your park or in whatever place shall please Your Excellency, to whom I commend myself with all possible humility. [2]

1. What does this document indicate about the realities of everyday life and the concerns of the state during the Renaissance?

2. As a representative of the Italian Renaissance, how do Leonardo's concerns differ from those of Petrarch two centuries earlier?

Burckhardt

The following is an excerpt from Jacob Burckhardt's classic, *The Civilization of the Renaissance in Italy.*

In the Middle Ages both sides of human consciousness — that which was turned within as that which was turned without — lay dreaming or half awake beneath a common veil. The veil was woven of faith, illusion, and childish prepossession, through which the world and history were seen clad in strange hues. Man was conscious of himself only as member of a race, people, party, family, or corporation — only through some general category. In Italy this veil first melted into air; an *objective* treatment and consideration of the state and of all the things of this world became possible. The *subjective* side at the same time asserted itself with corresponding emphasis; man became a spiritual *individual,* and recognised himself as such. In the same way the Greek had once distinguished himself from the barbarian, and the Arabian had felt himself an individual at a time when other Asiatics knew themselves only as members of a race. It will not be difficult to show that this result was owing above all to the political circumstances of Italy. . . .

Despotism . . . fostered in the highest degree the individuality not only of the tyrant or Condottiere himself, but also of the men whom he protected or used as his tools —

[2] Jean Paul Richter, *The Literary Works of Leonardo da Vinci* (Oxford: Phaidon Press Ltd., 1939), pp. 92–93.

the secretary, minister, poet, and companion. These people were forced to know all the inward resources of their own nature, passing or permanent; and their enjoyment of life was enhanced and concentrated by the desire to obtain the greatest satisfaction from a possibly very brief period of power and influence. . . . [3]

1. For Burckhardt, what is the most important distinction between the spirit of the Renaissance in Italy and the spirit of the Middle Ages?

Meaning of the Renaissance

In the following selection, John Addington Symonds presents an interpretation of the Renaissance similar to that of Burckhardt.

By the term Renaissance, or new birth, is indicated a natural movement, not to be explained by this or that characteristic, but to be accepted as an effort of humanity for which at length the time had come, and in the onward progress of which we still participate. The history of the Renaissance is not the history of arts, or of sciences, or of literature, or even of nations. It is the history of the attainment of self-conscious freedom by the human spirit manifested in the European races. It is no mere political mutation, no new fashion of art, no restoration of classical standards of taste. The arts and the inventions, the knowledge and the books which suddenly became vital at the time of the Renaissance, had long lain neglected on the shores of the Dead Sea which we call the Middle Ages. It was not their discovery which caused the Renaissance. But it was the intellectual energy, the spontaneous outburst of intelligence, which enabled mankind at that moment to make use of them. The force then generated still continues, vital and expansive, in the spirit of the modern world. . . .

Thus what the word Renaissance really means is new birth to liberty—the spirit of mankind recovering consciousness and the power of self-determination, recognising the beauty of the outer world and of the body through art, liberating the reason in science and the conscience in religion, restoring culture to the intelligence, and establishing the principle of political freedom. The Church was the schoolmaster of the Middle Ages. Culture was the humanising and refining influence of the Renaissance. [4]

1. How objective is this interpretation? Does it imply a negative view of the Middle Ages?

SPECULATIONS

1. The fourteenth and fifteenth centuries have been described as a period of political, economic, and social turmoil and disaster. Yet, it was also a period of extraordinary cultural creativity. How can you explain this apparent contradiction?

[3] Jacob Burckhardt, *The Civilization of the Renaissance in Italy,* trans. S. G. C. Middlemore (New York: The Macmillan Company, 1890), pp. 129–131.

[4] John Addington Symonds, *Renaissance in Italy. I, The Age of the Despots* (London: Smith, Elder and Company, 1898), pp. 2–4.

2. Considering his designs for the airplane, tank, and submarine, should Leonardo da Vinci be considered as important as an inventor as he was an artist? Why?

3. How do you imagine a noble from one of the northern courts would react upon visiting Florence in the mid-fourteenth century? Why?

TRANSITIONS

In "The West in Transition: Economy and Institutions 1300–1500," the economic depressions, social disasters, political instability, and religious disunity of the fourteenth and fifteenth centuries were examined. The picture at that period was gloomy compared to the thirteenth century.

In "The West in Transition: Society and Culture 1300–1500," we see that the same period was also one of extraordinary cultural creativity. In Italy a humanistic and artistic culture, responding to the new social needs of the dominant literate lay aristocracy, grew. In the North a more conservative and pietistic culture, clinging to the ideals of chivalry still prevalent among the lay aristocracy but nevertheless borrowing from Italian culture, evolved.

In "Overseas Expansion and a New Politics 1415–1560," Europe experiences a political, economic, and geographic revival characterized by the growth of monarchical power and overseas expansion.

THIRTEEN
OVERSEAS EXPANSION AND A NEW POLITICS
1415–1560

MAIN THEMES

1. In the sixteenth century, Europeans, led by the Portuguese and then the Spaniards, started expanding over the globe. At the same time Europe experienced a rapid economic growth that was of uneven benefit to its populations.
2. "New monarchies" in Western Europe increased their authority and territorial control.
3. In Italy and Eastern Europe, central authority was unable to overcome forces that were splintering areas into small, relatively autonomous units.
4. Initiated in Italy, new theories and practices of diplomacy and statecraft, focusing on the realities of power, spread throughout Europe.

OUTLINE AND SUMMARY

I. Exploration and Its Impact.

With access threatened by the Ottoman Empire, Europeans began seeking an alternative sea route to Asia.

A. The Overseas Expansion.

1. *The Portuguese:* In the fifteenth century, Prince Henry the Navigator of Portugal, motivated by a mixture of profit, religion, and curiosity, patronized a major effort to explore Africa. Eventually, Portuguese explorers, such as Bartholomeu Dias and Vasco da Gama, sailed around Africa, reached India, and made discoveries that would make Portugal the leader in the establishment of sea routes and trade with India and Asia. The Portuguese avoided colonization, establishing instead trading posts from Africa to China. Thus the West, supported by driving ambition, technical superiority in guns and ships, tactical skills, commercial expertise, and careful planning, began its rise to worldwide power. This expansion was continually sustained by competition among the various European states.

2. *The Spaniards:* Spain became the other main participant in the early European expansion. Limited by the Treaty of Tordesillas (1494) to the West, explorers, such as Christopher Columbus, Vasco da Balboa, and Ferdinand Magellan, made the New World the focus of Spain's explorations. Men, such as Hernando Cortes and Francisco Pizzaro, led Spanish troops to victory in Mexico and South

America and turned the land over to Spanish administrators (viceroys). Local natives were exploited and inhumanely treated. In 1545 silver mines were discovered in Bolivia, creating treasures that enriched Spain, and in turn, the rest of Western Europe.

B. Economic Growth.

In the sixteenth century, Europe experienced rapid economic growth, evidenced by inflation of prices, increase of population (especially in cities), expansion of trade, and prosperity in such industries as linen, cloth, silk, armaments, and glass. Precious metals played a role here, but more important was a revival of confidence, based upon political stability and the demand created by a growing population. Italian and German financial firms, such as the Fuggers, invested in trade and made close ties to leading monarchs. The guild system expanded, and the notion of a business enterprise as an abstract entity was established.

C. Social Change.

Food producers and landowners benefited from economic prosperity, but wages lagged far behind prices. Combined with an increasing population, this created large numbers of rural and urban poor, who resorted to wandering, crime, begging, and revolt. A few enterprising individuals were able to take advantage of economic opportunity and gain new wealth, title, and prestige; this period marks the growth of a new aristocracy.

II. The "New Monarchies."

Toward the end of the fifteenth century, new kings who effectively asserted royal authority came to power in Western Europe.

A. Tudor England.

English kings drew support from three sources: an effective administrative structure staffed by the powerful gentry, a strong but subordinate Parliament, and a uniform system of justice based upon common law.

1. *Henry VII:* Henry VII triumphed in the War of the Roses and founded the Tudor dynasty in 1485. By efficiently managing finances, strengthening the justices of the peace, making the council a more powerful judicial institution (in Star Chamber), and conducting foreign affairs shrewdly, he increased royal authority and political stability in England.

2. *Henry VIII and His Successors:* Henry VIII was a much bolder king than his father. With the aid of his strong chief minister, Cardinal Wolsey, he gained military success and consolidated his royal power at home. The inability of Wolsey to obtain from the pope a divorce for Henry, who wanted a son, caused his downfall. His replacement, Thomas Cromwell, encouraged Henry to break with the pope and head the English Church himself. Henry did this in 1534, adding wealth to the crown through collection of ecclesiastical fees and sale of monastic lands. The ability of the king and Parliament to bring this about increased the power and prestige of both institutions. Attempts by the nobility to regain lost power under Edward VI (1547–1553) and the Catholic Mary I (1553–1558) were short lived, as Elizabeth assumed power and increased monarchical authority.

B. Valois France.

In the fifteenth century, France's administrative system was less centralized than England's. Her lands were larger, her nobles were stronger, and local representative assemblies were more independent. French kings, however, took advantage of taxes (*aide, taille, gabelle*) to support an increasingly costly but powerful standing army, and of Roman law to issue ordinances and edicts, thereby strengthening royal authority.

    1. *Louis XI and Charles VIII:* Louis XI added to French power and territories by defeating the Duke of Burgundy and annexing most of his vast lands (1477). Thanks to clever diplomacy and luck, he gained further territories in the south and elsewhere. Charles VIII continued the pattern but also initiated a series of wars in Italy (1494) that lasted for sixty-five years.

    2. *The Growth of Government Power:* Although France was a rich country, governmental expenses were high, and nobles, many towns, royal officeholders, and clergy were exempt from some taxes. Louis XII (1498–1515) and Francis I (1515–1547) tried to solve this problem by selling administrative offices. This created new dynasties of noble officeholders, a new administrative class, and a growth of bureaucracies. In 1516 Francis gained the right to appoint France's bishops and abbots, another source for patronage. He centralized royal control into an inner council and asserted more strongly his legal powers (*lit de justice*). After Francis, the Reformation and civil wars reduced royal authority again.

C. United Spain.

The marriage of Isabella of Castile and Ferdinand of Aragon in 1469 led to the union of these two powerful kingdoms in the Iberian peninsula.

    1. *Ferdinand and Isabella:* By 1500 these monarchs had dramatically increased royal power in Spain. They reduced the power of the nobility, imposed law and order in Castile, acquired the dependence of lesser aristocrats (*hidalgos*), spread a centralized bureaucracy, gained authority over justice, drove Moors and Jews from the country, and employed the Inquisition to secure religious and political unity.

    2. *Foreign Affairs:* Ferdinand extended his kingdom with diplomatic and military skill. With the most effective standing army of the age, Spain became a major power in Italy. Her diplomatic corps had no equal.

    3. *Charles V, Holy Roman Emperor:* Charles inherited Spain, and as a Hapsburg, was elected Holy Roman Emperor (1519). Initially, because Charles was not Spanish, there was much hostility in Spain, which resulted in a number of revolts. Order was soon restored under the leadership of nobles and a detailed Spanish administration was shaped by Francisco de los Cobos. Spain became a vast federation of territories controlled by departmental and territorial councils and powerful viceroys, with Castile at the heart of power. This allowed for some local flexibility, while giving the crown the power it wanted.

4. *The Financial Toll of War:* Almost ceaseless wars drained the Hapsburgs and Spain financially. Much of this burden was supported by bullion from Latin America and loans from Italian and German financiers, who monopolized most of Spain's trade with the New World. In 1557 the monarchy declared the first of a series of bankruptcies.

III. The Splintered States.

Areas to the east of England, France, and Spain did not experience the same pattern of centralization.

A. The Holy Roman Empire: Autonomous Princes.

Here, weak institutions prevented the emergence of a strong central government. Most of these lands remained divided into numerous autonomous principalities, towns, and ecclesiastical units. The stronger princes continued to dominate most of these lands and the major central representative institution, the Diet.

B. Eastern Europe: Resurgent Nobles.

In Eastern Europe, the Hungarian and Polish patterns of a loss of power by the monarch, a growth of authority by the landowning aristocrats, and a revival of serfdom prevailed.

C. Italy: Independent City-States.

In 1494 a series of wars between Italian states, leading to continual involvement of the French and Hapsburgs, was initiated. By 1559 the Hapsburgs controlled most of Italy, with the exception of Venice and the Papal States. The small Italian political units were unable to survive onslaughts from large, centralized kingdoms.

IV. The New Statecraft.

Theorists and historians gained a new understanding of diplomacy and political leadership.

A. International Relations.

The Italians led in the establishment of resident ambassadors, a practice that was copied and expanded in the sixteenth century. The Italian wars also led to the rudiments of a balance of power system. In military affairs costly advances in arms, organization, defense, and logistics were made throughout Europe.

B. Contemporary Appraisals: Machiavelli and Guicciardini.

Political commentators turned from arguments based on divine will or contractual law to those based on pragmatism, opportunism, and effective government to explain political events, especially in Italy. Machiavelli analyzed power. In *The Prince,* he told the prince how to acquire and maintain power, recommending methods to inspire fear and respect when useful. This "Machiavellianism" was officially rejected, but it reflected many political realities of the times. In *Discourses,* he developed a cyclical theory of government (from tyranny to democracy and back again) and argued that the failure of ordinary citizens to participate actively in civic and military affairs had caused the Italians' defeat. Another Italian, Guicciardini, focused on the failure to unify Italy. In *History of Italy* he took a national perspective and rested his argument on original documents—the first major historian to do this. Both Machiavelli and Guicciardini reflected a pessimism about public affairs, which were characterized by an obsession with power and pragmatism.

Experiences of Daily Life: Settlers Overseas.

Most settlers faced great hardships in going overseas. Large numbers were forced by circumstances or authorities to make the dangerous move overseas.

SIGNIFICANT INDIVIDUALS

Explorers

Henry the Navigator (1394–1460), prince of Portugal, patron of explorers.

Vasco da Gama (1469?–1524), Portuguese, route around Africa to the East.

Christopher Columbus (1451–1506), Genoese, discoverer of America.

Ferdinand Magellan (1480–1521), Portuguese, circumnavigated the world.

Conquerors

Hernando Cortes (1485–1547), Spanish, conqueror of Mexico.

Francisco Pizzaro (1470?–1541), Spanish, conqueror of Peru.

Political Leaders

Henry VII (1485–1509), first Tudor king of England.

Henry VIII (1509–1547), king of England.

Cardinal Thomas Wolsey (1515–1529), chief minister of England.

Thomas Cromwell (1532–1540), chief minister of England.

Louis XI (1461–1483), king of France.

Charles VIII (1483–1498), king of France.

Francis I (1515–1547), king of France.

Isabella (1474–1504), queen of Castile.

Ferdinand (1479–1516), king of Aragon.

Charles V (1516–1556), king of Spain, (1519–1556), Holy Roman Emperor.

Matthias Corvinus (1458–1490), king of Hungary.

Cultural Figures

Niccolò Machiavelli (1469–1527),
Italian political philosopher.

Francesco Guicciardini (1483–1520),
Italian historian.

CHRONOLOGICAL DIAGRAM

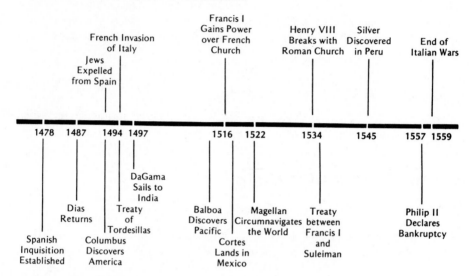

IDENTIFICATION

viceroys
audiencia
justices of the peace
the council (in Star Chamber)
Estates General
taille
standing army
sale of offices

"new monarch"
gentry
hidalgo
Moriscos
Diet
resident ambassador
balance of power
The Prince

MAP EXERCISE

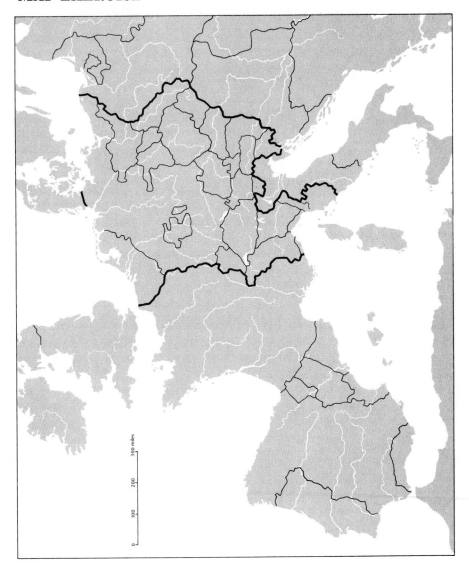

1. Label the *main* political divisions of Europe in the mid-sixteenth century.
2. Indicate the areas ruled by Charles V.

PROBLEMS FOR ANALYSIS

I. *Exploration and Its Impact.*

1. Distinguish between the Portuguese and Spanish patterns of exploration and expansion. What part did the size of Spain and of fifteenth-century political and military developments play in this difference?

2. What developments in prices, commerce, and industry evidenced economic growth? Why? What were the social consequences of this?

II. The "New Monarchies."

1. What developments and policies characterized the "new monarchies" of Western Europe?
2. Compare any two "new monarchies," focusing on the developments that distinguished the two, despite their similarities.

III. The Splintered States.

1. What is the historical significance of the failure of central authority to grow in Italy and Eastern Europe? Who became the holders of power in these areas? What were the consequences for the lower classes?

IV. The New Statecraft.

1. What distinguished diplomacy during the sixteenth century from that of previous times? Why did Italy play such an important role in this?
2. Machiavelli and Guicciardini were original observers of contemporary political events. What was so importantly new about their observations? In what ways did their observations reflect the events of their times?

DOCUMENTS

The Prince

Niccolò Machiavelli (1469–1527) was both a practical Italian statesman and a political philosopher. In the following excerpt from *The Prince*, he makes recommendations about how a prince can maintain his position.

> It now remains for us to consider what ought to be the conduct and bearing of a Prince in relation to his subjects and friends. And since I know that many have written on this subject, I fear it may be thought presumptuous of me to write of it also: the more so, because in my treatment of it I depart from the views that others have taken.
>
> But since it is my object to write what shall be useful to whosoever understands it, it seems to me better to follow the real truth of things than an imaginary view of them. For many Republics and Princedoms have been imagined that were never seen or known to exist in reality. And the manner in which we live, and that in which we ought to live, are things so wide asunder, that he who quits the one to betake himself to the other is more likely to destroy than to save himself; since any one who would act up to a perfect standard of goodness in everything, must be ruined among so many who are not good. It is essential, therefore, for a Prince who desires to maintain his position, to have learned how to be other than good, and to use or not to use his goodness as necessity requires.

Beginning then, with the first of the qualities above noticed, I say that it may be a good thing to be reputed liberal, but, nevertheless, that liberality without the reputation of it is hurtful; because, though it be worthily and rightly used, still if it be not known, you escape not the reproach of its opposite vice. Hence, to have credits for liberality with the world at large, you must neglect no circumstance of sumptuous display; the result being, that a Prince of a liberal disposition will consume his whole substance in things of this sort, and, after all, be obliged, if he would maintain his reputation for liberality, to burden his subjects with extraordinary taxes, and to resort to confiscations and all the other shifts whereby money is raised. But in this way he becomes hateful to his subjects, and growing impoverished is held in little esteem by any. So that in the end, having by his liberality offended many and obliged few, he is worse off than when he began, and is exposed to all his original dangers. Recognizing this, and endeavouring to retrace his steps, he at once incurs the infamy of miserliness.

A Prince, therefore, since he cannot without injury to himself practise the virtue of liberality so that it may be known, will not, if he be wise, greatly concern himself though he be called miserly. Because in time he will come to be regarded as more and more liberal, when it is seen that through his parsimony his revenues are sufficient; that he is able to defend himself against any who make war on him; that he can engage in enterprises against others without burdening his subjects; and thus exercise liberality towards all from whom he does not take, whose number is infinite, while he is miserly in respect of those only to whom he does not give, whose number is few.[1]

1. In what ways has Machiavelli separated the question of political power from ethics and morality here?
2. What does this document imply about the history of Italian politics?

The Courtier

The following is a selection from the work of Machiavelli's contemporary, Baldassare Castiglione (1478–1529).

I wish, then, that this Courtier of ours should be nobly born and of gentle race; because it is far less unseemly for one of ignoble birth to fail in worthy deeds, than for one of noble birth, who, if he strays from the path of his predecessors, stains his family name, and not only fails to achieve but loses what has been achieved already; for noble birth is like a bright lamp that manifests and makes visible good and evil deeds, and kindles and stimulates to virtue both by fear of shame and by hope of praise. . . .

But to come to some details, I am of opinion that the principal and true profession of the Courtier ought to be that of arms; which I would have him follow actively above all else, and be known among others as bold and strong, and loyal to whomsoever he serves. And he will win a reputation for these good qualities by exercising them at all times and in all places, since one may never fail in this without severest censure. And just as among women, their fair fame once sullied never recovers its first lustre, so the reputation of a gentleman who bears arms, if once it be in the least tarnished with cowardice or other disgrace, remains forever infamous before the world and full of ignominy. Therefore the more our Courtier excels in this art, the more he will be

[1] Niccolò Machiavelli, *The Prince,* trans. N. H. Tomson (Oxford: The Clarendon Press, 1897), pp. 109–110, 113–115.

worthy of praise; and yet I do not deem essential in him that perfect knowledge of things and those other qualities that befit a commander; since this would be too wide a sea, let us be content, as we have said, with perfect loyalty and unconquered courage, and that he be always seen to possess them. . . .[2]

1. According to Castiglione, what are the qualities of an ideal Renaissance courtier?
2. What similarities in advice and style are there between Castiglione and Machiavelli?

Columbus' First Voyage

In 1493 Christopher Columbus wrote a letter reporting on his first voyage, from which the following excerpts have been taken.

Sir, — Believing that you will take pleasure in hearing of the great success which our Lord has granted me in my voyage. I write you this letter, whereby you will learn how in thirty-three day's time I reached the Indies with the fleet which the most illustrious King and Queen, our Sovereigns, gave to me, where I found very many islands thickly peopled, of all which I took possession without resistance for their Highnesses by proclamation made and with the royal standard unfurled. To the first island that I found I gave the name of *San Salvador,* in remembrance of His High Majesty, who hath marvelously brought all these things to pass; the Indians call it *Guanaham.* To the second Island I gave the name of *Santa-Maria de Concepción*; the third I called *Fernandina,* the fourth, *Isabella*; the fifth, *Juana*; and so to each one I have a new name. When I reached *Juana,* I followed its coast to the westward, and found it so large that I thought it must be the mainland—the province of Cathay; and, as I found neither towns nor villages on the sea-coast, but only few hamlets, with the inhabitants of which I could not hold conversation, because they all immediately fled, I kept on the same route, thinking that I could not fail to light upon some large cities and towns. At length . . . [having] learned from some . . . Indians whom I had seized, that this land was certainly an island . . . I followed the coast eastward for a distance of one hundred and seven leagues, where it ended in a cape. From this cape, I saw another island to the eastward at a distance of eighteen leagues from the former, to which I gave the name of *La Española* [Hispaniola]. Thither I went, and followed its northern coast to the eastward . . . one hundred and seventy-eight full leagues due east. This island, like all the others, is extraordinarily large. . . . The lands are high, and there are many very lofty mountains . . . covered with trees of a thousand kinds of such great height that they seemed to reach the skies. Some were in bloom, others bearing fruit. . . . The nightingale was singing . . . and that, in November. . . . In the interior there are many mines of metals and a population innumerable. *Española* is a wonder. Its mountains and plains, and meadows, and fields, are so beautiful and rich for planting and sowing, and rearing cattle of all kinds, and for building towns and villages. The harbours on the coast, and the number and size and wholesomeness of the rivers, most of them bearing gold, surpass anything that would be believed by one who has not seen them. There is a great difference between the trees, fruits, and plants of this island and those

---

[2] Baldassare Castiglione, *The Book of the Courtier,* trans. Leonard E. Opdycke (1903), pp. 22, 25.

of *Juana.* In this island there are many spices and extensive mines of gold and other metals. The inhabitants of this and of all the other islands I have found or gained intelligence of, both men and women, go as naked as they were born, with the exception that some of the women cover one part only with a single leaf of grass or with a piece of cotton, made for that purpose. They have neither iron, nor steel, nor arms, nor are they competent to use them, not that they are not well-formed and of handsome stature, but because they are timid to a surprising degree. . . . It is true that when they are reassured and have thrown off this fear, they are guileless. . . . They never refuse anything that they possess when it is asked of them; on the contrary, they offer it themselves . . . and, whether it be something of value or of little worth that is offered to them, they are satisfied. . . . They are not acquainted with any kind of worship, and are not idolators; but believe that all power and, indeed, all good things are in heaven, and they are firmly convinced that I, with my vessels and crews, came from heaven, and with this belief received me at every place at which I touched, after they had overcome their apprehension. . . . On my reaching the Indies, I took by force . . . some of these natives, that they might learn our language and give me information in regard to what existed in these parts; . . . [they] are still with me, and, from repeated conversations . . . I find that they still believe that I come from heaven. [3]

1. What was Columbus expecting to find?
2. What was Columbus most concerned with? What did he feel his superiors would be most concerned with?

Expansion to Africa

In the following selection, Robert Collins traces the historical background of the fifteenth-century European expansion into Africa.

Africa first came under the European sphere of influence in antiquity when the Mediterranean coast of northern Africa was incorporated into the Hellenistic and Roman empires. During those centuries North Africa was exposed to European culture, government, and religion, and the northern littoral of Africa became more closely associated with Europe than with the vast sub-Saharan regions to the south. In the seventh century the European influence in North Africa was suddenly broken when Muslim armies swept out of Arabia on their holy mission to spread Islam. Advancing along the coast, the Arabs conquered all of North Africa and laid siege to Europe itself. Isolated from Africa and the Middle East by the Arabs, Europe turned in upon itself, more concerned with recapturing the order and the security that had vanished with the Roman empire than with expending its energies and resources in foreign lands. As power and prosperity returned to Europe, however, the interests of Europeans in Africa revived. With power came the desire to spread the teachings of Christ among the heathens. With prosperity came the demand for, and the resources to acquire, African and Oriental products. In the past the Europeans had been forced to deal with the Arabs, who not only held North Africa, but also controlled the trade routes

[3] R. H. Hajor, ed., *Selected Letters of Christopher Columbus* (London: Hakluyt Society, 1847), pp. 6–10.

to the Orient. Impervious to Christianity, the Arabs were not prepared to give up control of trade with the East to European merchants. Hoping to circumvent Arab middlemen, Europeans, particularly the Portuguese, began their tentative explorations along the African coast in search of an alternate route to the East. Led by a new and vigorous dynasty, the House of Aviz, the Portuguese were ready to carry the Christian crusade against Islam to Africa and to convert the Africans to Christ for the spiritual and material profit of the Portuguese nation.

The Portuguese crusade was not an immediate success. In 1415 a Portuguese expeditionary force captured Ceuta, across from Gibraltar, but the Portuguese were unable to penetrate farther into the Muslim states of North Africa. Nevertheless, the governor of Ceuta, Prince Henry, the third son of King João I of Portugal learned of the Sudanic states across the Sahara, speculated on their wealth, and pondered on their relations with the pagan Africans farther south who bartered gold and slaves for the salt and Mediterranean products of the Muslim merchants. Unable to defeat the Muslims of Morocco, Prince Henry sought to outflank them, and from 1415 until 1460 he organized the systematic exploration of the Atlantic coast of Africa.

There has always been a demand in Europe for Asian and African products— spices, sugar, silk, gold, and ivory. As the feudal and city-states of medieval Europe experienced economic growth, the demand for Oriental products sharply increased among an expanding leisure class. The supply seldom met this demand, inflating the price and stimulating merchants to deal in Asian and African goods at high risk but higher profits. The leading Christian merchants came from the maritime city-states of northern Italy, particularly from Genoa and Venice. By the end of the fourteenth century the Venetians had come to dominate the Eastern trade at the expense of their Genoese rivals. Throughout the fifteenth century Genoese navigators, sailors, and merchants therefore searched for new opportunities to gain control of the trade. They were experienced, highly skilled, and aware of the earlier expeditions which had hesitantly probed the inhospitable coast of Morocco and had landed in the Canary Islands. As a result, Prince Henry employed them to conduct his expeditions down the coast of Africa. [4]

1. According to Collins, what explains the European interest in Africa during the fifteenth century?

SPECULATIONS

1. If Machiavelli were alive today, what kinds of recommendations would he make to someone who wanted to gain and retain political office?
2. If you were advisor to Charles V, what policies would you suggest to retain the wealth coming from South America within Spain? What factors would you have to consider in making your recommendations?
3. What do you think motivated the explorers and conquerors? What kind of evidence would support your argument?

[4] Robert O. Collins, *Europeans in Africa* (New York: Alfred A. Knopf, 1971), pp. 3–5.

TRANSITIONS

In "The West in Transition: Society and Culture 1300–1500," the dynamic cultural developments of the fourteenth and fifteenth centuries and the social conditions supporting those developments were examined.

In "Overseas Expansion and a New Politics 1415–1560," Europe recovered from its political and economic contractions and expanded geographically throughout the world. This expansion was supported by economic growth and the establishment of powerful "new monarchies" in Western Europe. Lacking such strong, unifying central governments, the Germans, Italians, and Eastern Europeans fell behind. Yet poverty grew with the population, resentment with political centralization, and bewilderment with change.

In "Reformations in Religion 1500–1570," the great religious upheavals that destroyed religious unity in the West will be analyzed.

FOURTEEN
REFORMATIONS
IN RELIGION
1500–1570

MAIN THEMES

1. Discontent with the Church and a growing demand for spiritual consolation combined to set the stage for the Reformation.
2. Northern humanists, such as Thomas More and Erasmus, combined themes of Italian Humanism with religious concerns, creating an intellectual environment for the Reformation.
3. Lutheranism, based upon the doctrine of justification by faith and the idea that the Bible was the sole religious authority, grew within the politically divided Holy Roman Empire.
4. Zwingli and Calvin led new reform movements, and other groups, such as the Anabaptists and the Melchiorites, led more radical breaks from established religion.
5. Led by Pope Paul III, the Council of Trent, and the Jesuits, the Catholic Church reformed itself and initiated a revival of Catholicism.

OUTLINE AND SUMMARY

I. *Dissent and Piety.*

Religious dissatisfaction with the Church, which had been growing for some two centuries, came to a head in the early sixteenth century.

A. *Sources of Malaise.*

The main source of discontent leading to the Reformation was religious. The Church seemed to be declining, as evidenced by the Babylonian captivity in Avignon, the Great Schism, the Conciliar Movement, the secularization of the papacy and high Church officials, the sale of offices and indulgences, and the emphasis on outward works and ceremonies. At the same time, a demand grew for spiritual consolation not provided by the Church, as evidenced by the movements of John Wycliffe and John Huss, the emphasis on personal piety, the growth of mystical and lay religious fraternities (the brotherhood of the Eleven Thousand Virgins in Germany), and the ascendancy of Savonarola in Florence. The Church ignored the growing feeling of anticlericalism and demand for reform, except in

Spain under Cardinal Francisco Ximenes de Cisneros, until the mid-sixteenth century, when it was too late.

B. Piety and Protest in Literature and Art.

The invention of the printing press, the subsequent publication of the Bible in vernacular languages, and the popularity of critical literature (Brant, Rabelais, propaganda pieces) reflected the growth of popular piety and of dissatisfaction with the Church, especially in northern Europe. Similar spiritual themes were evident in the work of northern artists, such as Bosch, Grünewald, and Dürer.

II. The Northern Humanists.

The northern humanists adopted many of the themes of the earlier Italian humanists but added a strong religious concern with early Christian literature.

A. Christian Humanism.

Christian Humanism, originating in northern centers, such as the University of Heidelberg, was represented by scholars, such as Reuchlin and Lefèvre, and spread by the growing number of printing presses. It applied analysis of ancient texts, language, and style to early Christian (especially St. Paul) and Jewish writings in an effort to better understand the religious problems of the day.

B. Thomas More and Erasmus.

More (1478–1535, *Utopia*) and Erasmus (1466?–1536, *The Praise of Folly*) were the greatest of the Christian humanists. More argued that a religious person should participate in society, and that society can promote the truly Christian life, if properly organized and based on ascetic Christian principles. Erasmus strove for common sense and a revival of early, pure Christian faith based upon the life of Jesus. His biblical translations, books, and letters were tremendously influential, yet he refused to join either the Protestant or Catholic side in the growing struggle.

III. The Lutheran Reformation.

The religious and political environment of the Holy Roman Empire was well-suited to the success of a determined reformer, such as Martin Luther.

A. Martin Luther.

After experiencing personal crises and wrestling with a continuing sense of sinfulness, and despite almost superhuman efforts to lead a worthy monastic and scholarly life, Martin Luther came upon an interpretation of religion that would become the core of Lutheranism: "that justification—expiation of sin and attainment of righteousness through the infusion of grace—is achieved by faith alone."

1. *The Indulgence Controversy:* In 1517 Luther publicly challenged a Dominican monk, Tetzel, for selling indulgences (remissions for punishments in purgatory). Over the next three years, this act and subsequent publications brought Luther into conflict with the Dominicans, the pope (who excommunicated the defiant Luther), and the Holy Roman Emperor, Charles V (who condemned Luther at the Diet of Worms). Luther, then clearly a heretic, was saved by a politically independent German prince, Elector Frederick III of Saxony.

2. *Lutheran Doctrine and Practice:* Lutheranism was religiously revolutionary in a number of ways. The two fundamental assertions, partially derived from earlier nominalism, were that the individual could be justified by faith alone — not good works or the sacraments — and that the Bible was the sole religious authority — not tradition or pronouncements. These beliefs, along with other interpretations, such as the absence of free will, led to many changes in doctrine and practice: the importance of priests and the Church in general was diminished, most of the sacraments were denied, celibacy was rejected, the mass was altered, ritual was simplified, and the laity was encouraged to read the translated version of the Bible. Luther immediately gained considerable support, especially in northern and eastern Europe, but at the same time, more radical reformers and doctrines arose that Luther strongly opposed.

B. Disorders in the Name of Religion.

The Lutheran religious revolt became entwined with political matters. For a variety of reasons, Luther became allied with powerful German princes and with the kings of Denmark and Sweden against the Holy Roman Emperor and Catholic princes. At the same time, Luther opposed a peasant uprising in 1525, in the name of political and social order. By 1529 Lutheran princes had allied formally, and by mid-century, approximately half the population of the Empire was Lutheran. Despite military losses in the 1540s, the Protestants gained a compromise allowing each ruler to determine the religion of his territory (Diet at Augsburg, 1555).

IV. The Growth of Protestantism.

Shortly after Luther's stand in 1517, a variety of different forms of heresy arose in Europe, revealing both deep religious piety and discontent.

A. Zwingli.

Ulrich Zwingli led a successful reform movement in parts of the Swiss Confederation in the 1520s. Although in doctrine and practice Zwingli agreed in great part with Luther, his divergences from Luther were many: he emphasized simplicity, individualism, the need to educate and discipline all men, the unimportance of mystery and ritual, and a lack of distinction between secular and religious authority. In a civil war between Swiss Catholics and followers of Zwingli (1531), Zwingli was killed, and eventually his following was reduced and absorbed into Calvinism.

B. The Radicals.

More radical sects, such as the Anabaptists and the Melchiorites, formed in the 1520s and 1530s, but the more established Zwinglian, Calvinist, and Lutheran churches proved as intolerant of them as they were of the Catholics.

C. John Calvin and His Church.

John Calvin (*Institutes of the Christian Religion*) developed the most systematic form of Protestantism. In most matters, Calvinism resembled Lutheranism but stressed the overwhelming power of God, predestination, the union of secular and religious authority, and the importance of hierarchy and structure within the Church. From their base in Geneva, organized disciples with missionary zeal spread Calvinism to Scotland and parts of England, Germany, Switzerland, the Low Countries, and Hungary.

V. The Catholic Revival.

In the 1530s, in part as a reaction to the Protestant Reformation, in part as an internal movement, the Catholic Church started to purify itself.

A. Crisis and Reform in the Church.

Pope Paul III deserves much of the credit for the revival of the Catholic Church. Between 1534 and 1549 he set into motion a major church council to reexamine traditional theology, founded a Roman Inquisition to uproot heresy, attacked abuses within the Church, appointed cardinals of high quality, and paved the way for the succession of unusually successful popes.

B. The Council of Trent.

At the ecumenical council at Trent, 1545–1563, religious doctrine was debated and finally established, vigorously affirming the traditional Catholic position on most matters. The Catholic Church chose to hold its own ground, while aligning itself with many of the secular trends of the times, and its policies were in striking contrast to the austerity, sternness, and predestination stressed by the Protestants.

    1. *The Aftermath of Trent:* There was a strong revival of Catholic faith both within the institution of the Church and among believers, political leaders, artists, and writers.

C. Ignatius Loyola: The Making of a Reformer.

Loyola, after having a deeply moving religious experience, dedicated himself to a religious life within the Catholic Church. In his great work, *Spiritual Exercises,* he emphasized absolute discipline and the efficacy of free will and good works for attaining personal grace. In 1540 the papacy approved his plans for the founding of a new order, the Jesuits.

    1. *The Jesuits:* Through preaching, hearing confessions, teaching, and founding missions, the extremely knowledgeable, talented, and disciplined followers of

Loyola (Jesuits) gained tremendous success in stemming the tide of Protestantism. In many cases they returned great numbers into the Catholic fold. Jesuits established the most respected schools in Europe, gained considerable influence in important courts, and conducted successful missionary projects.

Experiences of Daily Life: Village Gatherings.

News, stories, and religious views were spread through regular village gatherings throughout Europe.

SIGNIFICANT INDIVIDUALS

Reformers and Protestants

Savonarola (1452–1498), Italian religious reformer.

Martin Luther (1483–1546), German Protestant.

Philipp Melanchton (1497–1546), German Protestant.

Ulrich Zwingli (1484–1531), Swiss Protestant.

John Calvin (1509–1564), French, Swiss Protestant.

Catholics

Paul III (1468–1549), reforming pope.

Ignatius Loyola (1491–1556), Spanish founder of the Jesuits.

Francis Xavier (1506–1552), Jesuit missionary.

Humanists

Sebastian Brant (1457?–1521), German.

François Rabelais (1494?–1553), French.

Johann Reuchlin (1455–1522), German.

Jacques Lefèvre d'Etaples (1450?–1537), French.

Sir Thomas More (1478–1535), English.

Desiderius Erasmus (1466?–1536), Dutch.

Artists

Hieronymus Bosch (1450–1516), Dutch painter.

Albrecht Dürer (1471–1528), German engraver.

CHRONOLOGICAL DIAGRAM

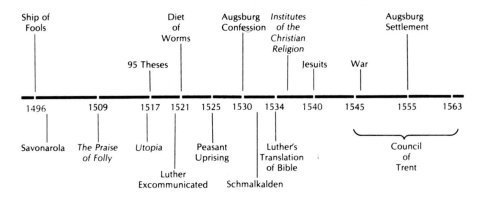

IDENTIFICATION

indulgences
lay religious fraternities
printing press
justification by faith
ninety-five theses
Index of Forbidden Books
Jesuits

Diet of Worms
priesthood of all believers
Augsburg Confession
predestination
Council of Trent
good works
village gatherings

MAP EXERCISE

1. Indicate the main Lutheran, Calvinist, and Anglican areas in 1560.

PROBLEMS FOR ANALYSIS

I. *Dissent and Piety.*

1. What were the sources of religious discontent that preceded the Reformation? What evidence is there for this?

II. The Northern Humanists.

1. Compare northern and Italian Humanism.
2. In what ways is it appropriate to focus on Thomas More and Erasmus and representatives of northern Humanism?

III. The Lutheran Reformation.

1. What were the main differences in doctrine and practice between Catholicism and Lutheranism?
2. "Despite his revolutionary actions, Martin Luther was quite authoritarian and conservative." Do you agree? Explain.

IV. The Growth of Protestantism.

1. "Protestantism was not simply a single movement away from the Roman Catholic Church; it was a series of separate and often conflicting movements." Do you agree? Explain.
2. Why did Calvinism develop into the most dynamic of the Protestant forces during the mid-sixteenth century?

V. The Catholic Revival.

1. In what ways was the Catholic revival of the sixteenth century both a Counter Reformation and a Catholic Reformation?
2. How did Pope Paul III, the Council of Trent, and the Jesuits contribute to the Catholic revival?

DOCUMENTS

Christian Humanism

The great Christian humanist Desiderius Erasmus (1466?–1536) never broke with the Catholic Church, but his writings criticizing the Church and contemporary mores were influential throughout the Reformation era.

> But why should I launch into so wide a sea of superstition? . . . Almost all Christians are wretchedly enslaved to ignorance, which the priests are so far from preventing or removing that they blacken the darkness and promote the delusion; wisely foreseeing that the people (like cows, which never give down their milk so well as when they are gently stroked) would part with less if they knew more. Now if a wise man should stand up and unseasonably speak the truth, telling everyone that a pious life is the only way of securing a happy death; that the best way to a pardon of our sins is a hearty abhorrence of our guilt and sincere resolutions of amendment; that the best devotion which can be paid the saints is to imitate their lives: if he were to proceed thus, many people would be vexed to lose the satisfaction they had had in tears, vigils, masses, fasting and like severities. . . .

Now as to the Popes of Rome who pretend themselves Christ's vicars, if they would but imitate his exemplary life, his poverty, labors, teaching and contempt of this world; if they did but consider the meaning of the word Pope, which signifies a father, or if they did but practice their surname of Most Holy, who on earth would be in worse condition? There would be no vigorous buying of votes in the conclave upon the vacancy of that see: who would retain the office by force and violence? How much of their pleasure would be abated if they were endowed with one dram of wisdom? Wisdom did I say? Nay, with one grain of that salt which our Saviour bid them not lose the savour of. It would deprive them of all their riches, honour, holdings, offices, dispensations, licenses, indulgences, their long train of attendance (see in how short a compass I have abbreviated all their marketing of religion); in a word all their perquisites would be lost. In their place would succeed vigils, fasts, tears, prayers, sermons, studies, repenting sighs, and a thousand such like penalties: nay, what's yet more deplorable, all their clerks, notaries, advocates, secretaries, grooms, servingmen, pimps (and somewhat else, which for modesty's sake I shall not mention); in short all these troops of attendance, which depend on His Holiness, would all lose their employments. This indeed would be hard, but what yet remains would be more dreadful: the very Head of the Church would be reduced from all his splendor to a purse and a staff. . . .[1]

1. According to Erasmus, what was wrong with Christianity and the Catholic Church?
2. Is he writing from an antireligious perspective? Explain.

Luther's Ninety-five Theses

On October 31, 1517, Luther posted his famous ninety-five theses, which ultimately led to his break with the Catholic Church and to the Reformation. The following are excerpts from those theses.

1. Our Lord and Master Jesus Christ in saying: "Repent ye," etc. intended that the whole life of believers should be penitence.

. . .

6. The Pope has no power to remit any guilt, except by declaring and warranting it to have been remitted by God; or, at most by remitting cases reserved for himself; in which cases, if his power were despised, guilt would certainly remain.

. . .

26. Thus those preachers of indulgences are in error who say that, by the indulgences of the Pope, a man is loosed and saved from all punishment.
27. They preach mad, who say that the soul flies out of purgatory as soon as the money thrown into the chest rattles.
28. It is certain that, when the money rattles in the chest, avarice and gain may be increased, but the suffrage of the Church depends on the will of God alone.

. . .

35. They preach no Christian doctrine, who teach that contrition is not necessary for those who buy souls out of purgatory or buy confessional licenses.
36. Every Christian who feels true compunction has of right plenary remission of pain and guilt, even without letters of pardon.

[1] Desiderius Erasmus, in *Praise of Folly* (London: n.d.), pp. 86–87, 157–159.

37. Every true Christian, whether living or dead, has a share in all the benefits of Christ and of the Church, given him by God, even without letters of pardon.

. . .

62. The true treasure of the Church is the Holy Gospel of the glory and grace of God.

. . .

65. Hence the treasures of the Gospel are nets, wherewith of old they fished for the men of riches.

66. The treasures of indulgences are nets, wherewith they now fish for the riches of men.

. . .

86. Again; why does not the Pope, whose riches are at this day more ample than those of the wealthiest of the wealthy, build the one Basilica of St. Peter with his own money, rather than with that of poor believers?

. . .

94. Christians should be exhorted to strive to follow Christ their head through pains, deaths, and hells.

95. And thus trust to enter heaven through many tribulations, rather than in the security of peace. [2]

1. What is Luther's greatest concern here?

2. Why might something like this lead to a break with the Church and to the Reformation?

Justification by Faith

Here, Luther recounts the crucial religious and theological turning points of his life.

> Though I lived as a monk without reproach, I felt that I was a sinner before God with an extremely disturbed conscience. I could not believe that he was placated by my satisfaction. I did not love, yes, I hated the righteous God who punishes sinners, and secretely, if not blasphemously, certainly murmuring greatly, I was angry with God, and said, "As if, indeed, it is not enough, that miserable sinners, eternally lost through original sin, are crushed by every kind of calamity by the law of the decalogue, without having God add pain to pain by the Gospel and also by the Gospel threatening us with his righteousness and wrath!" Thus I raged with a fierce and troubled conscience. Nevertheless, I beat importunately upon Paul at that place, most ardently desiring to know what St. Paul wanted.
>
> At last, by the mercy of God, meditating day and night, I gave heed to the context of the words, namely, "In it the righteousness of God is revealed, as it is written, 'He who through faith is righteous shall live.'" There I began to understand that the righteousness of God is that by which the righteous lives by a gift of God, namely by faith. And this is the meaning: the righteousness of God is revealed by the Gospel, namely, the passive righteousness with which merciful God justifies us by faith, as it

[2] H. Wace and C. Buchleim, eds., *Luther's Primary Works* (London: Hodder and Stoughton, Ltd., 1896), pp. 81–86.

is written, "He who through faith is righteous shall live." Here I felt that I was altogether born again and had entered paradise itself through open gates. There a totally other face of the entire Scripture showed itself to me. . . . [3]

1. Why is justification by faith so central to Luther's religious beliefs?

Luther's Political and Economic Views

John F. H. New interprets Luther's political and economic views, which would prove influential in the future development of Germany.

> Luther must be considered as a consummate theological politician. His ultimate concerns were inner, yet he had to take political stands to protect the Reformation he desired. Although not excusing them, political needs go far to explain his dubious moral stands on this and other issues. Above all he was fearful for the future, and his siding with the princes was a frank recognition that it was only in their support that the Reformation had any chance of success. Social revolution, chaos. Anabaptism, and even Judaism were threats to the cause that he was swift to denounce. His anti-Semitism was religiously rather than racially determined, but here, as in other matters, he failed to rid himself of the current prejudices of his place and time.
>
> Happily, the dictates of political realism coincided with the ethical consequences of his doctrines. Man was such that he needed the civil sword to contain him in order and tranquility and to bind him in a tolerable state of social cohesion. His liberty was a purely spiritual freedom from the duress of death. It was an inner grace that enabled man to fulfill the law because he had been made righteous by the free gift of God. So Luther preached absolute and unconditional obedience. He refused to condone even passive resistance to the secular arm except by princes. He did nothing to alter the habit of the authoritarian conscience. Indeed, he regarded wicked rulers as God-sent scourges. Lutheranism exchanged obedience to the Pope for abject obedience to the State.
>
> Luther's economic ethics were equally conservative, and in this shared the resentments of his petty bourgeois background. He did not visualize money as a productive thing in itself and therefore forbade all usury. This was to be more medieval than the schoolmen. Like St. Thomas, he believed that each person had his proper place in society and should keep it, and he used the word "calling" to suggest that God wants a Christian to be dedicated to his vocation.
>
> If this was old-fashioned, his appeal to German nationalism was radical and modern, foreshadowing the virulent German-consciousness of the 19th and 20th centuries. The Imperial Knights had early rallied to his standard, prepared to do battle for the emancipation of Germany from the Roman yoke. Although this was one of Luther's themes, his hopes were for peaceful reformation. But his vigorous German style and his outcries against the exploitation of Germany by foreigners were calculated to raise feelings of outraged patriotism. [4]

[3] "Preface to the Complete Edition of Luther's Latin Writings, Wittenberg, 1545," in *Luther's Works,* XXXIV, trans. L. W. Spitz, Sr. (Philadelphia: The Muhlenberg Press, 1960), pp. 337–338. Copyright © 1960 by Muhlenberg Press, reprinted by permission of Fortress Press.

[4] John F. H. New, *The Renaissance and Reformation: A Short History* (New York: John Wiley and Sons, Inc., 1969), pp. 127–128.

1. What form of political rule did Luther favor? Should he be considered a champion of the common people in politics?
2. Does this interpretation of Luther's economic views indicate that he was more open to modern capitalism and to the new economic developments of the sixteenth century?

Luther and Germany

Here, A. J. P. Taylor comments on Luther's place in the course of German history.

> No man has ever been so representative of the German spirit, and no man has had such a deep and lasting effect on German history. Germany is the Germany of Luther to this day. He was a man of great intellectual and of supreme literary ability, with a readiness to maintain his convictions to the death. But he turned with repugnance from all the values of Western civilization. He owed his breach with Catholicism to a visit to Rome, when he had seen, and rejected, the greatest glories of the Renaissance. He hated art, culture, intellect, and sought an escape into an imagined Germany of the past, romantic, irrational, non-European. In Luther was implicit the emotionalism of the Romantic movement, the German nationalist sense of being different, above all the elevation of feeling over thinking, which is characteristic of modern Germany. In Luther, German sentiment first asserted itself, and it asserted itself against reason, against civilization, against the West. In the rest of Europe religious reform implied going forward; with Luther it meant going back, repudiating everything which was carrying civilized life beyond barbarism. As once the German conquerors of Rome had prided themselves on being simpler, purer, than the heirs of Cicero and Virgil, so now Luther set himself up against Michael Angelo and Raphael. Even the technical occasion of his breach with Rome was symbolic; he objected to the sale of indulgences in order to raise money for the building of St. Peter's—if it had been for the purpose of massacring German peasants, Luther might never have become a Protestant. [5]

1. In what ways was Luther representative of the German spirit? Do you agree with this interpretation?

The Weber Thesis

Over seventy years ago, the German sociologist Max Weber argued that there was a relation between Protestantism and capitalism. This has remained a topic of debate for historians ever since. In the following selection, G. R. Elton describes Weber's argument.

> It all started with the German sociologist Max Weber's famous *The Protestant Ethic and the Spirit of Capitalism* (1904; Eng. trans. 1930). This argued that the particular state of mind which produced the "modern world" was a manifestation of the same mind as underlay the Protestant revolution. The brilliant essay introduced historians to the concept of the "calling" in Lutheran and Calvinist usage (since demonstrated to have been known to late medieval writers): the treatment of worldly avocations as God-created

[5] A. J. P. Taylor, *The Course of German History* (London: Hamish Hamilton Ltd., 1945; New York: Coward, McCann & Geoghegan, Inc., 1946), pp. 18–19.

and fulfillable in a spirit of worship. This concept, it was alleged, enabled the Protestant to see in his ordinary daily work an activity pleasing to God and therefore to be pursued as actively and profitably as possible. On the other hand, medieval and Roman Catholic Christianity were held to have condemned the world, with consequent hostility to economic activity and especially to that essential capitalist ingredient, the taking of interest on money lent. Protestantism—or rather, more particularly Calvinism and the later free sects such as the Quakers and Methodists—were therefore asserted to have been the necessary precondition of the growth of modern industrial capitalism; the ethos of Protestantism promoted—nor could anything else have promoted—the spirit of the entrepreneur; and for that reason capitalism is found flourishing in reformed countries, while the Reformation is found spreading among the commercial and industrial middle classes.[6]

1. How does the concept of the "calling" connect Protestantism and capitalism?
2. How would you go about attacking this argument?

SPECULATIONS

1. Suppose you were the pope in 1515 but had the hindsight of a historian living in the 1980s. What might you have done to prevent the Reformation? Do you think your efforts would have had a good chance of succeeding?
2. How important was Martin Luther to the Reformation? Do you think the Reformation would have occurred without him?
3. Which do you think was more compatible with the Renaissance and the secular developments of the early sixteenth century, Catholicism or Protestantism? Explain.

TRANSITIONS

In "Overseas Expansion and a New Politics 1415-1560," the growth of political authority around the "new monarchies" of Western Europe, the economic advances between the last quarter of the fifteenth century and the middle of the sixteenth century, and the process of European expansion were examined.

In "Reformations in Religion 1500-1570," the shattering of religious unity in Europe during the first half of the sixteenth century is analyzed. The fundamental religious issue of the Reformation was how could sinful humans gain salvation. Increasingly, the Catholic Church answered this question by emphasizing the role of the Church. Reformers reversed this trend by emphasizing the inward and personal approach. But spiritual conflict quickly evolved into fanatical attacks on all sides; moderation and tolerance failed almost everywhere.

In "A Century of War and Revolt 1560-1660," the international and domestic upheaval, inflamed by religious tensions, will be examined.

---

[6]G. R. Elton, *Reformation Europe, 1517-1519* (New York: Harper & Row, 1963), pp. 312-313. Copyright © Harper & Row, 1963.

SECTION SUMMARY
TRANSITION, RENAISSANCE, AND REFORMATION
1300–1559
CHAPTERS 11–14

CHRONOLOGICAL DIAGRAM

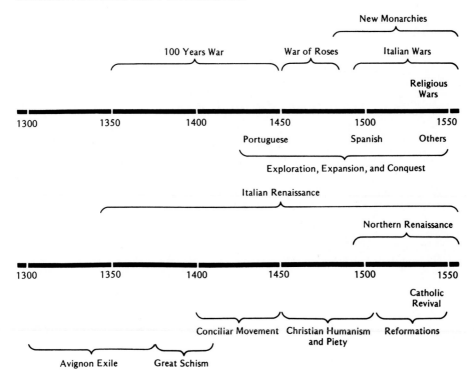

MAP EXERCISE

1. Indicate the following:
    a. The areas controlled by the various "new monarchies," and the approximate date of the establishment of the "new monarchies."
    b. The areas ruled by Charles V ca. 1550.
    c. Religious divisions ca. 1550.

BOX CHARTS

Reproduce the Box Charts in a larger format in your notebook or on separate sheets of paper.

Chart 1

	England 1300 → 1559	France 1300 → 1559	Spain 1300 → 1559	Italy 1300 → 1559	Holy Roman Empire 1300 → 1559
Cultural Values and Productions					
Religious System and Characteristics					
Social System and Characteristics					
Economic System and Characteristics					
Political Institutions and Developments					

Chart 2

Europe

	1300	1350	1400	1450	1500	1559
Political Leaders						
Explorers and Conquerors						
Religious Leaders						
Humanists						
Philosophers						
Writers						
Painters						
	1300	1350	1400	1450	1500	1559

FIFTEEN
A CENTURY OF
WAR AND REVOLT
1560–1660

MAIN THEMES

1. A series of costly, devastating wars raged in Europe in the period between 1560 and 1660.
2. While religious motives inflamed the violence, political and other motives came increasingly into play.
3. The Peace of Westphalia signified major international changes and a new period of relative control.
4. Throughout Europe tensions created great internal unrest, often breaking out in revolt and civil war.
5. By the mid-seventeenth century most countries had gained a new constitutional stability.

OUTLINE AND SUMMARY

I. *Warfare.*

The period between 1560 and 1660 was marked by almost constant violence.

A. *The Military Revolution.*

During the sixteenth century important changes in military equipment, organization, and tactics took place. Gunpowder came into general use. Sieges became more complicated and costly. The infantry, organized in huge squares, gained dominance over the cavalry. Standing armies grew in numbers and cost. Between the 1590s and 1630s Maurice of Nassau and Gustavus Adolphus developed new tactics emphasizing mobility, the salvo, and the use of light cannon to counter the dominance of the Spanish infantry. Increasingly large permanent professional armies caused a rapid growth of supporting administrative personnel, an increase in taxation, and a new opportunity for social mobility in the officer corps. A strategy of devastation came to characterize warfare in this age.

B. *The Wars of Religion.*

Religion was the most emotional issue underlying the wars that took place between the 1560s and 1640s.

1. *Spain's Catholic Crusade:* Philip II of Spain (1556–1598) ignited the conflicts. He succeeded against the Muslim fleet at Lepanto in 1571 but failed against Protestantism in France, the Low Countries, and England. His most stunning defeat was the loss of his Armada to the tactically superior British and bad weather.

2. *The Dutch Revolt:* Philip's religious intolerance helped provoke a reaction and then revolt in the Netherlands in the 1560s and 1570s. Despite ruthless suppression of this revolt by the Spanish governor (the duke of Alva), the Dutch, led by William of Orange, successfully resisted. After decades of fighting, the independence of the United Provinces was finally recognized in 1648.

3. *Civil War in France:* After the death of Henry II in 1559, France became divided into two warring parties: the Catholics, led by the Guise family, and the Calvinists (Huguenots), led by the Bourbon family. Catherine de Médicis, the real power behind the weak sons of Henry II, was unable to control the nobles led by these two families. The rise to power and conversion to Catholicism of the Bourbon Henry IV, the assassination of the duke of Guise, the weakening of the Catholics' main ally (Spain), and a weariness of war led to the defeat of the Catholic League. In 1598 the fighting ended and Henry granted toleration to the Huguenots. These decades of strife influenced political thought. Both Huguenots and Catholics developed contractual theories of government to justify revolt against the king. Nevertheless, more moderate political theorists (the politiques), notably Jean Bodin (*The Six Books of the Republic*), gained dominance by emphasizing peace, unity, and national security through an equilibrium between control and freedom.

C. The Thirty Years' War.

Between 1618 and 1648 the Holy Roman Empire suffered through a series of encounters known as the Thirty Years' War. Initially religion was the chief issue, but politics and international affairs became entwined with and sometimes prevailed over religious issues. Between 1618 and 1630 the Catholic Hapsburgs, led by Emperor Ferdinand, Maximilian of Bavaria, and Albrecht von Wallenstein, prevailed. Intervention by Protestant Sweden, led by Gustavus Adolphus, and by France in the 1630s and 1640s turned the tide. In 1648 peace was achieved, but only after great loss of life (more than a third of Germany's population) and economic dislocation. Wars in the Spanish Netherlands and around the Baltic did not end until 1661.

D. The Peace of Westphalia.

The Peace of Westphalia in 1648 was a landmark. For the first time, all participants came together at a peace conference and decided all outstanding issues. France, Sweden, the United Provinces, the Swiss Confederation, and German princes gained at the cost of the House of Hapsburg. France replaced Spain as the dominant Continental power. Economic leadership shifted northward, from the Mediterranean to England and the Netherlands. The settlement at Westphalia was regarded as the basis for all international negotiations for more than a century. After Westphalia, wars would continue—but for nonreligious purposes, at lesser human cost, and with more sense of control.

II. Revolts.

Warfare seriously affected domestic affairs in Europe during this period.

A. England.

Despite relative calm, tensions in England ultimately led to revolution.

1. *Elizabeth I:* Little affected by war, unified by a national reformation and Parliament, and led by an extraordinarily clever monarch, England was relatively calm between the 1560s and the 1630s. Elizabeth I (1558–1603) was strong, popular, and usually well advised. Yet the growth of a court patronage system became a cause for discontent after her death.

2. *Economic and Social Change:* During the sixteenth century the power and wealth of the great nobles (some sixty in number) was declining relative to the rise of the gentry (some 20,000), landowners who were benefiting from governmental service, agricultural wealth, increasing prices, and commercial investment. At the same time merchants led in England's commercial and industrial expansion. Trade increased, companies were formed that founded colonies in India and America, and manufacturing grew. Merchants and gentry gained cohesion and a sense of leadership; they resented interference by Elizabeth's successors. Puritans also became disgruntled with the monarchy.

3. *Parliament and the Law:* The gentry increased their influence and power through the House of Commons, which they controlled. They used their revenue powers and the common-law tradition to counter the policies of the financially pressed James I.

4. *Rising Antagonisms:* Under Charles I (1625–1649) conflict between Parliament, Puritans, common lawyers, and disenchanted country gentry on the one hand and the crown on the other intensified, leading Charles to rule without Parliament for eleven years. A religion-sparked invasion by the Scots required Charles to call on Parliament for help.

5. *The English Civil War:* From 1640 to 1642, under the leadership of John Pym and Oliver Cromwell, Parliament asserted itself against the king and the Anglican Church. A royalist party formed and by 1642 civil war was under way. Historians have difficulty interpreting the causes for this, because Parliament, the Puritans, and the gentry were split. While a small group of radical Puritans kept up the momentum, the influence of local circumstances (regional factors and allegiance to influential men) was probably most important.

6. *The Course of Conflict:* The antiroyalists, supported by the Scots, were at first successful. Antiroyalist forces then split; the Independents (more radical and favoring the congregational system), under the leadership of Oliver Cromwell and his New Model Army, succeeded over the allied royalists, Scots and Presbyterians in 1647. The remaining members of Parliament (the Rump Parliament) tried Charles, who continued to plot against them, and had him executed (1649).

7. *England Under Cromwell: The Interregnum:* Cromwell faced factions on all sides, including such groups as the egalitarian Levellers and Diggers. Unable to secure a new constitutional structure for government, he reluctantly took personal command as Lord Protector in 1653. After his death in 1658 his son Richard took over but was not strong enough to prevail against General George Monck. Monck brought Charles II to power in 1660.

8. *The Results of the Revolution:* Other than establishing the political power of the gentry, only relatively minor changes resulted from the revolution. The increased power of the gentry would be illustrated by the bloodless coup against the king in the 1680s.

B. France.

Resistance to the growing power of the monarchy continued in the 1600s until a final confrontation at mid-century ended in victory for the crown.

1. *Henry IV:* By his death in 1610 Henry had succeeded in reestablishing royal authority by manipulating the aristocracy and increasing his revenues through new sales of offices and an officeholder's fee (the *paulette*).

2. *Economic Affairs:* Merchants and peasants suffered from the religious wars; French trade did not completely recover for a century. The crown, adopting a set of attitudes called mercantilism, took increased responsibility for commerce, industry, and the promotion of prosperity.

3. *The Regency and Richelieu:* Between 1610 and 1624 Marie de Médicis and later the young Louis XIII managed to hold the weak monarchy together in the face of unrest of nobles and Calvinists. After 1624 the talented minister Cardinal Richelieu reasserted royal power. He utilized the powerful bureaucracy, undermined the nobility, increased the power of the *intendants,* and crushed the Huguenots at La Rochelle. Yet because of increasing taxes and resentful local nobles, France experienced almost continual peasant uprisings between the 1620s and 1670s.

4. *The Fronde:* Between 1648 and 1652 the upper levels of French society—the nobles, townsmen, and members of Parliaments—struggled to wrest power from the monarchy. Despite temporary losses (especially in Bordeaux), the monarchy, led by Cardinal Mazarin, was victorious. When Louis XIV took personal control in 1661, the monarchy was strong and stable.

C. Spain.

After the upheavals of the mid-seventeenth century Spain was no longer the most powerful state in Europe.

1. *Stresses in the Reign of Philip II:* Disunity among Spain's vast domains, from the Low Countries to the New World, was Philip's chief problem. Decisions came slowly, and the standing army proved costly and often unpopular. Philip's emphasis on the Catholic faith stimulated cohesion within the Iberian peninsula.

2. *Economic Problems:* Spain's American treasure and lucrative domestic wool industry benefited only small groups, mostly foreigners. Overspending brought the crown to bankruptcy. Moreover Spain suffered a serious decline of population during the seventeenth century. These problems made Spain unable to support her renewed involvement in the Thirty Years' War.

3. *Revolt and Secession:* Reacting against Olivares' program (the Union of Arms) to unify or "Castilianize" Spain, Catalonia, Portugal, Naples, and Sicily revolted in the 1640s. The great period of Spain's cultural brilliance and international domination was over by mid-century.

D. The United Provinces.

After a period of war and domestic tensions, the United Provinces became a unique state.

1. *The Structure of the United Provinces:* The United Provinces was more socially homogeneous and politically democratic than any other republic. The Dutch quickly gained economic mastery over European finance and trade (especially in Amsterdam). The wealth, openness, and religious tolerance of the Dutch supported an explosion of cultural creativity.

2. *Domestic Tensions:* Through most of the seventeenth century there was tension between the mercantile party, which dominated the Estates General, and the House of Orange. In times of peace, particularly under the leadership of Jan De Witt between 1653 and 1672, the more pacific and economically oriented mercantile party prevailed. In times of war, authority shifted to the centralizing House of Orange under such leaders as Maurice of Nassau, William II, and William III.

E. Sweden.

The Swedes made basic political and administrative decisions in the mid-seventeenth century.

1. *The Achievement of Gustavus Adolphus:* Gustavus Adolphus (1611–1632) led Sweden from a second-rate position to dominance in northern Europe. He unified the nobles, organized an efficient bureaucracy, and supported economic development (copper mining, iron mining and smelting, trade, and finance).

2. *The Role of the Nobles:* Under Queen Christina the nobility threatened to gain control in Sweden. In 1650, with the help of townsmen and peasants in the Riksdag, she restrained the nobles, and her successor Charles X Gustavus consolidated Gustavus Adolphus' gains.

F. Eastern Europe.

1. *The Ottoman Empire:* Supported by military might, Turkish rulers controlled a powerful though declining empire during the late sixteenth and seventeenth centuries.

2. *Poland:* This large kingdom was internally weak, thanks to religious differences and dominance of the Diet by the aristocracy. A mid-century revolt caused the loss of the Ukraine.

3. *Russia:* Reacting to the ruthless assertion of autocratic control by Ivan IV (1547–1584), the boyars revolted against his successors (Time of Troubles). Finally Mikhail Feodorovich (1613–1645) founded the Romanov dynasty, reorganized Russia administratively and legally, and extended central control. The boyars, however, imposed serfdom on the peasants, initiating a half-century of regional unrest and revolt (Stenka Razin). A schism between the Old Believers and the established church ultimately resulted in even greater control by the state over the church.

Experiences of Daily Life: The Soldier.

The reality of life for most soldiers during the 1600s had little to do with adventure, courage, or easy living.

SIGNIFICANT INDIVIDUALS

Political and Military Leaders

Elizabeth I (1558–1603), queen of England.

James I (1603–1625), king of England.

Charles I (1625–1649), king of England.

John Pym (1584–1643), English parliamentary leader.

Oliver Cromwell (1599–1658), English revolutionary, lord protector.

Catherine de Médicis (1519–1589), regent and power in France.

Duke of Guise (1550–1588), powerful French Catholic noble.

Henry IV (1589–1610), king of France.

Louis XIII (1610–1643), king of France.

Gustavus Adolphus (1611–1632), king of Sweden.

Ferdinand II (1619–1637), Holy Roman Emperor.

Cardinal Richelieu (1624–1642), chief minister in France.

Cardinal Mazarin (1642–1661), chief minister in France.

Philip II (1556–1598), king of Spain.

Duke of Alva (1508–1583), Spanish general.

Philip III (1598–1621), king of Spain.

Philip IV (1621–1665), king of Spain.

Count of Olivares (1621–1643), chief minister in Spain.

William of Orange (1533–1584), Dutch leader.

Maurice of Nassau (1587–1625), Dutch leader.

Jan De Witt (1625–1672), Dutch statesman.

Albrecht von Wallenstein (1583–1634), imperial general.

Ivan IV (1547–1584), Russian tsar.

Mikhail Feodorovich (1613–1645), Russian tsar.

Political Theorists

Jean Bodin (1530–1596), French politique.

CHRONOLOGICAL DIAGRAM

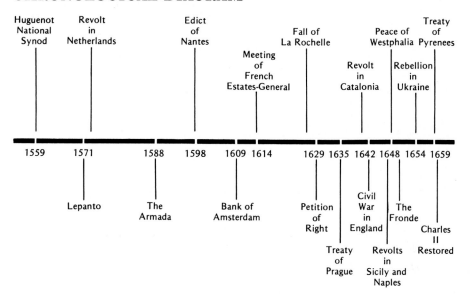

IDENTIFICATION

the salvo

the Armada

the Catholic League

Edict of Nantes

Huguenots

politiques

Edict of Restitution

the gentry

Grand Remonstrance

New Model Army

Rump Parliament

Levellers

mercantilism

the Fronde

Union of Arms

Time of Troubles

MAP EXERCISE

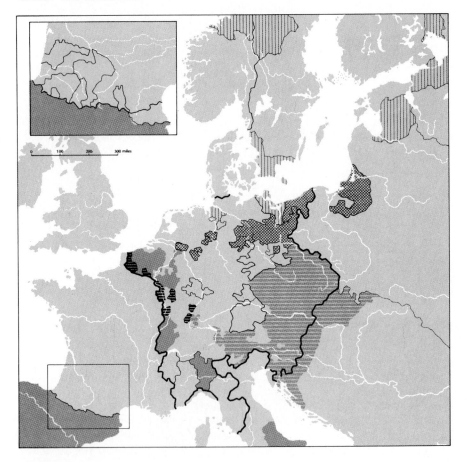

1. Indicate the lands controlled by the Austrian Hapsburgs, the Spanish Hapsburgs, France, Brandenburg-Prussia, and Sweden in 1660.

PROBLEMS FOR ANALYSIS

I. Warfare.

1. What changes in military equipment, organization, and tactics took place during the sixteenth and seventeenth centuries? What were some of the social and economic consequences of these changes?
2. Evaluate the relative weight of religious and political factors underlying the wars between the 1560s and 1640s. What kinds of actions evidence political rather than religious concerns?
3. What was the significance of the Peace of Westphalia? Did it result in peace for decades to come? What political changes resulted? Can it be considered a diplomatic triumph?

II. Revolts.

1. How do you explain the civil war and revolution in England? Were opponents clearly split along religious or social lines? What role did Cromwell play?
2. Compare the issues that caused discord in France and England. Is it fair to consider the Fronde similar to the English revolution? Why?
3. How do you explain Spain's decline in the seventeenth century? Evaluate the role economic factors played in this decline.
4. What was so unusual about the United Provinces? How was this small area able to defend itself against Spain? How would you explain its rapid economic and cultural success?
5. How was Sweden able to rise from a second-rate power to a position of dominance in the Baltic during the seventeenth century? What policies did Gustavus Adolphus follow to this end?
6. Compare the general nature of constitutional settlements reached throughout Europe at mid-century. In what areas did monarchical power prevail? In what areas was monarchical power weakened?

DOCUMENTS

Monarchical Authority

King James I (1603–1625) argued strongly for monarchical authority, as is illustrated in the following selection.

> The state of monarchy is the supremest thing upon earth; for kings are not only God's lieutenants upon earth, and sit upon God's throne, but even by God himself are called gods. There be three principal similitudes that illustrate the state of monarchy: one taken out of the word of God; and the two other out of the grounds of policy and philosophy. In the Scriptures kings are called gods, and so their power after a certain relation compared to the divine power. Kings are also compared to fathers of families: for a king is truly *Parens patriae,* the politique father of his people. And lastly, kings are compared to the head of this microcosm of the body of the man.
>
> Kings are justly called gods, for that they exercise a manner or resemblance of divine power upon earth: for if you will consider the attributes to God, you shall see how they agree in the person of a king. God hath power to create or destroy, make or unmake at his pleasure, to give life or send death, to judge all and to be judged nor accountable to none; to raise low things and to make high things low at his pleasure, and to God are both souls and body due. And the like power have kings: they make and unmake their subjects, they have power of raising and casting down, of life and of death, judges over all their subjects and in all causes and yet accountable to none but God only. . . .
>
> I conclude then this point touching the power of kings with this axiom of divinity, That as to dispute what God may do is blasphemy. . . . so is it sedition in subjects to dispute what a king may do in the height of his power. But just kings will ever be willing to declare what they will do, if they will not incur the curse of God. I will not be content that my power be disputed upon; but I shall ever be willing to make the reason appear of all my doings, and rule my actions according to my laws. . . . I would wish you to be careful to avoid three things in the matter of grievances:

First, that you do not meddle with the main points of government; that is my craft . . . to meddle with that were to lessen me. . . . I must not be taught my office.

Secondly, I would not have you meddle with such ancient rights of mine as I have received from my predecessors. . . . All novelties are dangerous as well in a politic as in a natural body, and therefore I would be loath to be quarreled in my ancient rights and possessions; for that were to judge me unworthy of that which my predecessors had and left me.

And lastly, I pray you beware to exhibit for grievance anything that is established by a settled law, and whereunto . . . you know I will never give a plausible answer; for it is an undutiful part in subjects to press their king, wherein they know beforehand he will refuse them. [1]

1. What is the basis of James' argument for enhanced monarchical authority?
2. According to James, what would be the proper role of Parliament?

Daily Life

Paul Zumthor presents a picture of daily life in Holland during the seventeenth century.

The businessman's office was usually situated in the basement of his house, or occasionally in the loft next to his warehouse, where it would not disturb domestic harmony. He called it his *Kantoor* (a corruption of the French *comptoir*), and the choice of site was dictated less by considerations of comfort than by the wife's refusal to allow the living-rooms to be used for business purposes. So that although a Dutch businessman had his living quarters and his offices under the same roof they were kept rigorously separate, and when the volume of business demanded expanded accommodation, interior walls were put up forming corridors that gave access to the premises, and a special entrance door was let into one of the outside walls—all this to avoid creating any disturbance in the living rooms!

The merchant's working day started at about ten in the morning. Actual trading activities were only conducted during four hours of a single day. From ten until midday the merchant presided over his office and the apprentices and clerks who had arisen earlier from the attics where they slept and were waiting to start work. Offices were furnished with utmost simplicity: a few sturdy desks, with lead inkwells nailed to them, chairs with leather seats, bookshelves laden with registers, a sand-glass. The boss sat at a raised desk, wearing a night-cap; the clerks sat two by two beneath him, wearing protective oversleeves.

At midday the Stock Exchange opened and was soon crowded with the town's merchants, plus a good number of onlookers and idlers. All important business was conducted here. Brokers hurried to and fro inside the building, carrying a portable writing-desk, and prepared contracts; when two merchants had struck a bargain— perhaps one of them had assigned a cargo of copper still in transit on the high seas at the time, in exchange for a cargo of precious wood plus a cash sum—they signed a contract, went straight off to the bank where their funds were deposited and arranged the transfer of this sum from one account to the other. They had perhaps completed a deal involving thousands of florins, without having had to handle a single coin. All

[1] King James I, *Works* (1609).

business had to be completed by two o'clock when the Stock Exchange closed. If urgent business demanded a return to the building a little after that time, a fine was levied. This arrangement permitted an advantageous centralisation of major commerce, helped speed up its operations and consequently facilitated credit.

A certain proportion of the population was threatened with penury at frequent intervals, as we have already seen. But more unfortunate even than these casual workers were those existing on the fringes of society in a state of permanent economic hardship. The frequency of unemployment and the nomadic tendencies of some work-men made it impossible to distinguish clearly between underprivileged workers and true vagabonds, but together they constituted a collection of humanity sprinkled with antisocial elements whose common denominator was the supreme, ever-present men-ace of hunger.

This segment of the nation, rejected by the very society whose economic shortcom-ings had provoked its existence, made its existence known through begging, a curse which afflicted town and country equally and grew worse as the century progressed. The provincial States proscribed mendicancy at regular intervals, but it was a scourge that no edicts could halt. Amsterdam swarmed with beggars and with a horde of imaginary cripples, and after the truce and the disbanding of the mercenaries the evil increased. Bands of dubious characters, leading a wandering existence or living here and there in improvised slums, exercised a variety of minor illegal trades, stole and even killed if necessary, were hunted from one province to another as a result of the banishment pronounced on them at regular intervals, and spoke an incomprehensible thieves' cant that impressed someone sufficiently for him to publish a vocabulary in 1613. It was impossible to distinguish brigands from honest wretches, and the scene was further confused by the presence of gipsies practising palmistry, drawing horo-scopes and — reputedly — stealing children. However often the gipsies were imprisoned or expelled they always came back. The forces of law and order were powerless to deal with this situation.

The municipalities were more or less aware of the economic origins of this disorder-liness and made a practice throughout the century of distributing free rations in years when famine struck or the cost of living suddenly increased. In such cases a shipload of wheat or rye was ordered and a rough bread baked and given away to needy people. In Leyden, in 1634, twenty thousand people received free bread. In Amsterdam, an official allocation of alms to the poor took place once a week. The Reformed Church also dispensed charity at a local level, but only to the needy who had at least a pro-visional domicile; an official appointed by the deacon or the town provided these deserving poor in winter with a little butter, cheese, bread and peat. But during the summer months these supplies were discontinued and they were left to fend for themselves.

The municipalities and the Church organised regular collections for aid to the poor. Bourgeois citizens were often generous contributors, and a properly launched collec-tion in a large town could well bring in fifteen or even twenty-five thousand florins. Tradition demanded the giving of alms on special occasions such as marriages in wealthy families. In several towns the poor were presented with the pall from the catafalque after a funeral ceremony, and it was rare for a prosperous citizen to die without bequeathing a sum of money for works of charity. The reputation of the Dutch for charity was acknowledged throughout Europe, and Louis XIV himself, on the eve of his invasion of the Netherlands, reassured Charles II in these terms: "Have no fear for the fate of Amsterdam. I live in the certain hope that Providence will save that city, if only in consideration of her charity."

To deal with its large industrial proletariat, Leyden had instituted a body of inspectors of paupers with large assistance funds at its disposal. During the second half of the century cottages were built in several towns with private funds and rented to poor people at very low rates. Poor-houses existed everywhere, some of them taken over from the previous religious orders and now administered by the State, and the largest towns boasted several institutions serving different categories of the needy: Leyden, for example, had an almshouse for homeless paupers, another for old folk, and an orphanage as well. But the main function of these poor-houses since the beginning of the seventeenth century was the rehabilitation of vagabonds. In most districts of any importance tramps could find a reception centre, sometimes attached to the local hospital, where they received free board and lodging for three days; on the morning of the fourth day they were sent on their way again. But in some towns the influx of vagabonds was so great that the poor-houses were closed from June to October. Amenities were rudimentary in these establishments: a large communal hall, heated and provided with benches, and two dormitories, one for men, the other for women. At the end of each meal the knives were counted and locked away for safety, and at night the dormitory doors were bolted securely.

Besides a large hospital, Amsterdam possessed several orphanages, and an almshouse providing lodging for as many as four hundred aged female paupers. In 1613 a "House of Charity" was founded to provide shelter for paupers who lived by begging, though to be eligible for admission they had to prove several years' domicile in the town. But this poor-house did provide needy travellers with a cash subsidy. A provost accompanied by officials attached to the institution scoured the town every day, rounding up beggars. At a later date the institution also housed children that the orphanage could not accommodate, and became responsible for carrying out free burials.

The administration of these various houses of refuge was vested by the town in committees of distinguished citizens, both men and women, who considered the appointment an honour. Although the day-to-day running of these charitable institutions by the junior personnel often left much to be desired, the administration at top level was usually remarkably efficient. They were often financed out of the revenues from former ecclesiastical properties, and especially in the second half of the century, benefited from foundations and legacies. Door-to-door collections were taken once a month, and the churches held a collection every Sunday. In addition, alms-boxes were to be found at various sites in the town. The municipality put aside the income it derived from its taxes on imported cereals, auction sales, banquets and deluxe funerals for the benefit of the various institutions. And finally, charity lotteries were organised periodically and were extremely popular with the public; on one occasion, a ticket costing two stuivers won first prize of a thousand florins.

Towards the end of the century the charitable institutions became too small and their revenue insufficient. Various remedies had to be devised, including the creation of special taxes, an increase in the number of lotteries, and sending paupers back to their place of birth. [2]

1. Describe the daily life of a Dutch businessperson.
2. How did the authorities deal with the poor?

[2] Paul Zumthor, *Daily Life in Rembrandt's Holland,* trans. Simon Watson Taylor (New York: Macmillan, 1962), pp. 141–148, 248–256. Reprinted with permission of Georges Borchardt, Inc.

SPECULATIONS

1. How might Charles I have prevented the English civil war and revolution?
2. As a political leader in the early seventeenth century, would you use religion for your own ends? What are the dangers in doing or not doing this?
3. As advisor to Philip II of Spain, what policies would you recommend to prevent the eventual decline of Spanish power? Why?

TRANSITIONS

In "Reformations in Religion 1500–1570," the religious revolutions that tore Europe apart during the sixteenth century were examined.

In "A Century of War and Revolt 1560–1660," we see this period dominated by war and internal revolt. At the base of these wars and revolts were the reactions to the upsetting changes occurring the previous period: the Reformation, the centralized "new monarchies," the rise in prices, and the social changes. More immediate circumstances leading to many of the wars were the dynastic commitments and ambitions of the Hapsburgs. Intensifying the level of violence was the emotional impact of religious differences. The period ends with a relative sense of constitutional and military stability almost everywhere, which was to last for a century.

In "Culture and Society in the Age of the Scientific Revolution 1540–1660," the social, cultural, and intellectual patterns paralleling these political and international trends during the sixteenth and seventeenth centuries will be explored.

SIXTEEN
CULTURE AND SOCIETY
IN THE AGE OF THE
SCIENTIFIC REVOLUTION
1540–1660

MAIN THEMES

1. A small number of thinkers overturned accepted ideas about nature and laid the foundations for modern science in the period from the mid-sixteenth to the mid-seventeenth century.
2. Major breakthroughs in physics, astronomy, mathematics, and anatomy rested on the new scientific principles of reason, doubt, observation, generalization, and testing by experiment.
3. Cultural styles evolved, from the distortion of mannerism to the drama of the Baroque and the discipline of Classicism.
4. Seventeenth-century society was hierarchical, with mobility a rarity for the lower orders.
5. Although peasants retained old, fatalistic attitudes, the traditional village was changing and being pulled into the activities of the territorial state.

OUTLINE AND SUMMARY

I. The Scientific Revolution.

In the sixteenth and seventeenth centuries a handful of scholars and experimenters created a revolution in ideas about nature.

A. Origins of the Scientific Revolution.

A number of factors supported the scientific revolution. Accepted theories of ancient Greek scholars, such as Aristotle in physics, Ptolemy in astronomy, and Galen in medicine, did not cover all the facts. Other Greek writings were discovered that indicated disagreement. Various magical beliefs, such as alchemy, reflected a growing view that there were simple, comprehensive keys to nature. A belief in the importance of careful measurement and observation had been growing, as illustrated by the invention of such instruments as the telescope, thermometer, barometer, and microscope. These combined to support the intellectual breakthroughs of the scientific revolution.

B. The Breakthroughs.

In 1543 Vesalius (*The Structure of the Human Body*) published important advances in anatomy. In the same year Copernicus (*On the Revolutions of the Heavenly Bodies*) published a mathematically sophisticated theory of planetary movement, placing the sun rather than the earth at the center of the universe.

1. *Kepler:* Relying on mathematics, Kepler discovered three laws of planetary motion (1609–1619) that were of theoretical importance for astronomers and of practical benefit to navigators. These discoveries further undermined Ptolemaic cosmology.

2. *Galileo:* Galileo combined mathematics, technical observation, and logic to reveal major new discoveries. He confirmed the earth as simply another revolving body, subject to the same laws of motion as the rest of the universe. He proposed the principle of inertia to explain all motion. He argued that every physical law is equally applicable throughout the universe. His rejection of authority and the argument that the earth moved (*Dialogue on the Two Great World Systems,* 1632) caused the famous condemnation by the Inquisition in 1633. By mid-century the new findings in physics, astronomy, and anatomy (enlarged by Harvey's discovery that the blood circulates) created a new, influential kind of certainty.

3. *Isaac Newton:* Newton became the great idol and genius of the scientific revolution. He united physics and astronomy in a single system to explain motion throughout the universe; he helped transform mathematics by the development of calculus; and he established some of the basic laws of modern physics. He represented the power of mathematics and experimentation against the methods of Descartes. His masterpiece was the *Principia* (1687); his most dramatic findings, the three laws of motion. He saw the universe as a system of impersonal, uniform forces—a vast, stable machine. Newton dominated physics and astronomy for more than a century.

C. Scientific Method: A New Epistemology.

Scientists moved toward a new theory of how to obtain and verify knowledge—a theory that was based on experience, reason, and doubt, rather than on authority. After formulation of a hypothesis, the process had three parts: observation, generalization, and testing. The language of science was mathematics.

D. The Wilder Influence of Scientific Thought.

Propagandizers helped spread acceptance of scientific methods.

1. *Francis Bacon:* Bacon was the greatest of these propagandizers, picturing scientific research as a collective enterprise gathering information that would lead to practical universal laws (*New Atlantis,* 1627).

2. *René Descartes:* The French philosopher Descartes applied the scientific method of doubt to all knowledge, relying on logical thought rather than on authority or the senses (*Discourse on Method,* 1637). He made an influential distinction between spirit and matter and founded analytical geometry.

3. *Thomas Hobbes:* Imitating scientific methods, Hobbes constructed an original political theory from a few limited premises about human nature (*Leviathan,* 1651). Applying a mechanistic view, he argued that people, by a social contract, remove themselves from a warlike state of nature to a peaceful society dominated by a sovereign power.

4. *Blaise Pascal:* A brilliant mathematician and experimenter, Pascal became influenced by Jansenism, a pious form of Catholicism that emphasized human weakness. He argued (*Pensées*) that scientific truths were less important than religious truths, a unique protest.

E. Science Institutionalized.

A number of scientific societies, such as the Lincean Academy (Rome, 1603), the Royal Society (London, 1660), and the Royal Academy of Sciences (France, 1666), were established as headquarters and clearing centers for research. Supported by royal patronage, these societies published scientific journals (*Philosophical Transactions,* 1665) and helped elevate their members in prestige and influence. The understanding and the sense of order, harmony, and reason that science was creating were influencing the leaders of society.

II. Literature and the Arts.

Changes in culture paralleled the evolution from disorder to order in other areas.

A. The Culture of the Late Sixteenth Century.

Artists reacted to the upheavals of the sixteenth century by attempting to escape reality through distortion.

1. *The Mannerists:* From about 1520 to 1610 the Mannerists, such as Parmigianino and El Greco, emphasized theatrical and disturbing qualities in their painting.

2. *Michel de Montaigne:* Montaigne, the greatest humanist and philosopher of the late sixteenth century, created the essay form ("An Apology for Raymond Sebond"). He emphasized Skepticism and the search for self-knowledge. This was a radical, totally secular individualism.

3. *Cervantes and Shakespeare:* Cervantes (1547–1616) captured the disillusionment accompanying Spain's decline in his novel *Don Quixote.* He satirized the chivalry of the nobles while portraying the often hypocritical lives of ordinary people. His contemporary William Shakespeare was the greatest creative artist of the English-speaking world. In such plays as *Richard II, Julius Caesar, Hamlet,* and *The Tempest,* Shakespeare reflects not only the tensions of his own times but timeless human problems of love, hatred, violence, and morality.

B. The Baroque and Classicism.

After 1600 the Baroque and then Classicism gained prominence in the arts and literature.

1. *The Baroque: Grandeur and Excitement:* The qualities of the Baroque — passion, drama, mystery, and awe — are primarily but not exclusively visual. Flourishing most in Rome and at the leading Catholic courts in Munich, Prague, Madrid, and Brussels, the Baroque is best exemplified by the grandiose paintings of Rubens, the court paintings of Velázquez, and the elaborate sculpture and architecture of Bernini. In music, new instruments (keyboard and string families) and forms (opera) were developed. Monteverdi made great innovations in the operatic form (*Orfeo,* 1607) and in the orchestra.

2. *Classicism: Grandeur and Restraint:* The Classical style of the seventeenth century aimed at grandiose effects—but through restraint and discipline, and within the bounds of a formal structure. This style, as exemplified by subdued scenes of Poussin and the dignified portraits of the Dutch painters, was an attempt to recapture the aesthetic values of ancient Greece and Rome. By the middle of the seventeenth century the Classical style spread to literature; examples are the dramas of Corneille (*Le Cid,* 1636), Racine, and Molière. Their dramas conformed to the ancient unities of place, time, and action, reflecting the new sense of calm during this period.

III. Social Patterns and Popular Culture.

While there were connections with intellectual trends, popular culture had roots of its own.

A. Hierarchy and Rank in the Social Order.

Seventeenth-century society was composed of relatively fixed ranks and orders of men, in clear hierarchies. The four main hierarchies were organized around occupations on the land, in the clergy, in commerce, and in the professions, with those connected to the land most important.

1. *Mobility and Privilege:* Wealth and education were gaining in social importance, indicating that mobility to desirable positions of prestige and privilege was possible. In the colonies, often surrounded by natives and supported by slavery, societies were more rigid; dominant groups reflected the situation and concerns of the mother country. In most areas mobility was a rarity for the lower levels of society. Some peasants were able to avoid the increased taxes, rising rents, and additional demands of the late sixteenth and seventeenth centuries by escaping to the cities or into the army, but poor wages, crime, and an early death were commonly their fate.

B. Demographic Patterns.

Population remained relatively stable in the seventeenth century. People usually married late, died young, and could expect only one out of two children to reach adulthood. Thus the extended family was uncommon. Famine, poor nutrition, disease, and war directly affected these patterns, especially among the lower classes and in areas racked by war.

C. Popular Culture.

Peasants, reflecting their dependence on unpredictable nature, assumed that outside forces controlled their destinies. The world was occupied by powerful spirits, both good and evil. These assumptions found expression in special processions, holidays, violent demonstrations (often led by women), and peasant uprisings (yearly in France until 1675). The great witch craze of the sixteenth and seventeenth centuries, which epitomizes the worst of this fear-ridden era, resulted in thousands of deaths until it faded away toward the end of the century. Urbanization contributed to a general drift away from magical beliefs in the middle and upper levels of society.

D. Change in the Traditional Village.

The traditional village in the West was changing from a closed, self-sufficient, and cohesive unit. Agricultural changes increased differences in the wealth of the villagers. Village councils started to disappear. Merchants organized the cottage industry system, thereby redirecting patterns of life. Cities grew, linking villages to the national market. Nobles stayed away, attracted to central courts and capital cities. Priests and ministers represented outside interests and learning. Governmental representatives (tax collectors, recruiting officers, army suppliers) appeared with increasing frequency. Slowly villages were becoming part of the territorial state.

Experiences of Daily Life: The Witch.

Old, poor women were usually the victims of witchcraft accusations.

SIGNIFICANT INDIVIDUALS

Scientists

Andreas Vesalius (1514–1564), Belgian anatomist.

Nicolaus Copernicus (1473–1543), Polish astronomer.

Johannes Kepler (1571–1630), German astronomer.

Galileo Galilei (1564–1643), Italian astronomer, physicist.

William Harvey (1578–1657), English anatomist.

Isaac Newton (1642–1727), English astronomer, physicist, mathematician.

Philosophers

Francis Bacon (1561–1626), English philosopher.

René Descartes (1596–1650), French philosopher, mathematician.

Thomas Hobbes (1588–1679), English political theorist.

Blaise Pascal (1623–1662), French mathematician, experimenter.

Mannerists

Parmigianino (1503–1540), Italian painter.

El Greco (1548?–1625?), Greek-Spanish painter.

Baroque

Peter Paul Rubens (1577–1640), Flemish painter.

Diego Velázquez (1599–1660), Spanish painter.

Giovanni Lorenzo Bernini (1598–1680), Italian sculptor, architect.

Rembrandt van Rijn (1606–1669), Dutch painter.

Claudio Monteverdi (1567–1643), Italian composer.

Classicism

Nicholas Poussin (1594–1665),
French painter.
Pierre Corneille (1606–1684), French
dramatist.

Jean Racine (1639–1699), French
dramatist.

Writers

Michel de Montaigne (1533–1592),
French essayist.
Miguel de Cervantes (1547–1616),
Spanish novelist.

William Shakespeare (1564–1616),
English dramatist, poet.

CHRONOLOGICAL DIAGRAM

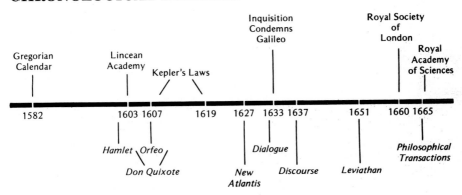

IDENTIFICATION

alchemy
scientific method
social contract
Skepticism
three unities
seigneurial reaction

Jansenism
Royal Society of London
Philosophical Transactions
great witch craze
cottage industry
three laws of motion

PROBLEMS FOR ANALYSIS

I. The Scientific Revolution.

1. Explain the origins of the scientific revolution. Were the theories of the ancient
   Greeks a hindrance or a support? What role did magical beliefs play?
2. What was the essence of the conflict between Galileo and the Church? Do you
   think it was in the Church's interest to condemn Galileo? Why?
3. Use examples to demonstrate the principles of the scientific method. How
   does the scientific method differ from earlier methods of obtaining and veri-
   fying knowledge?

4. Compare the methods emphasized by Francis Bacon, René Descartes, Thomas Hobbes, and John Locke. Do you think that Blaise Pascal would disagree with the methods and concerns of these four men? Why?

II. Literature and the Arts.

1. Compare the Baroque and Classical styles. In what ways did they reflect other developments in sixteenth- and seventeenth-century Europe?
2. It has been argued that Cervantes and Shakespeare reflected the historical concerns of their own societies as well as timeless human concerns. Use examples to support this argument.

III. Social Patterns and Popular Culture.

1. How was seventeenth-century society organized? Compare the possibilities for social mobility among various social groups.
2. Population remained relatively stable in the seventeenth century. How do you explain this? What were some of the demographic characteristics of seventeenth-century society?
3. How did popular culture reflect a dependence on nature and the conditions of life among the peasantry? How does the great witch craze fit into this situation?
4. What were the causes for change in the traditional village? Were most of these causes internal, or were they a result of intrusions from the outside?

DOCUMENTS

Descartes

René Descartes (1596–1650) was one of the great thinkers of the scientific revolution. He is best known for his ideas on how to seek truth and how to reason deductively with mathematical precision. The following is a selection from his most important work, *Discourse on the Method of Rightly Conducting the Reason and Seeking Truth in the Sciences* (1637).

In place of the multitudes of precepts of which logic is composed, I believed that the four following would prove perfectly sufficient for me, provided I took the firm and unwavering resolution never in a single instance to fail in observing them.

The FIRST was never to accept anything for true which I did not clearly know to be such; that is to say, carefully to avoid precipitancy and prejudice, and to comprise nothing more in my judgment than what was presented to my mind so clearly and distinctly as to exclude all ground of doubt.

The SECOND, to divide each of the difficulties under examination into as many parts as possible, and as might be necessary for its adequate solution.

The THIRD, to conduct my thoughts in such order that, by commencing with objects the simplest and easiest to know, I might ascend by little and little, and, as it were, step by step, to the knowledge of the more complex; assigning in thought a certain order even to those objects which in their own nature do not stand in a relation of antecedence and sequence.

At the LAST, in every case to make enumerations so complete, and reviews so general, that I might be assured that nothing was omitted.

. . . For, in fine, whether awake or asleep, we ought never to allow ourselves to be persuaded of the truth of anything unless on the evidence of our Reason. And it must be noted that I say of our REASON, and not of our imagination or of our senses: thus, for example, although we very clearly see the sun, we ought not therefore to determine that it is only of the size which our sense of sight presents; and we may very distinctly imagine the head of a lion joined to the body of a goat, without being therefore shut up to the conclusion that a chimera exists; for it is not a dictate of Reason that which we thus see or imagine is in reality existent; but it plainly tells us that all our ideas or notions contain in them some truth; for otherwise it could not be that God, who is wholly perfect and veracious, should have placed them in us. And because our reasonings are never so clear or so complete during sleep as when we are awake, although sometimes the acts of our imagination are then as lively and distinct, if not more so than in our waking moments, Reason further dictates that, since all our thoughts cannot be true because of our partial imperfection, those possessing truth must infallibly be found in the experience of our waking moments rather than in that of our dreams. . . .[1]

1. What are the advantages of this method of thought? How does it compare to Scholastic thinking?
2. How would an empiricist argue with Descartes' method of thought? How would you argue with it?

A Psychological Interpretation of the Scientific Revolution

The following is an unusual interpretation of the rise of science in the seventeenth century, from a psychological perspective.

The rise of science is the great distinctive intellectual phenomenon of modern times. The scientific movement that emerged in the seventeenth century brought a promise of progress and of the realization of man's deepest hopes. It proposed not only to liberate men from ignorance but also to free them from superstition, religious hatred, irksome toil, and war. For science was then not the pursuit of technicians; it was the "new philosophy," as Francis Bacon called it, the "active science," the first genuine alternative that had been contrived to dogma, myth, and taboo. The world of medieval gloom that denigrated the powers of man gave way to an optimistic faith in his capacities. The scientist of the seventeenth century was a philosophical optimist; delight and joy in man's status pervaded his theory of knowledge and of the universe. And it was this revolution in man's emotions which was the basis for the change in his ideas.

Behind the history of ideas lies the history of emotions. Every major intellectual movement is preceded by the advent of new kinds of feelings that shape the new mode in which reality is to be intellectually apprehended. Emotions determine the perspective, the framework, for the explanation of the perceived world. Whatever the social and economic forces that are operative in the background of people's lives, they impinge on men's ideas through the intervening channel of feeling and emotion. The categories and forms of explanation that characterize the thinking of any given era are thus intimately connected with its underlying emotional structure.

That the scientific revolution was the outcome of a liberation of curiosity all would agree. The question, however, remains unsettled: What was the emotional revolution in seventeenth-century thinkers which turned them into men of science? What was the psychological revolution upon which the scientific revolution was founded?

[1] René Descartes, *Discourse on Method and Meditations,* trans. John Vietch (Washington, D.C.: Dunne, 1901), pp. 160–162, 176–177.

In this study, I shall try to show that the scientific intellectual was born from the hedonist-libertarian spirit which, spreading through Europe in the sixteenth and seventeenth centuries, directly nurtured the liberation of human curiosity. Not asceticism, but satisfaction; not guilt, but joy in the human status; not self-abnegation, but self-affirmation; not original sin, but original merit and worth; not gloom, but merriment; not contempt for one's body and one's senses, but delight in one's physical being; not the exaltation of pain, but the hymn to pleasure—this was the emotional basis of the scientific movement of the seventeenth century. Herbert Butterfield has spoken of "a certain dynamic quality" which entered into Europe's "secularization of thought" in the seventeenth century. What I shall try to show is how the hedonist-libertarian ethic provided the momentum for the scientific revolution, and was in fact the creed of the emerging movements of scientific intellectuals everywhere.

The scientists of the seventeenth century swept away the miserable universe of death, famine, and the torture of human beings in the name of God. They took a world that had been peopled with demons and devils, and that superstition had thronged with unseen terror at every side. They cleansed it with clear words and plain experiment. They found an ethic that advised people to renounce their desires, and to cultivate in a hostile universe the humility which befitted their impotence, and they taught men instead to take pride in their human status, and to dare to change the world into one which would answer more fully to their desires. . . .

The scientific movement in the seventeenth century was not the by-product of an increase of repression or asceticism. It was the outcome of a liberation of energies; it derived from a lightening of the burden of guilt. With the growing awareness that happiness and joy are his aims, man could take frank pleasure in the world around him. Libidinal interests in external objects could develop unthwarted; the world was found interesting to live in—an unending stage for fresh experience. Energies were no longer consumed in inner conflicts. With an awakened respect for his own biological nature, self-hatred was cast off. Empiricism was the expression of a confidence in one's senses; the eyes and ears were no longer evidences of human corruption but trusted avenues to a knowledge of nature. The body was not the tainted seat of ignorance, but the source of pleasures and the means for knowledge. Human energies, hitherto turned against themselves, could reach out beyond concern for exclusive self. [2]

1. In what ways was the rise of science related to a revolution in man's emotions?

2. What was the "hedonist-libertarian" ethic?

The following is a selection from Arthur Lovejoy's classic, *The Great Chain of Being.*

The truly revolutionary theses in cosmography which gained ground in the sixteenth and came to be pretty generally accepted before the end of the seventeenth century were five in number, none of them entailed by the purely astronomical systems of Copernicus or Kepler. In any study of the history of the modern conception of the world, and in any account of the position of any individual writer, it is essential to keep these distinctions between issues constantly in view. The five more significant innovations were: (1) the assumption that other planets of our solar system are inhabited by living, sentient, and rational creatures; (2) the shattering of the outer walls of

---

[2] Lewis S. Feuer, *The Scientific Intellectual: The Psychological and Sociological Origins of Modern Science* (New York: Basic Books, 1963), pp. 1–19. Copyright © 1963 by Basic Books Publishing Co., Inc., New York.

the medieval universe, whether these were identified with the outermost crystalline sphere or with a definite "region" of the fixed stars, and the dispersal of these stars through vast, irregular distances; (3) the conception of the fixed stars as suns similar to ours, all or most of them surrounded by planetary systems of their own; (4) the supposition that the planets in these other worlds also have conscious inhabitants; (5) the assertion of the actual infinity of the physical universe in space and of the number of solar systems contained in it. [3]

1. In your own words, what were the five significant innovations in cosmography that gained acceptance by the end of the seventeenth century?

SPECULATIONS

1. The scientific revolution profoundly changed the ways in which people thought. It was difficult for many to accept this change. Today scientific ways of thinking are as accepted and taken for granted as were traditional ways of thinking in the sixteenth century. What might a future change in the ways of thinking be like, and do you think such ways of thinking would be accepted without too much difficulty?
2. What would a debate between Galileo and the head of the Inquisition be like?
3. Are there any parallels between the great witch craze of the seventeenth century and more recent historical occurrences? Explain.

TRANSITIONS

In "A Century of War and Revolt 1560–1660," a period of violence and upheaval marked by unusually brutal warfare, was examined. It was not until the mid-seventeenth century that the violence subsided and a new sense of order was attained.

In "Culture and Society in the Age of the Scientific Revolution 1540–1660," cultural and social patterns are shown to reflect this progression from uncertainty to stable resolution. This is clearest in the triumph of the scientific revolution — the revolutionary discoveries of a handful of men who laid the foundations for modern science — but it is also apparent in the evolution from Mannerism to the Classical style and in the increased control over people's lives gained by central governments. The upper classes throughout Europe benefited most from these trends.

In "The Triumph of Aristocrats and Kings 1660–1715," the course of European history during the second half of the seventeenth century will be explored. In this period absolutist kings continue the process of state-building within a European society and culture dominated by the aristocracy.

[3] Arthur O. Lovejoy, *The Great Chain of Being: A Study of the History of an Idea* (Cambridge, Mass.: Harvard University Press, 1936), pp. 108–109.

SEVENTEEN
THE TRIUMPH OF
ARISTOCRATS AND KINGS
1660–1715

MAIN THEMES

1. Louis XIV, by making his court at Versailles the center of society and building the state's power through financial, domestic, and military policies, epitomized the absolutist monarchs of the late seventeenth century.
2. The governments of England, the United Provinces, Sweden, and Poland were dominated by aristocrats or merchants. With the exception of England, these countries suffered a decline in power and influence.
3. The aristocratic culture of the period was organized in the academies and salons. Style and taste were dominated by grace, order, decorum, and regularity.
4. Scientists, with their appeal to order, reason, and logic, became heroes of their age; John Locke, who applied scientific ideas in philosophy and political theory, became a celebrated theorist of politics and human nature.

OUTLINE AND SUMMARY

I. The Absolute Monarchies.

Absolutist monarchs made their great courts the center of society.

A. Louis XIV at Versailles.

Louis XIV (1643–1715) built his elaborate court at Versailles and used it to impress the world and help domesticate the nobility. He justified his supremacy by emphasizing the divine right of kings to rule.

1. *Government and Foreign Policy:* Louis, as his own first minister, built the state's power by winning final control over the use of armed force, the formulation and execution of laws, and the collection and expenditure of revenue. His active, direct power over an effective, increasingly trained bureaucracy was crucial to this endeavor. His two leading ministers, Colbert in finance and Louvois in war, influenced Louis to pursue mercantilist economic policies and aggrandizing military actions against the Hapsburgs. Neither policy was particularly successful; Louis failed against the Dutch in the 1670s and against various combinations of allies (League of Augsburg, Grand Alliance) from the 1680s to the treaties of

Utrecht (1713, 1714). Yet his subjects endured these and other hardships without revolt; the authority of the French state was unquestioned.

2. *Domestic Affairs:* Louis further unified his country by revoking the toleration granted to the Huguenots in the Edict of Nantes (1685) and suppressing Jansenism. Economically, he and Colbert made efforts to stimulate manufacturing, agriculture, and trade. Luxury industries and trade with the West Indies gained most. Yet the famines (1690s and 1709) and the wars were costly, particularly for the lower classes. Nevertheless the eighteenth century was a period of relative economic and demographic growth, bringing to an end cycles of famine and plague and initiating strong urbanization.

B. The Hapsburgs at Vienna and Madrid.

To a lesser degree, the Hapsburg Leopold I (1658–1705) followed the pattern set at Versailles in Vienna (Schönbrunn). Relying on a small number of aristocrats in the Privy Council, he governed the lands with caution. At the urgings of Prince Eugène, he laid the foundations for the Austro-Hungarian Empire to the East. Spain declined rapidly. She lost control over many of her lands outside of the Iberian peninsula, and internally the nobles gained considerable autonomy.

C. The Hohenzollerns at Berlin.

By allying himself with the nobles, creating a strong army, and organizing his country to support the military, elector Frederick William (1640–1688) built Brandenburg-Prussia into the dominant principality in northern Germany. The Prussian landed nobility (Junkers) reimposed serfdom and made their estates profitable. Though he began to develop Berlin physically and culturally, it was his son Frederick (he succeeded his father as elector of Brandenburg in 1688, took the title of King of Prussia in 1701, and reigned until 1713) who made the city a focus of society and an intellectual and artistic center.

D. Peter the Great at St. Petersburg.

The ruthless Peter I (1682–1725) transformed Russia politically and socially. He simplified Russia's social order by reducing peasants and serfs to near uniformity under the heel of the aristocracy. The aristocracy was made into a service class, required to hold positions in the bureaucracy. He took over the Russian Orthodox Church and ignored representative institutions (the Duma). He built an entirely new capital, St. Petersburg, making it the cultural and social center of Russia. Whenever necessary, he imported experts from the West. By the end of his reign, Russia had expanded to dominance in the Baltic and was highly regarded throughout Europe.

II. The Anti-Absolutists.

Other late-seventeenth-century governments were dominated by aristocrats or merchants.

A. The Triumph of the Gentry in England.

The gentry, supported by custom, law, and the House of Commons, was independently powerful in England. Charles II (1660–1685) managed to rule England effectively, but when his son, James II, encouraged Catholicism against the wishes of Parliament, leading members of the gentry invited William III to invade the country. James fled, and William and Mary were proclaimed monarchs in 1689. William ruled authoritatively but with clear limitations (the Bill of Rights, the Act of Toleration).

   1. *Politics and Prosperity:* The crown remained a dominant partner in government throughout the eighteenth century but shared that power with the gentry, now divided into two parties: the Whigs, usually in power and favoring more limited royal prerogatives, and the Tories, favoring royal independence and traditional Anglicanism. England (Great Britain after union with Scotland in 1707) prospered economically, as evidenced by the success of the Bank of England (1694), the rise of the navy, and the overseas expansion. Even the lower classes benefited. England's taxes were relatively low, her society was somewhat mobile, her judiciary was comparatively impartial, and her people were uniquely free from governmental interference.

B. Aristocracy in the United Provinces, Sweden, and Poland.

The Dutch republic fell increasingly under the power of the merchant oligarchy and provincial leadership in the Estates General. This elite was more restrained, egalitarian, and oriented toward economic goals than other elites in Europe. In the face of English competition, Dutch power declined in the eighteenth century. Initially Swedish kings continued the tradition of absolutism; but military defeats in the early eighteenth century resulted in the loss of Sweden's Baltic empire, and a resurgent nobility created a system, similar to England's, that gave them political and social power. Poland suffered from continued dominance of the old landed aristocracy, which eventually resulted in the dismemberment of this decentralized state in the late eighteenth century.

III. The Culture of the Age.

A quest for regularity, order, and decorum characterized the aristocratic culture of the late seventeenth century.

A. The Academy and the Salon.

Academies and salons organized French intellectual life and were imitated elsewhere. Official academies established under royal patronage, such as the French Academy and the Royal Academy of Painting and Sculpture, set standards for literature, art, and architecture. Salons, usually organized by women, were small, elite social gatherings that promoted culture and gentility. They complemented and sometimes competed with the courts as social and cultural centers.

B. *Style and Taste.*

Art and literature of the late seventeenth century were dominated by lightness, grace, elegance, order, and regularity; the emotional or exuberant vision was gone. The new ideal is illustrated in the literary criticism of Boileau (*Poetic Art,* 1674), the poetry of Dryden, the paintings of Watteau, and the court drama of Racine (*Phèdre,* 1677). The middle and lower classes were more actively involved in the music and popular literature of the day, above all the comedies of Molière (*The Bourgeois Gentleman, 1670; Tartuffe*). His company, the Comédie Française, was a great success and gained acceptance even at court, despite the satiric nature of his plays.

C. *Science and Thought.*

The late seventeenth century was the age of the virtuoso — nobles who dabbled in experiments and sought friendships with scientists. Scientists, with their appealing values of order, reason, and logic, became heroes of their age; they had clearly surpassed the Ancients in prestige (Battle of the Books) and achievements.

   1. *John Locke:* Locke applied his belief in the scientific method, empiricism, and order to explain human understanding (*Essay Concerning Human Understanding,* 1690). He argued that we are born with the mind a clean slate (*tabula rasa*). By reasoning with data derived from the senses, we gain understanding. He applied these principles to politics, systematizing the views of the English gentry and many European aristocrats (*Second Treatise of Civil Government,* 1690). He used Hobbes' notion of the creation of a sovereign power through a social contract ending the state of nature, but he reserved the rights of life, liberty, and property to the individual. His emphasis on property made him a spokesman for the elite.

Experiences of Daily Life: The Peasant Household.

Most peasant households in Western Europe were organized around subsistence agricultural production.

SIGNIFICANT INDIVIDUALS

Political Leaders

Louis XIV (1643–1715), king of France.

Peter I (1682–1725), tsar of Russia.

Charles II (1660–1685), king of England

Charles II (1665–1700), king of Spain.

Frederick William (1640–1688), elector of Brandenburg.

Frederick III, elector of Brandenburg (1688–1701) and first king of Prussia under the name and title of King Frederick I (1701–1713).

Leopold I (1658–1705), Hapsburg Holy Roman Emperor.

William III (1672–1702), stadholder of Holland (1689–1702), king of England

Charles XI (1660–1697), king of Sweden

Charles XII (1697–1718), king of Sweden.

Ministers and Generals

Jean-Baptiste Colbert (1619–1683),
French financial reformer.
Marquis of Louvois (1641–1691),
French minister of war.

Prince Eugène of Savoy (1663–1736),
Austrian general and minister.

Culture and Science

Nicolas Boileau (1636–1711), French
critic, poet.
John Dryden (1631–1700), English
poet.
Antoine Watteau (1684–1721),
French painter.
Jean Racine (1639–1699), French
dramatic poet.

Molière (1622–1673), French
dramatist.
John Locke (1632–1704), English
philosopher, political theorist.

CHRONOLOGICAL DIAGRAM

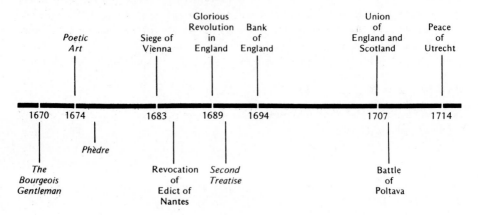

IDENTIFICATION

Grand Alliance	Exclusion Crisis
Peace of Utrecht	Bill of Rights
Whigs	the salon
Tories	French Academy
Schönbrunn	Battle of the Books
Junkers	*tabula rasa*
Battle of Poltava	

PROBLEMS FOR ANALYSIS

I. The Absolute Monarchies.

1. In what ways did the policies of Louis XIV build the state's power? What evidences success or failure of these policies?
2. How did the various absolutist monarchs use their great courts to support their own power while undermining that of their nobility?
3. What distinguished Peter the Great from other European monarchs? What different conditions did he face? How did his policies influence subsequent Russian history?

II. The Anti-Absolutists.

1. What developments support the argument that during the late seventeenth century the gentry triumphed in England? Does this mean that the crown became completely subservient to the English gentry? Explain.
2. Compare the decentralization of government and society that occurred in the United Provinces, Sweden, and Poland during the late seventeenth and early eighteenth centuries. Was this decentralization the sole cause for the comparative loss of power of these three countries? Explain.

III. The Culture of the Age.

1. What role did the academies and salons play in organizing intellectual life? Did they offer new opportunities to artists and thinkers or restrict what they could do?
2. Why has the culture of this age been characterized as aristocratic? Support your answer with examples.
3. What was so appealing about the scientist at this time? Why did Locke's answers and values fit so well with his times? Explain.

DOCUMENTS

John Locke

John Locke (1632–1704) is considered one of the great liberal political theorists. In the following selection from his *Second Treatise on Civil Government* (1690), he analyzes human beings in the state of nature as the starting point for his social contract theory of liberal government.

To understand political power [a] right, and derive it from its original, we must consider, what state all men are naturally in, and that is, a state of perfect freedom to order their actions, and dispose of their possessions and persons, as they think fit, within the bounds of the law of nature, without asking leave, or depending upon the will of any other man.

A state also of equality, wherein all the power and jurisdiction is reciprocal, no one having more than another; there being nothing more evident, than that creatures of the same species and rank, promiscuously born to all the same advantages of nature, and the use of the same faculties, should also be equal one amongst another without subordination or subjection, unless the lord and master of them all should, by any manifest declaration of his will, set one above another, and confer on him, by an evident and clear appointment, an undoubted right to dominion and sovereignty. . . .

But though this be a state of liberty, yet it is not a state of license: though man in that state have an uncontrollable liberty to dispose of his person or possessions, yet he has not liberty to destroy himself, or so much as any creature in his possessions, but where some nobler use than its bare preservation calls for it. The state of nature has a law of nature to govern it, which obliges every one, and reason, which is that law, teaches all mankind, who will but consult it, that being all equal and independent, no one ought to harm another in his life, health, liberty, or possessions: for men being all the workmanship of one omnipotent, and infinitely wise maker; all the servants of one sovereign master, sent into the world by his order, and about his business; they are his property whose workmanship they are, made to last during his, not one another's pleasure. . . .

If man in the state of nature be so free as has been said; if he be absolute lord of his own person and possessions; equal to the greatest and subject to no body, why will he part with his freedom? Why will he give up this empire, and subject himself to the dominion and control of any other power? To which 'tis obvious to answer, that though in the state of nature he hath such a right, yet the enjoyment of it is very uncertain and constantly exposed to the invasion of others; for all being kings as much as he, every man his equal, and the greater part no strict observers of equity and justice, the enjoyment of the property he has in this state is very unsafe, very insecure. This makes him willing to quit this condition which, however free, is full of fears and continual dangers; and 'tis not without reason that he seeks out and is willing to join in society with others who are already united, or have a mind to unite for the mutual preservation of their lives, liberties, and estates, which I call by the general name, property.

The great and chief end therefore, of men's uniting into commonwealths, and putting themselves under government, is the preservation of their property; to which in the state of nature there are many things wanting. . . .[1]

[1] John Locke, *The Works of John Locke* (London, 1812), Vol. V, pp. 339–341, 353–356, 411–412, 416, 423–424, 469–471.

1. According to Locke, what was life like in the state of nature? Why is this important?
2. For what reasons do individuals leave the state of nature and form commonwealths?

English Parliament's Bill of Rights

The triumphant Parliament presented its demands in the Bill of Rights of 1689, to which William of Orange assented as a condition of acquiring the English crown.

> . . . And whereas the said James the Second having abdicated the government, and the throne being thereby vacant, his highness the Prince of Orange (whom it hath pleased Almighty God to make the glorious instrument of delivering this kingdom from popery and arbitrary power) did (by the advice of the lords spiritual and temporal, diverse principal persons of the commons) cause letters to be written . . . for the choosing of such persons to represent them, as were of right to be sent to parliament . . . being now assembled in a full and free representative of this nation . . . do in the first place (as their ancestors in like case have usually done) for the vindicating and asserting their ancient rights and liberties, declare;
>
> 1. That the pretended power of suspending laws, or the execution of laws, by regal authority, without the consent of parliament, is illegal.
> 2. That the pretended power of dispensing with laws, or the execution of laws, by regal authority, as it hath been assumed and exercised of late, is illegal.
> 3. That the commission for erecting the late court of commissioners for ecclesiastical causes, and all other commission and courts of like nature are illegal and pernicious.
> 4. That levying of money for or to the use of the crown, by pretence of prerogative without the grant of parliament, for a longer time, or in other manner than the same is or shall be granted, is illegal.
> 5. That it is the right of the subjects to petition the King, and all committments and prosecutions for such petitioning are illegal.
> 6. That the raising or keeping of a standing army within the kingdom in time of peace, unless it be with the consent of parliament, is against the law.
>
> . . .
>
> 8. That election of members of parliament ought to be free.
> 9. That the freedom of speech, and debates or proceedings in parliament, ought not to be impeached or questioned in any court or place out of parliament.
> 10. That excessive bail ought not to be required, nor excessive fines imposed; nor cruel and unusual punishments inflicted. . . . [2]

1. How does Parliament justify its rights and demands?
2. What grievances did Parliament hold against James II?
3. How does this document relate to the ideas of John Locke?

---

[2] *Statutes of the Realm*, VI, p. 142.

Louis XIV

In the following selection, John B. Wolf interprets the rule of Louis XIV, particularly his military ambitions.

Louis XIV never intended to impose the balance of power upon Europe, and he never understood his historic role in the formation of the European community. He had been brought up to believe that he must achieve his *gloire,* that is to say, that he must fulfill his destiny; Mazarin had often impressed upon him that he had both the possibility of greatness and the responsibility to achieve it. It is therefore not surprising that, when Mazarin died leaving Louis to manage his own affairs, the young king inaugurated a period of intense activity. Cooperating with the advisors that he had inherited from the cardinal, Louis struck out in all directions to make his government strong and his reign notable; reforms in the army, in the administration of justice, in the organization of economic life followed one another with rapid succession. This was the period when the basic ordinances for the organization of the bureaucracies in France were promulgated; during the rest of the reign there were to be many edicts concerning governmental organization, but they were usually merely modifications of the earlier ordinances. Since France was the most populous and perhaps the richest of the kingdoms of Europe, this burst of energy was quickly transformed into real power. The army that Richelieu had started became, under Louvois, the foremost military instrument in Europe and at the same time, with Colbert attending to commerce, colonies, and finance, the king's treasury became the most prosperous on the continent. Louis did not need to build the great colonnade of the Louvre to prove to Europe that his reign was starting auspiciously; perceptive men understood that money and soldiers augured an era of French hegemony.

Since Louis and his whole generation were brought up during wars and taught that they in turn would wage wars, it was to be expected that the young French king would use these military resources, and since his government was now in full command of the kingdom, their use would unquestionably be applied beyond the frontiers. As he explained to his son in his *Mémoires,* he was confronted with the choice of making war on England as an ally of the Dutch or upon Spain to secure his wife's inheritance; as he tells it the problem was just that simple! In another place he adds that as soon as there was talk of war, his "court was flooded with gentlemen demanding employment." In other words the moral and political climate not only implied that the king would use the force that he had, but also encouraged him to do so. [3]

1. According to the standards of the seventeenth century, as interpreted here, should Louis XIV be condemned for his wars?

Science and Administration

James King points to the influence of scientific thinking in Louis XIV's administration.

In a brilliant period of accomplishment, between 1661 and 1683, Louis XIV and Colbert effected a veritable revolution in the techniques of government in France. Before

[3] John B. Wolf, "The Emergence of the European States-System," *Chapters in Western Civilization,* 3rd edition (New York: Columbia University Press, 1961), pp. 415-416.

the death of the great Minister, that government had already assumed many technical attributes suggesting the influence of the scientific spirit and commonly associated with the administration of modern states. Thus statistical and social surveys became a recognized and inseparable part of government. The functions of the intendancy were significantly extended into the field of statistics, and the canalization of these functions into the office of the *contrôleur général* pointed the way to the establishment of regular statistical bureaus. In a development analogous to the urge of contemporary scientists to give utility to the facts of nature by tabulation, arrangement, and classification, administrative archives were created for the collation, classification, and preservation of useful data. Along similar lines, the emphasis in seventeenth-century science and rationalism on the veracity of mathematics, its importance as a guide to reason and as a certain measure in quantitative calculation, was reflected in this new government by the vigorous application of accounting methods in reforming the financial structure. [4]

1. What was the "veritable revolution" in the techniques of government in France according to James King?

The French Peasantry

Pierre Goubert presents a different perspective on the era of Louis XIV, focusing on the peasantry.

Fifteen million peasants, therefore, together with a tenth or a twentieth of that number of workers (the title of journeyman had fallen into disuse) made up the productive force of the realm and made some kind of a living, mostly rather poor but occasionally quite good, punctuated every now and then by appalling periods of crisis. Taking into account time, place and attitude of mind, they should probably be regarded as among the more fortunate of the world's populations. If they did sometimes complain or resort here and there to active rebellion triggered off by a new tax, an unexpected shortage, a false rumour or some more or less well-founded apprehension, these revolts were never more than local or regional affairs, with little or no organization, and only became at all serious when some other sector of society — usually the nobility — began to take a positive interest.

These popular risings, the existence, duration and gravity of which is no longer in dispute, were regularly concluded by the triumph of order as symbolized by the king's army. They had no serious effect on the comparatively simple basis of society.

If, for the sake of brevity, we discount the middle class which was still very small although showing signs of development among the small shopkeepers, craftsmen and minor tradespeople, it would be fair to say that, as a general rule, nine out of ten of King Louis' subjects worked hard and thanklessly with their hands in order to permit the tenth to devote himself comfortably to the life of bourgeois, nobleman or mere idler. Directly or indirectly, this tenth of the population lived to a greater or lesser extent on the vast revenues of the land, scraped from the soil of the kingdom by the inhabitants of the countryside and swelled and transformed by their labour and those of the workers in the towns. To one of these numerous classes of *rentier* belonged nearly

[4] James A. King, *Science and Rationalism in the Government of Louis XIV, 1661–1683* (Baltimore: The Johns Hopkins University Press, 1949), pp. 310–312. Copyright © 1949 by The Johns Hopkins University Press.

all the nobility, most of the clergy and the whole of the bourgeoisie, all those privileged persons in fact who also enjoyed the benefits of their own special legal system, the *leges privatae.* [5]

1. What role did nine-tenths of the people play in French society in the second half of the seventeenth century, according to Goubert?

SPECULATIONS

1. First as an aristocrat, and second as a merchant, what were the advantages and disadvantages of living in a country dominated by an absolutist monarch at the end of the seventeenth century?
2. Would you rather be an artist or writer accepted into the Parisian salons at the end of the seventeenth century or an artist or writer in New York City during the 1980s? What would be the advantages and disadvantages?
3. If you were a religious authority at the end of the seventeenth century, would you feel threatened by the ideas of Locke? Why?

TRANSITIONS

In "Culture and Society in the Age of the Scientific Revolution 1540–1660," the fundamental scientific discoveries and the cultural creations of this period were examined. These achievements contributed to a sense of order by the mid-seventeenth century.

In "The Triumph of Aristocrats and Kings 1660–1715," the quest for order remained the underlying concern throughout Europe for the rest of the seventeenth century. Absolutist kings, epitomized by Louis XIV, rose to prominence. Those states (with the exception of England) which failed to focus power on the monarch declined. The aristocracy, to varying degrees, dominated the new, powerful, governmental administration as needed allies and agents of absolute monarchs or as direct controllers of events. Cultural styles reflected this enhanced position of the aristocracy.

In "Absolutism and Empire 1715–1770s," the eighteenth-century competition for power and authority on the Continent and in the colonial empires, which resulted in a mid-century conflagration, will be traced.

[5] Pierre Goubert, *Louis XIV and Twenty Million Frenchmen,* trans. Anne Carter (New York: Pantheon Books, Random House, 1969). Copyright © 1969 by Pantheon Books, Random House.